Дарагому Др. Янку За-
прудніку

ад Аўтара

+ Ч. Сіповіч

Лёндан, 10.I.79.

THE PONTIFICAL LITURGY

OF SAINT JOHN CHRYSOSTOM

A manuscript of the 17th Century in the

Slavonic text and Latin translation.

EDITED WITH EXPLANATORY LITURGICAL NOTES

by

CESLAUS SIPOVIČ

Bishop of Mariamme

Apostolic Visitor of Byelorussians

together with

THE LIFE OF THEODORE SKUMINOVIČ

Bishop of Gratianopolis

Suffragan and Archdeacon of Byelorussia.

The Francis Skaryna

Byelorussian Library and Museum

London 1978.

This edition is limited to 400 copies.

Cover by Veronica Kendle

Printed in the United Kingdom
by
Ukrainian Publishers Limited
200 Liverpool Road, London N1 1LF

Ord. No. 4783

To
the Apostles and Martyrs
for Church Unity in Byelorussia.

Acknowledgement

The author is grateful to all people who have offered their time and experience to make this edition possible. He is particularly indebted to Christopher Morris, Fr. A. Nadson, Guy de Picarda, Dr. Roger Renard, Vera Rich and Dr. W. Ryan.

INTRODUCTION

In making available to the general public the manuscript of the Slavonic-Latin Liturgy of St. John Chrysostom, the original of which is to be found in the Byelorussian Library of Francis Skaryna in London, we hope to acquaint a wider circle of liturgists with an authentic text of the pontifical celebration of the Divine Liturgy and its ceremonies which were celebrated according to the order (ustaŭ) of the Eastern Catholic Church of the Metropolitan See of Kiev and of the whole "Ruthenian land" in the sixteenth and seventeenth centuries.

This edition seeks to be one more concrete illustration of the Pontifical Liturgy preserved in the manuscript of the Byelorussian Library (referred to hereafter for convenience as MS BL), which, although it has many things in common with those already known through various publications[1], still has its own particular merit for Byelorussians and Ukrainians.

MS BL contains the text of the liturgy of the Eastern Church in Byelorussia and the Ukraine, which at the Council of Brest in 1596 submitted to the See of Rome in matters of faith, whilst maintaining its own distinctive traditional ritual. The Eastern rite, which came from Byzantium, was essentially the same for all Eastern and Southern Slavs. In time, however, there arose significant regional differences, especially between the rites of Muscovite Russia after the reforms of Patriarch Nikon (1652-1667) and the rites of the Byelorussians and Ukrainians living in the Grand Duchy of Lithuania. The latter were governed by the Metropolitan See of Kiev, with jurisdictional dependence first upon Constantinople, and after the Union of Brest upon Rome. That portion which did not unite with the Catholic Church, however, remained jurisdictionally dependent upon Constantinople.

The reforms of Patriarch Nikon were not introduced into Byelorussia until the time of the successive partitions of the Commonwealth (1772, 1793, 1795), which resulted in a persecution of the Catholic Church of both rites and the imposition on Byelorussians of everything that was Russian. This led to the final liquidation of the Catholic Eastern Church in 1839.

It is today a very rare occurrence to find printed liturgical books of Byelorussian origin; even more rare are manuscripts of Pontifical Service Books — works that are more native to the Slavonic genius than to the Greek, even though in essence the rite derived from the Greeks.

The value of MS BL is enhanced by the fact that it is the oldest of all currently known Pontifical Service Books or Archieratica printed in Byelorussia and the Ukraine. It contains two texts of the Liturgy of St. John Chrysostom: one in Old-Slavonic in the Byelorussian *svod* (edition), and a parallel version in Latin. It will be for linguists to analyse the subtleties of the language: what we have endeavoured to do is to ensure that the authentic text be printed correctly and to illustrate some of its liturgical particularities.

It is worthy of note that Metropolitan Macarius, in his well known compendious study *The History of the Russian Church*[2], already drew attention to "certain remarkable features" in the liturgical rites of the

Orthodox Church in Byelorussia and the Ukraine (which he called "the Western-Russian Church") in the sixteenth century.

The liturgist, A. Dmitrijevskij, examined the manuscripts of many Service Books (służebniki) of the sixteenth century containing the Liturgy of St. John Chrysostom which he compared with one another. For the Entrance Prayers of the first service book printed in Byelorussia (Vilna, 1583), however, he did not find an established group, and he placed it into a category apart, which corresponds fairly closely to MS BL[3].

Similarly, after studying the liturgical manuscripts of the Vilna Public Library, transferred there in the main from the Suprasl monastery, F. Dobrianskij states that "although they have no trace of confessional or doctrinal differences, there are at least local and national differences (in rites), and often purely philological ones. It is difficult to say whether they were translated directly from the Greek language into the local Byelorussian dialect, or whether they were compiled from translations that existed in Eastern Russia and were only revised in accordance with the needs of local speech"[4].

Again, the difference between the Byelorussian and Ukrainian service books did not escape the attention of Bishop Bocian, who drew a distinction between the Vilna and Kiev groups[5].

Cyril Korolevskij, who devoted much time to the study of various Eastern rites, more than once expressed some extreme views regarding Catholics of the Ukrainian and Byelorussian rites. When he came to study these rites more closely, he observed their originality and appreciated their value, and wrote that it would be indeed criminal if, for the sake of an illusory one-sided unity, the old and the original were to be destroyed[6].

We are convinced that MS BL, containing a detailed version of the Pontifical Liturgy according to the rite of the Kievan Metropolitan See, has preserved those liturgical values from which even today we draw spiritual sustenance. For this we are indebted to Bishop Theodore Skuminovič († 1668), Suffragan of Vilna and Byelorussia. He may well have been the author of the manuscript, which he presented to the Basilian Fathers in Rome as a lasting memorial of his respect — *aeternum obsequii monumentum.*

---

1) See bibliography: Dmitrievskij, A., Dobrianskij, F., Karataev, I., Nevostruev-Gorski, Petrovski, A., Rud, S.
2) SPb 1879, v. IX, pp. 296-7.
3) *Bogosluženije,* p. 60.
4) *Opisanije,* p. XLIX.
5) "Ex periodo schismatica quae promanarunt editionum familiae, sunt altera Vilnensis, altera Kioviensis", 'De modificationibus', pp. 944-45.
6) "Très peu ou point étudiés jusqu'à présent, même par les Ruthènes eux-mêmes, les livres ruthènes n'en représentent pas moins une tradition très ancienne, d'une valeur parfois supérieure à celle de la recension vulgate... quand on a procédé à quelques suppressions textuelles... on se trouve en présence d'une recension de haute valeur, qu'il serait vraiment criminel de vouloir supprimer sous prétexte d'uniformité". 'Le Pontifical', p. 203.

THE PONTIFICAL LITURGY OF SAINT JOHN CHRYSOSTOM IN A MANUSCRIPT OF THE XVII CENTURY THE SLAVONIC TEXT AND THE LATIN TRANSLATION

Божесьтвеньная Лутургия:

Иже во Святыхъ Отца Нашего
Іоанна Златоустаго
Егда Служитъ Святитель
По Уставу
Церкве Восточное Кафолическое
Митрополии Киевское
И всея Россійскія Земли

Divina Liturgia

Sancti Patris nri
Joannis Chrysostomi
Quando Celebrat Pontifex
Secundum Ordinem
Ecclesiae Orientalis Catholicae
Metropoliae Chiovensis
Et omnium Terrarum Russiae.

Eccle SS.tm Sergij et Bacchi in Urbe
offero diuturnum mei obsequij monumentum
Theodorus Skuminowicz Eps Gratianopolitanus
Suffrag. Viln. Albam Russiam

+

Святитель хотяй божественную совершати лит-
ургию, облечен весь [illegible] совлачится от мантии
святительския, и тако исходит во церкви. И изыш-
[illegible] диаконы совокупльшеся во [illegible] церковные
со паникадилом и кадилом, священницы же со священными
одеждами, сопровождающии его. Тогда Архидиакон
[illegible] фимиам и кадильницу главу преклонь глаголет;
Благослови владыко кадило.
Архиерей абие фимиама благословит глаголя; Кадило
приносим Ти Христе Боже во воню благоухания духовнаго, еже п-
риемь во святый и пренебесный, и мысленный твой жертвенник
возниспосли нам божественную благодать пресвят-
ого твоего духа, богатыя же милости твоя. и дару[illegible] на[illegible]
рабом твоим призывающым имя твое, Отца и Сына
и Святаго духа всегда ныне и присно и во веки веком
Аминь. Хвалите + отроцы Господа, хвалите им-
я Господне.
И тако Архидиакон глав паки преклонь идет пред
Святителем кадя, поюще стихъ: Буди имя Господне
благословенно есть ныне и до века.
Лик: Буди имя Господне г҃. и прочая пения.
Архиерей абие [illegible] благословляет люди, и [illegible] гла-
Прохождшася стопы моя во правде, Помянух Господ-
и возвеселихся со рекшими мне, в дом Господень пой-
дем. Азъ же множеством милости твоея вниду в до-
м твой и поклонюся ко церкви твоей во страсе твоем. Господи наставит мя правдою твоею враг моих ради, и
исправи пред собою путь мой.

PONTIFEX volens Diuinum absoluere Sacrificium, tempore iam instante, induitur Chlamyde Pontificali et ita procedit ad Ecclesiam. Et egressus inuenit Diaconos indutos amictu Ecclesiastico cum Thuribulo et Thymiamate, Ceroferarios autem cum Candelis accensis, illum expectantes. Tunc Archidiaconus tenendo Thymiama et Thuribulum caput inclinans dicit: Benedic Domine Thymiama.

Pontifex autem Thymium benedicit, dicens: Incensum tibi ✝ offerimus Christe Deus, in odorem suauitatis Spiritualis: quem suscipe Domine in Sanctum et Supercaeleste, et Intellectuale tuum Altare, et repende nobis opes misericordiae tuae, et miserationes tuas, et largire nobis ipsas Seruis tuis inuocantibus nomen tuum Patris, et Filij, et Sancti Spiritus, ubiq nunc et semper et in secula Seculorum. Amen. Laudate ✝ pueri Dominum, laudate nomen Domini.

S. Chrysostomus

Pontificale Sbt.ᵐ Atq ita Archidiaconus caput rursum inclinans, praeit Pontificem incensans, cantando versiculum: Sit nomen Domini benedictum, ex hoc nunc et vsq in Seculum. ~~Chorus Sit~~

Cho: Sit nomen Domini benedictum. ~~vel~~ vel alias Cantiones.

Pontifex autem eundo benedicit populum, et tacite dicit: Effusi sunt gressus mei in Iustitiam. memor fui Domini, et laetatus sum in his quae dicta sunt mihi in domum Domini ibimus. Ego autem in multitudine misericordiae tuae, introibo in domum tuam, et adorabo ad templum Sanctum tuum in timore tuo. Domine deduc me in Iustitia tua propter inimicos meos, et dirige ante te viam meam

+

И паки. Препрехвальная дево, преизнаменитая благословенная
Богородице дево, прими молитвы наша, и донеси я Сыну своему
и Богу нашему, да спасет тебе ради души наша.
Таже псалом кв. Господь пасет мя г.
И тако пришедъ пред святыя врата, творит поклон гла
голя стихъ: Боже милостивъ буди мне грешному.
И абие архидиаконъ сотворяет [illegible] пономарем при
емлет. Ко святителю, преклоньше главы и взяти с него [illegible]
сотворяет со престоящимъ. Архиерей же сотворив обычный глас
[...], и во святых вратех стояще знаменуяся глаголет:

Благословенъ Богъ нашъ всегда ныне и присно и во веки веки
Аминь. Царю небесный утешителю душе истинный, иже
везде сый, и вся исполняяй, сокровище благих, и жизни по
дателю, прииди и вселися в нас, и очисти нас от всякия
скверны, и спаси блаже души наша. Творит же поклон г
глаголя; Святый Боже, святый крепкий, святый безсмер
тный помилуй нас. Слава отцу и сыну и святому духу, и
и присно и во веки веком. Аминь. Пресвятая Троице помилуй
нас, Господи очисти грехи наша, Владыко прости безз
акония наша, святый посети, и исцели немощи наша, имене
твоего ради. Господи помилуй г. Слава отцу. И ныне.
Отче наш. Яко твое есть царство, и сила, и слава отц
и сына и святаго духа, ныне и присно и во веки веком. Аминь.
Господи помилуй вб. Слава отцу. И ныне. И паки твор
поклон трижды глаголя. Приидите поклонимся цареви на
шему Богу. Приидите поклонимся Христу цареви нашему
Богу. Приидите поклонимся и припадем к самому Госп
ду Иисусу Христу цареви и Богу нашему.

От Пасхи а до пятьдесятницы, иже глаголется Царю. + Но Христос воскресе.

12

ntificale Rutenu Et iterum. Impenetrabilis Porta, mystice designata, Benedicta Dei Genitrix Virgo, Suscipe preces nostras et presenta illas Filio tuo et Deo nostro, ut saluet propter te animas nostras.

Postea Psalmum 22 Dominus regit me &c.

Ac ita consistens ante Sacram Portam facit Adorationem dicens versiculum

Deus Propitius esto mihi peccatori.

Interim Archidiaconus reddito thuribulo Sacristae accedit ad Pontificem, inclinato vero capite, et deponens illi Caputium, redit circumstantibus. Pontifex vero aperto capite, et in medio portae Sanctae consistens, crucem sibi imprimendo, dicit: Benedictus Deus noster, ubiq nunc et semper, et in secula seculorum. Amen. Rex Caelorum Paraclete, Spiritus Veritatis, qui ubiq es, et omnia imples, qui es thesaurus bonorum, et vitae largitor, veni et habita in nobis, et purga nos ab omni macula, et salua optime animas nostras. Et facit adorationem ter dicens: Sancte Deus, Sancte fortis, Sancte immortalis, miserere nobis. Gloria Patri et Filio, et Sancto Spiritui, et nunc et semper, et in secula seculorum. Amen. Sanctissima Trinitas miserere nobis, Domine munda peccata nostra, Domine dimittas iniquitates nostras, Sancte visita, et sana infirmitates nostras propter nomen tuum. Domine miserere. ter. Gloria Patri, Et nunc. Pater noster. Quoniam tuum est Regnum, et Potentia, et Gloria Patris et Filij, et Sancti Spiritus nunc et semper et in secula seculorum. Amen. Domine miserere 12 Gloria Patri. Et nunc. Et iterum facit adorationem ter dicens: Venite adoremus Regem nostrum Deum. Venite adoremus Christum Regem nostrum Deum. Venite adoremus et procidamus ante ipsum Dominum Jesum Christum Regem et Deum nostrum.

S. Chrysostomus
~~A festo Pascha~~
~~lis usq ad Pen~~
~~tecosten pro dicit~~
~~Rex &~~
~~sed Christus surrexit~~

Pontificale Rutenu

Kyrie Eleyson

Kyrie Eleyson

Таже глаголетъ тропари сия.

Помилуй нас Господи, помилуй нас, всякаго бо отвѣта недоумѣюще, сию ти молитву, яко Владыцѣ грѣшнии приносимъ, помилуй нас Господи, помилуй нас.

Слава Отцу и Сыну и Святому Духу:

Господи помилуй нас, на тя бо уповахомъ, не прогнѣвайся на ны зѣло, ниже помяни беззаконий нашихъ, но призри нынѣ яко милосердъ, и избави нас отъ врагъ нашихъ. Ты бо еси Богъ нашъ, и мы людие твои, вси дѣло рукъ твоею, и имя твое призываемъ.

И нынѣ и присно и во вѣки вѣкомъ. Аминь.

Милосердия двери, отверзи намъ Благословенная Богородице, надѣющиися на тя да не погибнемъ, но да избавимся тобою отъ бѣдъ, ты бо еси спасение рода христианскаго.

Посемъ поклоняется иконѣ Спасовѣ глаголя;

Пречистому ти образу поклоняемся Благий, просяще прощения прегрѣшениямъ нашимъ Христе Боже: волею бо благоизволилъ еси плотию взыйти на крестъ, да избавиши отъ работы вражия, ихже создалъ, тѣмъ благодаряще вопиемъ ти: радости исполнилъ еси вся Спасе нашъ пришедый спасти миръ, слава тебѣ.

Поклоняется и иконѣ Богородичнѣ глаголя.

Милосердия сущи источникъ, милости сподоби нас Богородице, призри на люди согрѣшившия, яви яко присно силу твою. На тя бо уповающе радуйся вопиемъ ти, яко ве иногда Гавриилъ безплотныхъ архистратигъ.

И потомъ поклоняется ко престолу глаголя.

Боже ослаби грѣхи моя и помилуй мя.

+ 4

Postmodum dicit Antiphonas has: Miserere nostri Domine, miserere nostri, omne enim Responsum ignorantes, hanc tibi Supplicationem, sicut Domino, peccatores afferimus; miserere nostri Domine, miserere nostri.

Gloria Patri et Filio, et Sancto Spiritui. Domine miserere nostri, in te enim speravimus. Non irascaris nobis nimium, neque memor sis iniquitatum nostrarum, sed respice nunc sicut misericors, et libera nos ab inimicis nostris. Tu enim es Deus noster, et nos populus tuus, et omnes opus manuum tuarum, et nomen tuum invocamus

Et nunc et semper et in Secula Seculorum. Amen.

Misericordiae fores aperi nobis Benedicta Dei Genitrix, ut sperantes in te non pereamus, sed liberemur per te à periculis. Tu enim Salus generis Christianorum.

Postea facit venerationem ante imaginem Salvatoris dicens: Honorabilissimam tuam imaginem veneramur, ~~optime~~, rogantes indulgentiam delictorum nostrorum Christe Deus. Voluntarie enim bene elegisti secundum corpus ascendere in Crucem, ut liberares illos à servitute inimici, quos creasti. Propterea gratias agentes accinimus tibi: Gaudio universa implens Salvator noster, qui venisti ad salvandum Mundum, Gloria tibi.

Facit quoque Venerationem ante imaginem Deigenitricis, dicens:

Tu quae fons misericordiae existis, misericordia dignos nos facias Deigenitrix: respice populum qui peccavit, ostende, prout semper potentiam tuam. In te enim sperantes, Ave, accinimus tibi, sicut quondam Gabriel Incorporeorum Archangelus.

Postea facit adorationem versus Altare, dicens;

Deus mundo peccata mea & miserere mei.

+

И тако входит во олтарь диаконом что под руце держаще
Со священосвятителе пред царскими дверми стоящему, и глаго[лет]
молитву входя. Господи отими от мене вся безза[ко]
ния моя, и прегрешения моя, да достойно вниду во святи[ли]
ще святаго храма твоего. Господи Боже наш, ниспосли руку твою с высоты
святаго жилища твоего, и укрепи мя во предлежащую служ[бу]
твою, да неосужденно предстану страшному твоему олта[рю]
и безкровную жертву совершу. Яко твоя есть сила и слав[а]
во веки веком. Аминь.

Егда же пристъпит ко святому престолу, диакони отъ[ем]
ше и поднесше святое евангелие напрестольное, дают
целовати архиерееви нъчто сотворше.

Известно буди, яко иереи сослужители обретаются сто[я]
щые окрест престола, обретающе во всю службу иере[и]
совершенно все едино преображаеми на престоловнике
архипрезвитера, или единого от [illegible] иереи.

По целовании же святаго евангелия архидиакон или диа[кон]
взем служебник святительский, держит и приимо архи[ерей]
зстраны левое. тонце чтет сиа молитву сию.

Владыко Господи Вседержителю не хотяй смерти г[решни]
ком, но обращения их, и всем показа нам путь
жизни и спасения, и образ покаяния показав дарова нам врачев[ство]
и милостивецем, подавый врачевство источник слез.
Ты убо владыко и мене ущедри, не помяни моих безчи[сленных]
соблазн, но милостиво прости прегрешения моя. Ты бо
еси безгрешен, и милосерд, и премилостив, каяйся о злобах
человеческих, приемляй поклонение от всея твари твоея
хвалимый непрестанно невидимыми силами, и страшен
херувимом и серафимом, и от тех славы неизреченн[ыя]
приемляй. И паки на земли своею от девы рождся плотию.
исполнения прием, яко агнец незлобив своею кровию, осв[ятив]
шая весь мир, поставлей нам непостыдно рабом твоим
твоя от твоих ти тебе приносити.

Ты и ны[не]

16

Pontificale Ruthenorum

Atq ita ingreditur in Altare, Diaconis manus illius fulcientibus, Ceroferarijs autem ante Regiam Portam Stantibus, et dicit orationem istam:
Domine aufer a me omnes iniquitates meas, et delicta mea, ut digne ingrediar hereditatem Sancte domus tuæ. Domine emitte manum tuam de excelso habitaculo et corrobora me ad propositum ministerium tuum, ut indemnis adsistam tremendo tuo Altari, et incruentum Sacrificium peragam. Quoniam tua est potentia, et gloria in Secula Seculorum. Amen.

Deus noster Chrysostomus

Postquam vero accesserit ad Sacram mensam, Diaconi accepto Sancto Euangelio in mensa iacente, dant illud ad osculandum Pontifici, non aperientes. Sciendum quod Sacerdotes celebrantes in(?) Stantes circum mensam expectantes Pontificem, induti toto amictu Sacerdotali. Iam completo Offertorio in Altari Propositionis per Archipresbyterum, vel vnum ex Sacerdotib.
Post osculum vero S. Euangelij Archidiacony vel Diacony accepto Missali Pontificali tenet illud ex parte sinistra ante Pontificem, ille vero legit tacite orationem istam: Domine Domine omnipotens, qui non vis mortem peccatorum, sed expectas conuersionem illorum qui ostendisti nobis viam nouam et sanctam et exemplar pœnitentiæ demonstrasti antiquis peccatoribus et publicanis, dedisti peccatrici fontem lachrymarum. ijsdem etiam Domine et me parem facias, immemor meorum innumerabilium Scandalorum, sed transpiciens delicta mea.

P. Vit.

Tu enim Solus es Sine peccato et misericors, et totius miserationis, quem penitet super malitias hominum, qui adoraris ab omni Creatura tua, laudaris incessanter a Cælestibus virtutibus, quem timent Cherubim et Seraphim, cuiq illi indicibiliter exhibent famulatum. Atq iterum in terra per temetipsum obtulisti Sacrificium, occisionem Subiens, Sicut Agnus innocens tuo Sanguine Sanctificans totum mundum, iussisti nos indignos Seruos tuos, tua ex tuis tibi offerre.

Ты иныи владыко прѣжде моя прегрешения разрѣшивши вс[ѣ]
моя, и исполни мя твоего хваления. Сердце чисто созижд[и]
во мнѣ Боже и духъ правъ обнови во утробѣ моей, и приими м[я]
дерзающа внити во святилище твое, и вознести тебѣ т[…]
вотъ твоихъ. Яко же предалъ еси святымъ твоимъ ученикомъ
и иже отъ тѣхъ приявше, тайнъ твоей совершители бываютъ.
Не по нашему достоинству, но твоего ради милосердия, сот[…]
владыка чистоту души моея, и спасение отъ плоти моея, и[…]
мя отъ нынѣ сосуды твоего силою, и духовного дѣйствия.
Нѣсть бо ничто утаяющеся отъ тебѣ, но вся обнаженна и с[…]
провиденна яко предъ очима твоима суть. Вѣдая же владыко
яко несоглашанных моихъ зрита очи твои, и въ книгахъ тво[ихъ]
вся написашеся. Тѣмъже не отверзи моего недостоинства
и лица твоего не отвращати отъ мене, да не отвращуся по[…]
срамъ лицъ и стыдъ отъ тебѣ, но сподоби мя поработати
святымъ твоимъ тайнамъ. Яко подобаетъ ти всяка слав[а]
честь и поклонение Отцу и Сыну и Святому Духу. Нынѣ и[…]
Скончавъ же молитву и поклонъшеся исходитъ царскими две[рми]
и восходитъ на амвонъ: диакономъ [два] его подъ руцѣ держ[а]
щимъ: Иереомъ сослужителемъ послѣдствующимъ, ми[…]
тре же святителскую и посохъ носимомъ. И тако ставъ [на]
амвонѣ: Иереи окрестъ амвона станутъ порядъ, посту[пив]
ше ко священнодѣицамъ стоящимъ при царскихъ вратѣхъ. С[то]
ятъ же сами диакони при святителю. Архидиаконъ а[…]
преклонъ главу ко святителю, и взявъ снего мантию
отдаетъ со окрестъ стоящимъ, самъ же даетъ порядъ
одежды церковныя святителеви […] и нань во
возлагаетъ. Одежды же святителския вся прежде уготов:
ванна лежитъ на налоѣ со отъ иного святителя поставлен-
ному.
И абие святитель, знаменуяся глаголетъ: Благословенъ Б[огъ]
нашъ всегда нынѣ и присно и во вѣки вѣкомъ. Аминь.

Pontificale
Spitomum

Tu Domine nunc etiam despiciens mea delicta, aperi os meum, et impleas illud tua laude. Cor mundum crea in me Deus, et Spiritum rectum innoua in uisceribus meis, et Suscipe me qui audeo introire in Sancta tua, et offerre tua ex tuis tibi. Prout tradidisti Sanctis tuis discipulis, et nos ab illis Suscipientes, Sacramenti tui participes efficimur. Non secundum nostrum promeritum, sed propter tuam misericordiam ablue Domine turpitudinem animæ meæ, et maculam carnis meæ, et totum me exaltes, Sanctifices tua potentia, et spirituali dextera. Nihil enim est occultum coram te, sed omnia nuda et aperta coram oculis tuis sunt. Scis quoque Dñe, quia imperfecta mea viderunt oculi tui, et in libro tuo omnia inscribuntur. Propterea non abomineris meam indignitatem, neque faciem tuam auertas a me, ut non reuertar, confusione et sudore repletus à te, sed dignum me facias vt absoluam Sancta tua Sacramenta. Quoniam decet te omnis gloria, honor et adoratio, Patrem et Filium, et Sanctum Spiritum, nunc et semper, et in secula seculorum. Amen.

Finita uero oratione, et facta adoratione, egreditur per Regiam Portam, et ascendit Ambonam, Diaconis quidem manus ipsius fulcientibus, Sacerdotibus uero Concelebrantibus illum subsequentibus; Mitra etiam Pontificalis et Pedum defertur. Atque ita consistit in Ambona: Sacerdotes circumstant Ambonam per ordinem procedentes usque ad Ceroferarios stantes penes Sanctam Portam. Astant uero Pontifici Duo Diaconi. Archidiaconus ergo inclinato capite Pontificem uersus, et tollens ab illo Chlamydem reddit illam circumstantibus. Ipse uero ordine dat vestitum Ecclesiasticum Pontifici, manusque illius deosculans, et illum super imponens. Vestitus uero Pontificalis totus antea exaparatus iacet in pulpito, quod ex parte Sinistra Pontificis collocatur.

Et tunc Pontifex sese signans dicit: Benedictus Deus noster ✠ ubique nunc et semper et in secula seculorum. Amen.

+

Взем стихарь, благословляет, целует, и
возлагает глаголя: Да возрадуется душа моя о
Господе, яко облече мя в ризу спасения, и одеждою веселия одея мя, яко жениху возложи ми венец, и яко невесту
украси мя красотою.

Взем параманъ, глаголет: Рече Господь, иго мое благо,
бремя мое легко есть.

Взем епитрахиль, глаголет: Благословен Бог изли-
вая благодать Свою на иереи Своя, яко миро на главе
сходящее на браду, браду Аароню, сходящее на ометы
одежды его. Яко роса Аермонская сходящая на горы Си-
онские. Яко тамо заповеда Господь, благословение живот в ве[ки].

Взем пояс, глаголет: Благословен Бог препоясуя
мя силою, и положи непорочен путь мой, совершаяй ноз[и]
яко елени, и на высоких поставляяй мя.

Взем поручь десную глаголет: Десница Твоя Господи
прославися в крепости, десная Ти рука Господи со-
круши враги, и множеством славы Твоея стерл еси со-
постаты.

Взем в левою, глаголет: Руце Твои сотвористе мя
и создасте мя, вразуми мя и научуся заповедем Твоим.

Взем полицу прилагает ю ко поясу з десной страны
над коленом глаголя: Препояши меч Твой по бедре
Твоей, сильне, красотою Твоею, и добротою Твоею, и напряцы, и
успевай, и царствуй, истины ради и кротости и правды, и
наставит тя дивно десница Твоя.

Взем саккос [аще есть архиепископ] или фелонь [аще епи-
скоп] глаголет: Иереи Твои Господи облекутся в правду
и преподобнии Твои радостию возрадуются.

Взем омофор глаголет: Се есть образ Сына Божия
собствени действует и оставит овец на горах, и иде на взыс-
кание единой погибшия, и обрет ю взят на рамо свое
и по овцу принесе, и по своему хотению.

Пришитие митру глаголет: Положи на главе моей венец от
камене честна.

+

Sumens Tunicellam, benedicit illam, osculatur, et imponit dicens: Exultat anima mea in domino: induit me vestimento salutari, et tunica letitiæ circumdedit me, et tanquam Sponso imposuit mihi Coronam, et vt Sponsam decorauit me ornamento.

S. Chrysostomus

Sumens humerale dicit: Dixit Dominus † Iugum meum suaue, et onus meum leue est.

Sumens stolam dicit: Benedictus Deus † qui effundit gratiam suam super Sacerdotes eius, vt vnguentum super caput, quod descendit in barbam, barbam Aaron, quod descendit in oram vestimenti eius, vt ros Hermon, qui descendit in montem Sion, quoniam ibi mandauit Dominus benedictionem vitam vsque in seculum.

S. Chrysost.

Sumens Cingulum dicit: Benedictus † Deus, qui cingit me potentiâ et posuit immaculatam viam meam, perficiens pedes meos sicut ceruí, et in excelso collocauit me.

S. Chrysostomus

Sumens Manipulare dextrum dicit: Dextera tua † Domine glorificata est in virtute, Dextera tua manus Domine confregit inimicos, et plenitudine gloriæ tuæ conculcasti aduersantes.

S. Chrysost.

Sumens vero sinistrum dicit: Manus † tuæ fecerunt me et plasmauerunt me, da mihi intellectum, et scrutabor mandata tua.

S. Chrysost.

Sumens Genuale, applicat illud ad cingulum ex parte dextra supra genu dicens. Accingere gladio † tuo super femur tuum potentissime, specie tua et pulchritudine tua, et intende, et procede, et regna, propter veritatem, et mansuetudinem et Iustitiam, et deducet te mirabiliter dextera tua.

S. Chrysost.

Sumens Saccum [si est Archiepiscopus] uel Pluuiale [si Episcopus] dicit: Sacerdotes † tui Domine induentur Iustitiâ, et Iusti tui exultatione exultabunt.

S. Chrysost.

Sumens Pallium dicit: Hæc est † imago Filij Dei, qui dereliquit nonaginta nouem oues in montibus, et venit ad quærendam vnam quæ perierat, et inuenta illa accepit super humeros suos et ad Patrem detulit, et ad suum beneplacitum.

Suscipiens quoque Mitram dicit: Posuit in capite meo coronam de lapide pretioso.

Здѣ аще будут становленници, становит их святитель во диаконство раздѣлно.
Посем архидиакон отходит з амвона, и взем воду у ватных стоящих от олтаря, преходит пред святителя. Ту бо дают воду презвитером начальнейшим прямо себе стоящым, и еще диакони, салие возливает воду на р[уце] святителеви. И он же благословит воду, руце умывает, отирает глаголя.
Умыю в неповинных руце мои, и обыду олтарь твой Господи, еже услышати ми глас хвалы твоея, и повед[ати] вся чудеса твоя. Господи возлюбих благолѣпие дому тв[оего] и мѣсто селения славы твоея, да не погубиши со нечестив[ыми] души моея, и с мужи кровей живота моего, их же в руках беззакония, десница их исполнися мзды. Аз же не з[ло]бием моим ходих. Избави мя Господи и помилуй мя. Нога моя ста на правости во церквах благословлю тя Владыко Господи Боже мой, прости ми грѣшному, и непо[мя]ни беззаконий моих, и сподоби мя неосужденно предст[ати] святому твоему жертвенику, и принести тебе безкровн[ую] жертву. Яко благословен еси во вѣки. Аминь. ≡
Отнуд же руце отрев, возлагает на выю архидиакона держаща воду. Он же отходит во олтарь, и отдав ю понамарю, от него же приемлет кадилницу со фимиамом и став прямо архиерея, преклонь главу глаголет:
Благослови владыко кадило. Он же фимиама благословляет глаголя молитву выше писанную. Кадило ти приносим. Паки архидиакон: О предложенных честных дарех Господу помолимся. Архиерей же благословит предложенная и глаголет молитву сия.
Боже Боже наш, иже небесный хлѣб пищу всего мира Господа нашего и Бога Иисуса Христа, пославый Спаса, и Избавителя и благодѣтеля, благословяща и освящающа нас. Сам благослови предложение сие, и приими е во пренебесный твой жертвеник. Помяни яко благ и человѣколюбец принесших и за их же принесоша, и нас неосужденных сохрани во священнодѣйствии божественных твоих таин. Яко святися и прославися пречестное и великолѣпое имя тв[ое]

≡ Исповѣмь ти ся [illegible] законника честную си правою на царство приготовлен[illegible]
И [illegible] прободен[illegible] безсмертие и оставление еси человѣком, Спасе наш слава тебѣ.

ntificale Pont.mi Hic si adfuerint Ordinandi, ordinat illos Pontifex usque Diaconatum exclusive.
Tum Archidiaconus descendit ex Ambone, et accepta aqua praeparata Hanc extra Altare, accedit ad Pontificem. Tobalcam quidem dat duobus Sacerdotibus primis, ex opposito sibi consistentibus, et peluim Diacono, ipse vero infundit aquam in manus Pontificis. Ille vero benedicit aquam, manus lavat et abstergit, dicens:

S. Chrysost. Lavabo † inter innocentes manus meas, et circumdabo Altare tuum Domine, ut audiam vocem laudis tuae, et enarrem universa mirabilia tua. Domine dilexi decorem domus tuae, et locum habitationis gloriae tuae. Ne perdas cum impijs animam meam, et cum viris sanguinum vitam meam. In quorum manibus iniquitates, dextera eorum repleta est muneribus. Ego autem in innocentia mea ingressus sum, libera me Domine, et miserere mei, pes meus stetit in directo, in Ecclesijs benedicam te Domine. † Domine Domine Deus meus, dimittas mihi peccatori, et non recorderis iniquitatum mearum et dignum me facias irreprehensibiliter assistere sancto tuo Altari. Quonium benedictus es in secula Amen.

Abstersis vero manibus tobalcam imponit collo Archidiaconi tenentis aquam. Ille vero recedit ad Altare, et reddit illam Sacristae, ab illo autem recipit Thuribulum cum Incenso. Et consistens ante Pontificem inclinat caput dicens: Benedic Domine Incensum. Ille autem Thymiama benedicit, dicens orationem suprascriptam. Incensum tibi offerimus. Rursus Archidiaconus: Pro propositis honorabilibus donis Dominum deprecemur. Pontifex vero benedicit proposita et dicit has orationes: Deus Deus noster, qui Caelestem panem cibum totius mundi Dominum nostrum et Deum Jesum Christum misisti Salvatorem et Redemptorem, et benefactorem, benedicentem et Sanctificantem nos tu benedic † oblationem istam, et suscipe ipsam ad super caeleste tuum Sacrarium, memento ut bonus et clemens offerentium, et pro quibus obtulerunt, et nos indemnes custodias, in celebratione divinorum tuorum mysteriorum. Quoniam Sanctificatum et glorificatum est honorabile et magnificum nomen tuum, Patris et Filij et Spiritus Sancti, nunc et semper, et in secula seculorum. Amen.

[Margin:] Redemisti nos a maledictione legis pretioso tuo sanguine, cruci affixus, et lancea perforatus immortalitatem hominibus dedisti, Salvator noster gloria tibi.

S. Chrysost.

+

Владыко Господи Боже нашъ Животъ хотящымъ ми причас-
тити. Не страшнымъ симъ и божественнымъ Тайнамъ страхомъ и сокрушенiемъ
не смѣю ниже очію возвести, ни руцѣ воздвигнути на высоту
Божiю, ни дерзнути сотворити на молбу, и внити внутрь вн-
тонмо iерей единъ единою лѣта вхождаше служащы Священа-
служѣ. Бѣхъ хотѣлъ уподобитися и азъ, но не смѣю прибли-
житися ко Святѣй Трапезѣ сей на нейже хощетъ возлежати а-
гнецъ Сынъ Божiй Iисусъ Христосъ, и раздробитися, и податися въ
на оставленiе грѣховъ, на жизнь вѣчную. Сего ради дерза-
ю служити сему понеже Ты приятъ блуднаго Сына покая-
шагося, и слезами омывшаго стопы Твоея Спаса. И понеже
Ты приятъ разбойника вопиюща по Тебѣ: Помяни мя Господи во царствiи Своемъ, и не поноси ча[ ]ъ со всѣхъ соблазнъ
иныхъ его, но обрати его [illegible]. Да Тебѣ милосердишь и ми-
ложе милость, и приими мя хотящаго причаститися Святѣй Твоей Жертвѣ. Ей молютися Владыко прежде очисти
совѣсть мою, и отими грѣхъ душа моея, и всего мя [ ]
[ ]одъ освятити силою Твоею, да без осужденiя предстан[у]
предъ лицемъ славы Твоея, и достоинъ буду сопричастника
Единороднаго Сына Твоего. Ибоже слава со Отцемъ и
Святымъ Духомъ. Аминь.

Егдаже Святитель глаголетъ Молитвою сию: Архиерей
апонъ кадитъ Святую Трапезу Крестообразно, предло-
женiя, весь олтарь, иконы, Архиерея, всѣхъ сослужащи-
хъ iереовъ и люди, глаголя втай Тропарь сей. Во Гро-
бѣ плотскы, во адѣже со душею яко Богъ, в раиже съ раз-
бойникомъ и на престолѣ бяше Христе со Отцемъ и Духомъ вся
исполняя неописанный. Таже Псаломъ N.

Помилуй мя Боже.

И тако входитъ папа во Святый олтарь, и покадивъ
Святую Трапезу, [illegible] отдаетъ пономарю
Самъже исходитъ отъ олтаря, и [illegible] Святи-
телемъ станетъ [illegible] страны низъ презвитерей.

ntificale
...

Domine Domine Deus noster, nunc volens accedere ad tremendum tuum et mirabile mysterium, timore correptus, non audeo in Cælum oculos elevare, neq manus extendere in excelsa Dei, neq os aperire ad preces, et intrare in domum, quam tantum Sacerdos unus semel in anno ingrediebatur Sacrificium peragens. Cui vellem et ego assimilari. Sed non ausim approximare ad Sanctam mensam hanc, in qua vult reponi Unigenitus Filius Dei Jesus Christus, et frangi, et distribui fidelibus, in remissionem peccatorum in vitam æternam. Propterea Confidens accedo ad Sacrificium hoc. Quoniam tu Suscepisti Prodigum filium pænitentiam agentem, et lachrymis abluentem maculas suas: et quoniam tu Suscepisti Latronem clamantem ad te, memento mei Domine in Regno tuo, et non exprobrasti illi omnia scandala illius, sed induxisti illum in Paradysum. Eâdem ergo misericordia, et mecum facias misericordiam, et suscipe me volentem communicare Sanctum tuum Sacrificium. Ah Supplicio tibi Domine, ante omnia purifices conscientiam meam, et amoue turpitudinem animæ meæ, et totum me prorsus sanctifica potentia, ut irreprehensibiliter consistam ante faciem gloriæ tuæ, et dignus efficiar protectione Unigeniti tui Filij. Qui gloria cum Patre et Sancto Spiritu. nunc &c.

Pontifice vero absoluente orationes prædictas, Archidiaconus incensat S.^m mensam in modum Crucis, Proposita, totum Altare, Imagines, Pontificem, omnes concelebrantes, Ecclesiam et populum. Recitans tacitè Antiphonam hanc. In monumento

S. Chrysost. cum corpore, in Inferno vero cum anima ut Deus, in Paradyso vero cum latrone, et in throno eras Christe cum Patre et Spiritu, omnia implens incircumscriptus.

Dicit etiam psalm. 50. Miserere mei Deus. Atq ita ingreditur rursus Sanctum Altare, et incensat Sanctam Mensam. Thuribulum quidem reddit Sacristæ, ipse vero egreditur ex Altari et caput inclinans coram Pontifice consistit ex parte dextra post Presbyteros.

+

Архиерей же абие совершивъ молитвы преклонь главу
глаголетъ ко сослужителемъ: Простите мя честнии
отцы и благословите елика согрѣшихъ, словомъ, дѣломъ
и помышлениемъ и всѣми моими чювствы.
Иерей же преклоньше главы глаголютъ; Благодатию своею
Богъ да проститъ тя отче святый по вышеписанному.
Архиерей со сослужители знаменуяся глаголетъ по
вышеписанному. Благословенъ Богъ нашъ всегда нынѣ.
Царю небесный.
Творятъ же поклонения трие глаголюще; Слава въ вышнихъ
Богу. и на земли миръ во человецѣхъ благоволения. дважды
Господи устнѣ мои отверзеши и уста моя возвѣ-
стятъ хвалу твою. а҃
Посемъ ко архиерею приступаютъ вси сослужители,
священницы же и диакони порядъ, и на коегождо ихъ гла-
ву кладетъ архиерей руку десную, и тако приимаютъ прощ-
ния, целовавше же руку и поклонившеся отходятъ на мѣста
своя. глаголютъ же.
Сослужители: Время есть сотворити Господеви, владыко святый.
Архиерей. Благословенъ Богъ нашъ всегда нынѣ.
Сослужит. Помолися о мнѣ владыко.
Архиерей. Да исправитъ Господь стопы твоя.
Сослужит. Помяни мя владыко святый.
Архиерей. Да помянетъ тя Господь во царствии своемъ
Сослужители. Аминь.
И тако архипресвитеръ отходитъ во олтарь и ста-
нетъ предъ святою трапезою: архидиаконъ же предъ царски-
ми враты; прочии сослужители окрестъ архиерея
стоящемъ.

nti i cale R. [illegible]

Pontifex itaq completis orationibus, inclinato capite, alloquitur concelebrantes. Absoluite me Venerabiles Patres, et benedicite, in quibus, cunq peccaui, verbo, opere, et cogitatione, et omnibus meis sensibus. Sacerdotes uero inclinato capite dicunt: Gratia Sua Deus absoluat te Pater Sancte. Pontifex cum Concelebrantibus Signans sese dicit, secundum quod supra Scriptum est: Benedictus Deus noster ubiq, nunc. Rex Cælestis. vt supra

Facit quoq adorationes tres dicens Gloria in excelsis Deo et in terra pax hominibus Bonæ voluntatis: bis. Domine labia mea aperies, et os meum annunciabit laudem tuam. semel.

Postea ad Pontificem accedunt omnes Concelebrantes, Sacerdotes et Diaconi per ordinem, et supra cuiuslibet illorum caput ponit Pontifex manum dexteram, et ita accipiunt absolutionem: osculantes uero manum et caput inclinantes recedunt ad loca sua. Dicunt ergo:

S. Chrysost.

Concelebrans: Tempus faciendi Domino, Domine benedic.
Pontifex: Benedictus Deus noster, ubiq nunc.
Concelebrans: Ora pro me Domine.
Pontifex: Dirigat Dominus gressus tuos.
Concelebrans: Recordare mei Sancte Pontifex.
Pontifex: Recordetur tui Dominus in Regno Suo.
Concelebrans: Amen.

Atq ita Archipresbyter recedit ad Altare et consistit ante Sacram Mensam. Archidiaconus uero ante Regiam Portam, alijs Concelebrantibus circum Pontificem stantibus.

Служьба Божаи·
Sacrificium· Divinum·

Служител. Лик.

Архидиакон возглашает; Благослови Владыко.

Архипрезвитер возглас. Архиерей и Иерей ... Благословенно царство, Отца и Сына И Святаго Духа, ныне и присно и во веки веком. Аминь.

Архидиакон: Миром Господу помолимся. Господи пом.

~~[illegible]~~. О свышнем мире и Спасении душ наших Господу помолимся. Госп. Пом

Архиерей Стоящь на амвон. О мире всего мира, Благостояния Святых Божиих церквей и Соединении всех Госп. пом. Госп. П.

О Святом храме сем, и с верою, Благоговением, и страхом Божиим входящих в он Господу помолимся Госп. П.

О ~~[illegible]~~ Митрополите: или Со~~[illegible]~~ ~~[illegible]~~ Архиепископе или Епископе [имя есть слово] нашем Н. честнем презвитерстве, еже о Христе диаконстве, и всем причте и людех Госп. Помол. Госп. П.

О Благоверном и Богохранимом Народе ~~Царе~~ нашем Н. и о всей Палате и воех его Госп. Пом. Госп. П.

О поспешити и покорити под нозе его всякаго врага и супостата Госп. Пом. Госп. Пом.

О Святей обители сей и о всяком граде и стране и верою живущих в них Госп. пом. Госп. Пом.

О Благорастворении воздуха, о изобилии плодов земных и временех мирных Госп. пом. Госп. Пом.

О плавающих, путешествующих, недугующих, страждущихся, плененных и Спасении их Госп. Пом. Госп. Пом.

Chrysostomus 12

Celebrantes		Chorus.
		S. Chrysostomi
Archidiaconus alta voce:	Benedic Domine.	
Archipresbyter alta vo[ce] Pontifex et Sacerdotes missa:	Benedictum Regnum Patris et Filij, et Spiritus Sancti, nunc et semper et in secula seculorum.	Amen.
Archidiaconus:	In pace Dominum deprecemur.	Kyrie Eleyson.
Pontifex sedet in Ambona.	Pro pace quæ sursum est et salute animarum nostrarum Dominum deprecemur.	K. E.
	Pro pace totius mundi, stabilitate Sanctarum Dei Ecclesiarum, et unione omnium, Dñm deprecemur.	K. E.
	Pro Sancta domo ista, et cum fide, innocentia et timore Dei intrantibus in ipsam Dñm deprecemur.	K. E.
~~Illustrissimo~~ [qui celebrat]	Pro Metropolita, vel Archiepiscopo, vel Episcopo nostro N. Venerandis Præsbyteris in Christo Diaconis, pro universo Clero et populo Dñm deprecemur.	~~Reverendissimo~~ K. E.
	Pro Orthodoxo et à Deo custodito Rege nostro N. toto palatio et exercitu ipsius. Dñm deprecemur.	K. E.
	Ut debellet et subijciat sub pedes ipsius omnem inimicum et aduersarium. Dñm deprecemur.	K. E.
	Pro Sancto hoc habitaculo, omni urbe, et Regione, et cum fide habitantibus in ipsis. Dñm deprecemur.	K. E.
	Pro salubritate aëris, fertilitate fructuum terræ et temporibus pacificis Dñm deprecemur.	K. E.
	Pro navigantibus, itinerantibus ægrotantibus laborantibus, captiuis et salute ipsorum Dñm deprecemur.	K. E.

Служение

О избавитися нам от всякия скорби, гнева, беды и нужды, Господу помолимся. — Лики: Гос. пом.
Заступи, спаси, помилуй и сохрани нас, Боже, Твоею благодатию. — Гос. пом.
Пресвятую, пречистую, преблагословенную, славную Владычицу нашу Богородицу и Приснодеву Марию со всеми святыми помянувше, сами себе и друг друга и весь живот наш Христу Богу предадим. — Тебе Господи.

Архиерей и иереи в олтаре молитву. Егда архидиакон глаголет ектению.

Господи Боже наш, Егоже держава несказанна, и слава непостижима, Егоже милость безмерна, и человеколюбие неизреченно. Сам, Владыко, по благоутробию Твоему, призри на ны и на святый храм сей, и сотвори с нами, и с молящимися с нами, богатыя милости Твоя и щедроты Твоя.

Архипресвитер возглас.

Яко подобает Тебе всякая слава, честь и поклонение, Отцу и Сыну и Святому Духу, ныне и присно и во веки веков. — Аминь.

И тако архидиакон преклонь главу ко престолу и святителю, отходит и станет на месте своем. Лики же псалом: Благослови, душе моя, Господа, и вся внутренняя моя имя святое Его, и весь до конца.

Или уставныя антифоны.

Диакон глаголет.

Паки и паки миром Господу помолимся. — Господи пом.
Заступи, спаси... — Гос. пом.
Пресвятую, пречистую... — Тебе Господи.

Chrysostomus

Celebrantes		Chorus.
	Ut liberet nos ab omni tribulatione, ira, periculo et necessitate Dm deprecemur.	S. Chrysostomus Kyrie Eleyson.
	Adiuua, Salua, miserere, et conserua nos Deus tua gratia. Sanctissimæ Intemeratæ superbenedictæ Gloriosæ Reginæ nostræ, Deiparæ et semper Virginis Mariæ cum omnibus SS. memoriam recolentes, nosmetipsos, et inuicem, et totam vitam nostram Christo Deo committamus	K. E. Tibi Domine.
Pontifex et Sacerdotes secreto orat dum dicit Archidiaconus Litanias	Domine Deus noster cuius potentia incomprehensibilis, et gloria incomprehensibilis, cuius misericordia immensa, et pietas ineffabilis. Tu Domine per viscera misericordiæ tuæ, respice super nos, et super Sanctam domum istam, et fac nobiscum et cum orantibus nobiscum opes misericordiæ tuæ et miserationis tuæ.	
Archipresbyter altâ voce	Quoniam decet te omnis gloria, honor et adoratio Patrem et Filium, et Sanctum Spiritum nunc et semper, et in secula seculorum.	Amen.
	Et ita Archidiaconus capite inclinato versus Altare et Pontificem, recedit et stat in loco suo. Chorus autem Psalmum 102 Benedic anima mea Dominum, et omnia interiora mea &c vid. ante.	
Diaconus dicit:	Iterum et iterum in pace Dm deprecemur	Kyrie Eleyson.
	Adiuua, Salua, miserere et cons. &c.	K. E.
	Sanctissimæ intemeratæ &c.	Tibi Domine.

Святитель

Архиерей и Иереи в тай.

Господи Боже нашъ спаси люди своя и благослови достояние твое, исполнение церкви твоея сохрани, освяти любящая благолепие храма твоего. Ты тѣх возпрослави Божественною силою твоею, и не остави насъ уповающихъ на тя.

Архипресвитеръ возгласъ.

Яко твоя держава, и твое есть царство, и сила, и слава, Отца и Сына и Святаго Духа, нынѣ

Аминь

Затѣм Псаломъ Благослови душе моя Господа и весь до конца.

Егда же совершается Псаломъ вторый Иерей поклон сотворивши святителю и митру с него снимъ станет на левой сторонѣ.

Архиерей востав з сѣдалища, и знаменаяся со всеми иереи глаголет в тай [illegible] [illegible].

Пения.

Слава Отцу и Сыну и Святому Духу, и нынѣ и присно и во вѣки вѣковъ. Аминь. Единородный Сыне и Слово Божие, безсмертный сый и изволивый спасения нашего ради воплотитися от Святыя Богородицы и Приснодевы Марии, непреложно вочеловѣчивыйся, распныйся Христе Боже смертию смерть поправый, единъ сый Святыя Троица сопрославляемый Отцу и Святому Духу спаси насъ.

Пришедши митру Архиерей паки садится на сѣдалищи своемъ.

Диаконъ:

Паки и паки миромъ Господу помолимся.

Заступи, спаси.

Пресвятую, чистую.

Господу по[молимся]

Господи помилуй

Тебѣ Господи

Celebrantes

Pontifex et Sacerdotes secrete orant

Domine Deus noster salua populum tuum et benedic hereditati tuæ, plenitudinem Ecclesiæ tuæ custodi, sanctifica diligentes decorem domus tuæ, tu ipsos vicissim glorifica diuinâ tuâ potentiâ, et ne derelinquas nos sperantes in te.

Archipresbyter altâ voce

Quoniam tua potentia et tuum est Regnum, et potestas, et gloria, Patris et Filij et Spiritus Sancti, nunc &c.

Hic Chorus Psalmum 145. Lauda anima mea Dominum, et totum ad finem.

Cum vero finitur Psalmus Sacerdos secundus et Missam accipiens consistit in loco suo: Pontifex autem consurgens ex Faldistorio, et signans se cum omnibus sacerdotibus dicit:

Chorus idem canet: Gloria Patri et Filio et Spiritui Sancto, et nunc et semper, et in sæcula sæculorum Amen. Vnigenite Fili, et Verbum Dei, qui cum sis immortalis, dignatus es salutis nostræ causa, incarnari ex Sancta Dei genitrice, et semper Virgine Maria, incommutabiliter homo factus et crucifixus Christe Deus, morte mortem conculcans. Vnus cum sis ex Sancta Trinitate, con glorificaris Patri et Sancto Spiritui, salua nos.

Cantus

Suscipiens vero Missam Pontifex rursus considet in Faldistorio suo.

Diaconus

Iterum et iterum in pace Dominum populens.

Adiuua, salua &c.

Sanctissimæ, intemeratæ &c.

Chorus

Amen.

Dñe miserere.

Dñe miserere.

Tibi Domine.

Священнодейств.

Лист 4

Архиерей со иереи молитву 3-го

Иже общыя сия и согласныя нам даровавый молитвы, иже двема или трием согласующимся о имени твоем прошения дати обещавый. Сам и ныне раб твоих прошения к полезному исполни, подая нам в настоящем веце познание твоея истины, и в будущем живот вечный даруя...

Архипресвитер возглас. Яко благий и человеколюбец Бог еси и тебе славу возсылаем, Отцу и Сыну и Святому Духу и ныне...

Аминь

Глас ... Блаженна. Во царствии твоем помяни нас Господи. Блажени нищии духом, яко тех есть царство небесное. Блаженни.

Егда же поются Блаженна, диакони со священники поклоньшеся святителеви, исходят во олтарь. Святители и сослужащии ~~...~~ ся святый Параклиз. Архипресвитер взем святое Евангелие и целовав е, дает архидиакону: диаконове приемлют ~~...~~ и тако исходят северными дверьми. Сицевым образом. Предходят свещеносцы. Последствуют диакони пред святым Евангелием. Таже архидиакон идет держа святое Евангелие прямо себе обема руками. Но и архипресвитер поемь идет донележе приидет ко царским дверем. Таже поклоньшеся ко олтарю. Архидиакон со святым Евангелием идет ко святителю, ~~...~~ ~~...~~, целует святое Евангелие.

~~Архидиакон: Благослови владыко святый вход.~~

~~Архиерей: Благословен вход святых твоих всегда ныне.~~

36

Chrysostomus

Celebrantes.

tifex cum Sacerdotib. orat secreto.

Qui communes has et concordes nobis [illegible] gitus es Supplicationes, et qui duobus aut tribus convenientibus in nomine tuo, petitiones tribuere pollicitus es. Tu et nunc Servorum tuorum petitiones ad utilitatem expleas, tribuens nobis in praesenti Seculo cognitionem tuae veritatis, et in futuro vitam aeternam concedens.

chipraesbyter altâ voce.

Quoniam bonus, et pius Deus es, et tibi gloriam damus, Patri et Filio, et Spiritui Sancto nunc et semper et in secula seculorum.

Hic leguntur Beatitudines. In Regno tuo, cum veneris, memento nostri Domine. Beati pauperes Spiritu, quoniam ipsorum est Regnum Caelorum. Beati &c. Cum autem leguntur beatitudines, Diaconi cum Ceroferarijs, venerati Pontificem, ingrediuntur Altare Porta Sancta, et vniti cum Archipraesbytero, adorant Sanctam mensam. Archipraesbyter accepto S. Euangelio, et osculatus illud, dat Archidiacono. Diaconus autem accipit Thuribulum impletum thure. Ac ita egrediuntur Porta Boreali, hoc modo. Praecedunt Ceroferarij, Subsequitur Diaconus incensans ante S. Euangelium. Postea it Archidiaconus tenens S. Euangelium ante se vtraq manu. Sed et Archipraesbyter illum sequitur, donec peruenerint ad Regiam Portam. Vbi adorans Altare Archidiaconus cum S. Euangelio procedit ad Pontificem, ~~et [illegible]~~

~~Qui consurgens ex [illegible] osculatur S. Euangelium.~~

~~Archidiaconus~~ ~~Benedic Domine Sanctum ingressum~~

~~Pontifex~~ ~~Benedictus ingressus S.~~ ~~tuorum [illegible]~~

Chorus.

S. Chrysostomus

Amen.

15

+

Сослужители Лит.

Архиерей молитву от[...]: Владыко Господи Боже наш, поставивый на небесех чины и воинства Ангельская и Архангельская во служение твоея славы, сотвори с входом нашим вход святых Ангел быти, сослужащих нам и сославословящих твою благость.

Яко подобает ти всяка слава, ч[есть].

Таже целует святое Евангелие.

Архидиакон. Благослови владыко святый вход.

Архиерей. Благословен вход святых твоих всегда: и ныне:

Зде аще есть Монастырь и Братии хотящ иноком быти, или инокиня, облачатися иноцы.

Архидиакон же ставь прямо святых врат, возношает мало святое Евангелие:

Архидиакон велегласно. Премудрость, прости.

Зде поется. Приидите поклонимся и припадем ко Христу. Спаси нас Сыне Божий

Пение [аще неделя] Воскресый из мертвых.

[аще праздник] во святых дивен сый.

[аще за усопших] Животом и мертвыми обладаяй.]

Поющих ти Аллилуия, Аллилуия, Аллилуия.

Чтется же и тропари порядок.

Архиерей со всеми сослужителями входит во олтарь вратом под руку от Иерей начальнейших. Архидиакон святое Евангелие полагает на престол и стоит одесную святителя: Иереи окрест престола.

Архиерей молитву. Боже святый, иже во святых почиваяй, иже трисвятым гласом от Серафимов воспеваемый, и от всех небесных сил поклоняемый. Иже от несущаго во бытие приведый всяческая, создавый человека по образу твоему и по подобию, и всяким твоим дарованием украсивый:

Celebrantes		Chorus.
Pontifex secreto orat.	Domine Domine Deus noster, qui constituisti in Cælis ordines et Exercitus Angelorum et Archangelorum ad ministerium tuæ gloriæ, fac cum ingressu nostro ingressum Sanctorum Angelorum fieri, conservientium nobiscum, et simul glorificantium tuam bonitatem. Quoniam decet te omnis gloria &c.	S. Chrysostomus
	Postea osculatur S. Euangelium	
Archidiaconus:	Benedic Domine S. Ingressum.	
Pontifex:	Benedictus ingressus SS.[torum] tuorum, ubiq[ue] nunc &c.	
	Hic si est monasterium et volet esse monachus vel Monacha, induuntur habitu monastico.	
	Archidiaconus autem assistens ante Sanctam Portam elevat parum Euangelium.	
Archidiaconus altâ voce:	Sapientia, Recti.	
Cantus:	Hic canitur. Venite adoremus et procidamus ante Christum, Salua nos Fili Dei [si est dies Dominica] Qui resurrexisti à mortuis [si est alia dies] Qui in Sanctis mirabilis es. [si est pro defunctis] Qui viuorum et mortuorum dominaris] psallentes tibi Alleluia, Alleluia, Alleluia. Leguntur et antiphonæ ex ordine	R. R.
Pontificale Ruthenum		
	Pontifex cum omnibus concelebrantibus ingreditur Altare, fultus manibus Sacerdotum primariorum. Archidiaconus S. Euangelium reponit supra S. Mensam, et consistit ex parte dextra Pontificis, Sacerdotes vero circum Sacram mensam.	S. Cs.
S. Chrysostomus		
Pontifex orat secreto:	Deus Sancte, qui in Sanctis requiescis, qui ter Sancta voce à Seraphim celebraris, et à Cherubim glorificaris, et ab omni Supercælesti potestate glorificaris, Qui ex non ente ad esse produxisti vniuersa, qui creasti hominem ad imaginem tuam et similitudinem et omni tuo dono decorasti:	

Священник. дая просящым премудрость и разум, и непре-
зирая согрешающаго, но полагая на спасение
покаяние: сподобивый нас смиренных и не-
достойных раб твоих и во час сей стати
пред славою святаго твоего жертвенника,
и должное тебе поклонение и славословие
приносити. Сам владыко прими и от уст
нас грешных трисвятое пение, и посети
нас благостию твоею. Прости нам всякое прегрешение вольное и не вольное. Освяти
душа наша и телеса и даждь нам в преподобии
служити тебе во вся дни живота нашего;
Молитвами святыя Богородица, и всех святых от века тебе угодивших.

Прочтение же молитвы, взяв архидиакона:
ист в слананара(?) сосиалвеш(?) со двема све-
щама возжженнома, и дасть м в [illegible] десную
святителеви, целуя ю. И подносит мало святое евангелие. Святитель же благословляет е трижды.

Архиерей. Христе Боже наш Свет истинный, иже
просвещаяй всякаго человека грядущаго в мир.
Да знаменается на нас Свет лица твоего
яко да в нем узрим Свет неприступный.
Направи стопы наша на дело заповедей твоих.
Молитвами пречистыя ти матере и спаси мя(?).
И сотворит трисвятание(?).

Архидиакон. Благослови владыко время трисвятаго.
Святитель же знаменует святым евангелием десною.

Архиерей. Отца и Сына и Святаго Духа Един
Бог во трех лицах, во трех собствах и
составех, едино Божество и едино существо.
И абие архиерей целует святое евангелие
диакони же полагают е. потребою(?) на
святей трапезе.

Celebrantes. Qui das petenti Sapientiam et prudentiam et non despicis peccantem, sed constituisti ad salutem pænitentiam. Qui dignatus es nos humiles et indignos famulos tuos etiam in hora hac assistere in conspectu Gloriæ sancti tui Altaris, et debitam tibi venerationem et glorificationem proferre. Tu Domine suscipe etiam ex ore nostro qui peccatores sumus Trisagium hymnum, et respice nos bonitate tua, dimitte nobis omne delictum voluntarium et involuntarium, Sanctifica nostras animas et corpora et concede nobis in Sanctitate servire tibi omnibus diebus vitæ nostræ, precibus Sanctiss.[me] Deigenitricis, et omnium Sanctorum qui à seculo tibi complacuerunt. Chorus

Lecta vero oratione, accipit Archidiaconus apud Sacristiam Tricerio, cum duabus candelis accensis, et dat illud in manum dexteram Pontificis, osculans illum: et parum elevat S.[m] Euangelium Pontifex autem benedicit illud ter: P. Rus.

Pontificale Prut.

Pontifex. Christe ✝ Deus noster, Lux vera, illuminans omnem hominem venientem in hunc mundum. Signetur ✝ super nos lumen vultus tui, ut in illo videamus lumen inaccessibile. Dirige ✝ Gressus nostros in opus mandatorum tuorum, precibus intemeratæ tuæ matris et salva nos. I

Et reddit Tricerium.

Archidiaconus Benedic Domine Tempus Trisagy.

Pontifex vero signat S. Euangelium dexterâ

Pontifex Secreto Patrem ✝ et Filium et Sanctum Spiritum, simul, Deū adoramus. in tribus personis et subsistentys, unam divinitatem et unam ~~essentiam~~ substantiam.

Tunc Pontifex osculatur S. Euangelium, Diaconi autem reponunt illud prout et prius in sancta mensa

Служитель | Лик

Архидиакон: Господу помолимся | Господи помилуй

Святитель совращается лицем на запад, стоя во святых вратех:

Архиерей возглас: Яко свят еси Господи Боже наш и тебе славу возсылаем, Отцу и Сыну и Святому Духу ныне и присно

Архидиакон: И во веки веком. | Аминь.

Певчие: Зде поют трисвятое. Святый Боже, Святый Крепкий, Святый Безсмертный, помилуй нас.

Но и Святитель совращшеся ко олтарю три поклоны творит со сослужители, глаголя втай трижды: Святый Боже и пр. Тогда Архидиакон дает Святителю трисвещник со трема свещами возжженными и целует десницу его: Вси же сослужители поют, Святый Боже. Святитель же совращся на запад и став во царских вратех, трисвещнем благословляет вся люди, держа левою посох святительский.

Архиерей: Господи Господи призри с небесе и виждь, и посети виноград сей, и соверши его же насади десница твоя. Виждь [illegible] десная твоя на [illegible], и на Сына человеческаго его же утвердил еси себе. Господи Боже сил обрати ны просвети лице твое на ны и спасени будем. Троице Пресвятая, Отче, Сыне, и Святый Душе, призри с небесе святаго твоего и благослови всех нас

Святитель же совращается и отходит со трисвещником по горнему месту под [illegible] диакона:

Архидиакон: Повели владыко.

Архиерей: Повелением Господним небеса утвердишася.

Архидиакон: Благослови владыко престоловозношение сие.

Архиерей: Благословен грядый во имя Господне

Архидиакон: Благослови владыко горнее седалище.

Архиерей: Благословен еси на престоле славы царствия твоего, седяй на херувимех. Ныне [illegible]

Chrysost. +

Celebrantes		Chorus.
Archidiaconus	Dominum deprecemur.	S. Chrysostomus
	Tunc Pontifex conuersus facie ad Populum consistit in Sancta porta.	
Pontifex: altâ uoce	Quoniam Sanctus es Domine Deus noster, et tibi gloriam damus, Patri et Filio, et Sancto Spiritui nunc et semper.	
Archidiaconus:	Et in secula saeculorum.	Amen.
Cantus	Hic canitur ter: Sancte Deus, Sancte fortis, Sancte immortalis, miserere nobis.	
...ificale Ruthenum	Sed et Pontifex conuersus ad Altare adorationem exhibet ter et idem dicit Sancte Deus. Tunc Archidiaconus dat Pontifici Tricerium cum tribus candelis accensis, et osculatur manum illius dextram, omnes uero Concelebrantes canunt: Sancte Deus &c. Pontifex uero conuersus ad populum et consistens in Regia Porta ter benedicit candelis homines, tenens laeua manu Pedum Pontificale.	P. Rut.
Pontifex:	Domine ✝ Domine, respice de Caelo et vide et visita, vineam tuam et perfice, quam plantauit dextera tua. Sit manus illa dextera Supra virum, et Supra Filium hominis, quem confirmasti tibi. Domine ✝ Deus virtutum conuerte nos, illumines vultum tuum Super nos, et Saluabimur. Trinitas ✝ Sanctissima, Pater, Fili, et Sancte Spiritus, respice de Caelo Sancto tuo et benedic nos omnes.	
S. Chrysostomus	Pontifex uero reuertitur, et recedit cum Tricerio uersus Altare Propositionis, Subnixus manibus Diaconorum.	S. Ch.
Archidiaconus:	Iube Domine.	
Pontifex:	Iussu Domini Caeli firmati Sunt.	
Archidiaconus:	Benedic Domine hac proposita.	
Pontifex:	Benedictus ✝ qui venit in nomine Domini.	
Archidiaconus:	Benedic Domine Superiorem Sedem.	
Pontifex:	Benedictus ✝ es in Throno Gloriae Regni tui, qui Sedes supra Cherubim, nunc &c.	

Служитель.

Литъ:

Святителеви последствуютъ оси Іереи престо-
лообразно. Сирѣчь. Стоящіи одесныя страны престола, на лѣвою же царскими двери и
престоломъ цртъ, а з лѣвое наршеднию, и тако
станутъ сопристь Святителя, внутрь олтаря.
Внегда же отходитъ Святитель внутрь олтарь

Пѣние

Поется: Слава Отцу и Сыну и Святому Ду-
ху, нынѣ и присно и во вѣки вѣкомъ. Аминь.
Святый безсмертный помилуй насъ.
Паки Сослужители поютъ: Святый Боже. т҃і.
Святитель же ставъ предъ сѣдалищемъ своимъ,
Благословляетъ трижды престолъ трисвѣщ-
никомъ глаголя молитву вышеписанную:
Господи, Господи призри т҃і.

Пѣние.

Паки поется. Святый Боже т҃і.
Тогда диаконъ преклонь главу ко престолу
и Святителеви, держа въ рукахъ Апостолъ, исходитъ изъ олтаря. Сиверными дверми,
и ставъ предъ царскими поклонъ сотворяетъ.

Архидиаконъ возглашаетъ: Исъ полла ети деспота. Вонмемъ.

Архиерей. Миръ всѣмъ.

Диаконъ. И со духомъ твоимъ. Прокименъ г҃.

Пѣние. Поетъ же ся Прокименъ тогда [illegible].

Архидиаконъ. Премудрость. Диаконъ, надписание Апостола.

Архидиаконъ. Вонмемъ. Диаконъ четъ Апостолъ, и аще
служится праздникъ сей, два Апостола четъ.
Внегда же четъся Апостолъ, два священницы началнѣйшие приступаютъ ко Архиере-
ови: поклоньше же ся, и Омофоръ надъ поленома
цѣловавше снимаютъ и со Святителя.

Архи

Celebrantes. | Chorus.

Pontificale R. | P. Rut.

Pontificem uero subsequuntur omnes Sacerdotes in modum Crucis. Hoc est, qui stant ex parte dextra Sacrae mensae, ad sinistram per Sacram mensam et portam procedunt, ex parte sinistra ad dexteram, et ita circumsistunt Pontificem intra Altare.

Cum autem recedit Pontifex intra Altare, canitur: Gloria

Cantus: Patri et Filio, et Sancto Spiritui nunc et semper, et in secula seculorum. Amen. Sancte immortalis, miserere nobis. Tum concelebrantes canant semel:

Sancte Deus &c. Pontifex uero consistens ante sedem suam benedicit ter Altare Triceris dicens orationem suprascriptam:

Domine, Domine, respice &c. Et reddit Tricerium Archidiacono, hic autem Sacristae, et consedet.

Cantus: Canitur rursus Sancte Deus &c.

Tunc Diaconus capite inclinato uersus Sacram mensam et Pontificem habens in manibus librum Epistolarum, egreditur ex Altari Porta Septentrionali, et consistens ante Regiam facit adorationem

Chrysostomus | S. Chrysost.

Archidiaconus altâ voce: In multos annos Domine. Attendamus.

Pontifex: Pax omnibus.

Diaconus: Et cum Spiritu tuo. Versiculus.

Cantus: Canitur ter versiculus idem.

Archidiaconus altâ voce: Sapientia.

Diaconus: Titulum Epistolae.

Archidiaconus: Attendamus. Diaconus legit Epistolam. Et si festum aliquod occurreret etiam duas Epistolas legit. Cum autem legitur Epistola, duo Sacerdotes Primarii accedunt ad Pontificem; Veneratione vero exhibita et Pallium supra genua osculati deponunt illud ex Pontifice.

+

Служебник(?) — Литургие(?)

Архиерей Молитву. Господи Боже наш, благослови + Совершенныя Сия Царстия, и сподоби их во преподобии и правде славити тебе. Нын.

Целует Омофор Святитель, и приемше возлагает и на левое рамо Архидиакони. И там Совершается Апостол.

Архиерей. Мир + ти.

Архидиакон. И со духом твоим. Псалом Давидов Аллилуиа. — Аллилуиа трижды

И поклоньшеся паки возвращается во олтарь Совершенныи братии, и поклон сотворше Архиерею Апостол отлагает на место свое. Посем Архидиакон взем от пана- маре кадильницу и фимиам, приходит ко Святителеви.

Архидиакон. Благослови Владыко кадило.

Архиерей. Кадило ти + приносим. Х.

Взятоже прощения Архидиакон кадит по первому чину начинаем службу Божию.

Архиерей Молитву. Воссия во сердцех наших Человеколюбче Владыко нетленный свет Богоразумия твоего и мысленныя наша отверзи очи, во еже разумети евангельския твоя проповедания. Вложиже в нас и страх блаженных твоих заповедей да плотския похоти вся поправше, духовное жительство пройдем, вся яже ко благоугождению твоему и мудрствующе и деюще. Ты бо еси просвещение душ и телес наших Христе Боже наш, и тебе славу возсылаем со Отцем и Сыном и Святым Духом. Нын.

Архидиакон кадит и кадильницу отдав диакону станет у престола: и взем обема рукама Святое Евангелие, держит е прямо себе.

Celebrantes		Chorus.
Pontifex: Pontificale Ruthen.	Domine Deus noster benedic ✝ Reverendos hos Sacerdotes, et dignos illos facias in sanctitate et Justitia laudare te nunc &c.	P. Ruth.
	Osculatur Pallium Pontifex. Sacerdotes uero imponunt illud supra dextrum brachium Archidiaconi. Interim finit Epistola.	
Chrysostomus. Pontifex	Pax ✝ tibi.	S. Chry.
Diaconus	Et cum Spiritu tuo. Psalmus Dauid.	Alleluia, Alleluia Alleluia.
	Et exhibita adoratione recepti reuertitur ad altare sub... tronali porta, et capite inclinato versus Pontificem, Epistolarium ponit in loco suo. Tum Archidiaconus accipit apud Sacristam Thuribulum et Thymiama accedit ad Pontificem.	
Archidiaconus:	Benedic Domine Thymiama.	
Pontifex:	Incensum ✝ tibi offerimus. &c.	
	Et accepta benedictione Archidiaconus incensat secundum prius, prout, dum inciperet sacrificium Diuinum.	
Pontifex orat: S. Chrysostomus	Illucescat in cordibus nostris, Clementissime Domine incorruptibilis lux Diuinae scientiae tuae, et intellectuales nostros aperi oculos, ad intelligendum Euangelicam tuam praedicationem. Immitte quoque nobis timorem beatissimorum tuorum mandatorum, ut carnis concupiscentijs omnibus deuictis, spiritualem vitam transigamus omnia ad beneplacendum tibi et sapientes et facientes. Tu enim es illuminatio animarum et corporum nostrorum Christe Deus noster, et tibi gloriam damus, Patri et Filio et Sancto Spiritui. nunc &c.	S. Chrysost.
	Archidiaconus incensans et thuribulum reddens Diacono consistit ante mensam. Et accipiens utraque manu S. Euangelium tenet illud ante se.	

Святители Архидиакон возглашает. Благослови Владыко благовестити Святаго, Славнаго и всехвальнаго Апостола и Евангелиста Христова N. Аминь

Архиерей возглас. Бог за молитв Святаго Славнаго и всехвальнаго Апостола и Евангелиста Христова N. да даст ти глагол благовествующом силою многою во исполнение возлюбленнаго Сына своего, Господа нашего Иисуса Христа.

Архидиакон аки царь Святыми враты со Евангелием, предходящим ему Священослужителем, и диакон со кадилницею, и станет на амвоне, и полагает Святое Евангелие на налой, от Пономаря прежде приуготованном. Станут же вместо налоя Священослужители. Но и диакон надевает прямо Архидиакона и Евангелия. Архипресвитер митру со Святителя взяв держит ю аж до скончания Евангелия.

Диакон. Премудрость, прости, услышим Святаго Евангелия.

Архидиакон. От N. Святаго Евангелия чтение. — Слава тебе Господи

Диакон. Вонмем. Архидиакон чтет С. Евангелие. Архиерею стоящу и посох левою держащу.

Архиерей по Евангелии. Мир ти. И митру приимает от Архипресвитера.

Архидиакон. И со духом твоим. — Слава тебе Господи

И идет з амвона по Святителем вратам: Но и Архиерей исходит прямо ему и приимет Святое Евангелие, и целовав поставляет е. на престоле. Тогда Иереи идут Ко Святителю по первому чину образно ли- мо ходяще себе, межи престолом и Святилищем Святительским, и тако станут опрест престола. Архидиакон же поклон сотворивше обращается от царских врат и станет на амвоне.

Celebrantes.	+	Chorus.
Archidiaconus alta voce:	Benedic Domine Euangelizare Sanctum, gloriosum et laudabilissimum Apostolum et Euangelistam Christi N.	
Chrysostomi vero Pontifex alta voce:	Deus precibus Sancti gloriosi et laudabilissimi Apostoli et Euangelistae Christi N. det tibi verbum Annunciatori cum magna virtute ad complendum Euangelium dilecti Filij Sui Domini nostri Jesu Christi.	
... Euangelizanti		
	Et procedit per S. Portam cum Euangelio, antecuntibus Ceroferarijs, et Diacono cum Thuribulo. Et consistit in Ambona, et ponit S. Euangelium in pulpito à Sacrista priusquam veniret ibi collocato. Circumstant vero Pulpitum Ceroferarij. Sed et Diaconus incensat versus Archidiaconum et Euangelium. Archipresbyter Infula Pontificis aperta tenet illam usq ad finem Euangelij.	
...conus alta voce:	Sapientia recti audiamus Sanctum Euangelium.	
Archidiaconus:	Ex N. Sancti Euangelij Lectio.	Gloria tibi Dne.
Diaconus:	Attendamus.	
	Archidiaconus legit S. Euangelium: Et si fuerit festum aliquod, legit duo Euangelia. Pontifice stante et Pedum sinistra tenente.	
Pontifex post Euangelium:	Pax + tibi.	
Archidiaconus secreto	Et cum Spiritu tuo.	Gloria tibi Domine.
	Et procedit ex Ambona versus Sanctam Portam. Sed et Pontifex progreditur versus Archidiaconum. Et suscipiens sanctum Euangelium, et osculatus illud, collocat illud in S. mensa.	
	Tunc Sacerdotes procedunt ad Pontificem sicut prius in modum Crucis transeuntes semetipsos inter S. Mensam et Sedem Pontificis. Atq ita capite inclinato stabunt circum S. Mensam. Archidiaconus autem facta adoratione revertitur à S. Porta et stabit in Ambona.	

Сослужащіи
Архидіаконъ. Рцѣмъ вси по всѣхъ
от всея душа и от всего помышленія
нашего рцѣмъ вси

Литв. Господи пом.

Господи Вседержителю Боже отецъ нашихъ,
Молимъ тися услыши и помилуй. — Г. П.

Помилуй насъ Боже по велицѣй милости твоей
Молимъ тися Господи услыши и помилуй. — Г. П.

Госп. Пом. 3

Посемъ Архидіаконъ взявъ омофоръ з шийки
своея, приймаетъ и обѣма рукама и развширенъ
держитъ прямо себѣ.

Архидіаконъ. Еще молимся о благовѣрномъ и Богохранимомъ
великомъ Королѣ нашемъ Х. о державѣ, побѣдѣ,
пребываніи, мирѣ, здравіи, спасеніи, сохра-
неніи грѣховъ его. И о еже Господу Богу
нашему, наипаче поспѣшити и пособити ему
во всемъ, и покорити подъ нозѣ его всякого врага и супостата, Молимъ тися Господи услыши
и помилуй.

И абие сослужителіи поютъ во олтари три-
кратъ: Господи помилуй. — Госп. Поми

Святитель же пріимъ от діакона Сосудникъ
со обѣма свѣщама розвѣтвеныма обращаетъся
ко народу, и ставъ во святыхъ вратѣхъ, лѣвою убо
держитъ посохъ, а десною знаменуетъ осѣняя:
нимъ люди [трижды] по крестописаньно.

Архіерей. Господи † спаси царя и услыши его во онь
же день аще призовемъ тя.

Обращшися и ставъ у престола чтетъ молитву:

Господи Боже нашъ прилежное сіе моленіе
пріими от своихъ рабъ, и помилуй насъ по множеству милости твоея, и щедроты твоя низпосли на ны, и на вся люди твоя ожидающихъ
от тебе богатыя милости.

S. Chrysost.

Celebrantes.		Chorus.
		S. Chrysost.
Archidiaconus:	Dicamus omnes ad Dominum.	Kirie Eleyson.
	Ex tota anima, et ex tota mente nostra dicamus omnes.	K. E.
	Domine omnipotens Deus Patrum nostrorum quæsumus te exaudi et miserere.	K. E.
	Miserere nostri Deus, secundum magnam misericordiam tuam, quæsumus te Domine exaudi et miserere.	Kirie Eleyson 3
	Postea Archidiaconus tollens omoforion ex manu sua sinistra, suscipit illud utraque manu et extensum tenet ante se.	
Archidiaconus:	Etiam quæsumus pro orthodoxo, et a Deo custodito magno Rege nostro N. pro potentia, victoria, permansione, pace, sanitate, salute ipsius. Et ut Dominus Deus noster in maius cooperetur, et dirigat ipsum in omnibus, et subiciat sub pedes ipsius omnem inimicum et hostem. quæsumus te Domine exaudi et miserere.	
	Tunc concelebrantes canunt intra Altare ter: Kyrie Eleyson	Kyrie Eleyson. 3
	Pontifex vero accepto a Diacono Tricerio cum duabus tantum candelis accensis, convertitur versus populum. Et consistens in Sancta Porta, sinistra quidem tenet Dicerium, dextra vero benedicit Tricerio populum ter, secundum quod supra scriptum est.	
Pontifex: Pontif. Antonin	Domine ✠ salvum fac Regem N. et exaudi illum in die qua invocaverit te.	P. Ant.
	Conversusque et consistens ante Sacram Mensam legit orationem: Domine Deus noster, intensam hanc	S. Chry.
S. Chrysost.	supplicationem suscipe a servis tuis et miserere nostri secundum multitudinem misericordiæ tuæ, et miserationes tuas mitte super nos, et super omnem populum tuum expectantem a te opes misericordiæ.	

Служители.

Архидиаконъ: Еще молимся о ~~преосвященнѣйшемъ~~ Митропо-
литѣ: или ~~[illegible]~~ Архиепископѣ, или о
Епископѣ [что есть служба] нашемъ N. о еже избавитися ему отъ всякія скорби, гнѣва, бѣды
и нужды, всякія сопротивныя вещи, и проститися всякому прегрѣшенію его вольному и
невольному, Молимътися Господи услыши и помилуй. — Литія. Господи. пом.

Паки Служители поютъ трижды Господи помилуй.
~~Ар~~ Святитель же благословляетъ трапезу престолъ по предписанному.

Архиерей. Господи спаси + вселенскаго Архиерея [аще
служба есть Митрополита: аще ли инъ, глаголетъ]
преосвященнаго Митрополита] нашего N. и
услыши его во нь же день аще призовемъ тя.
И сконьчавъ отдаетъ остальнымъ диакономъ.
Архидиаконъ же паки омофоръ полагаетъ на
шею свою по первому. И аще есть Монастырь гдѣ служитъ Святитель.

Архидиаконъ. Еще молимся о ~~[illegible]~~ [честнѣйшемъ] отцѣ нашемъ
Архимандритѣ N. о здравіи и спасеніи, и
оставленіи грѣховъ его рцемъ вси. — Госп. пом.
Еще молимся о благочестивыхъ ктиторѣхъ:
~~дѣхъ~~ святыя обители сея, о давшихъ вклады
N.N. о здравіи и спасеніи. — Госп. Пом.
Служащіи глаголютъ всегда вспоминая:
бывшихъ Святителей.
Еще молимся о отцѣхъ нашихъ духовныхъ,
и всей еже о Христѣ братіи нашей о здравіи и спа[сеніи]. — Госп. Пом. г.
Еще молимся о всѣхъ служащихъ и послу-
жившихъ во святѣй обители сей, о здравіи и спа[сеніи]. — Госп. Пом. г.
Еще молимся о предстоящихъ людѣхъ, и
чающихъ еже отъ тебе богатыя милости,
о здравіи и спасеніи. — Госп. Пом. г.
Еще молимся за все братство наше за
творящихъ намъ милостыню, за вся православныя Христіаны о здравіи и спасеніи. — Госп. Пом. г.

Celebrantes. | Chorus.

Archidiaconus: Pontificale Ruthenorum

Etiam quæsumus pro Metropolita, uel, Archiepiscopo, uel, Episcopo [qui celebrat] nostro N. ut liberetur ab omni tribulatione, periculo, et necessitate, et ab omnibus contrarijs, et dimittantur omnia delicta illius, voluntaria et inuoluntaria, quæsumus te Domine exaudi et miserere.

Rursus Concelebrantes canunt ter: Kyrie Eleyson. — Kyrie Eleyson 3

Pontifex autem benedicit ter Sacram Mensam secundum prius scripta.

Pontifex: Domine Saluum fac œcumenicum Pontificem N. [Si celebrans est Metropolita. Quod si alius, dicit: Ill.^m Metropolitam] nostrum N. et exaudias illum in die qua inuocauerit te.

Quo finito reddit Tricerium Diacono. Archidiaconus autem rursus super humerale reponit supra brachium suum sinistrum secundum prius.

Quodsi uero sit Monasterium ubi celebrat Pontifex.

Archidiaconus: Etiam quæsumus pro R.^{do} Patre nostro Abbate N. pro Sanitate, et Salute et remissione peccatorum illius, quæsumus te Domine exaudi et miserere. — Kyrie Eleyson 3

Etiam quæsumus pro orthodoxis Fundatoribus Sanctæ habitationis huius, pro Seruis Dei N.N. pro Sanitate et Salute.

Hæc autem dicit ubique facta commemoratione Pontificis.

Etiam quæsumus pro Patribus nostris Spiritualibus et omnibus in Christo Fratribus nostris, pro Sanitate et Salute. — Kyrie eleyson 3

Etiam quæsumus pro omnibus inseruientibus, et qui inseruierunt in hoc Sancto Habitaculo pro Sanitate et Salute. — K. E. 3

Etiam quæsumus pro circumstante populo et expectante à te diuitem misericordiam, pro Sanitate et Salute. — K. E. 3

Etiam quæsumus pro tota confraternitate nostra pro benefactoribus nostris, pro omnibus orthodoxis Christianis, pro Sanitate et Salute. — K. E. 3

Служители.

Архиерей возглас. Яко милостив и человеколюбец Бог еси, и тебе славу возсылаем Отцу и Сыну и Святому Духу, ныне и присно и во веки веков. — Аминь.

Аще есть служба Божия за усопшаго. — Аминь.

Архидиакон. Помилуй нас Боже по велицей милости твоей, молимтися, Господи услыши и помилуй. — Господи помилуй.

Еще молимся о покои блаженныя памяти, и оставлении грехов, преждепочившаго и ныне поминаемаго раба Божия N. и о еже проститися ему всякому прегрешению вольному и невольному, рцем вси. — Госп. пом. г

Яко да Господь Бог учинит дух его идеже праведнии почивают, Господу помолимся. — Госп. пом. г

Милость Божию и царство небесное и оставление грехов испросивше ему, сами себе и друг друга, и весь живот наш Христу Богу предадим. — Тебе Господи

Господу помолимся. — Госп. Пом. [illegible]

Архиерей тайно молитву. Боже духов и всякия плоти, смерть поправый, диавола упразднивый, и живот миру твоему даровавый. Сам покой Господи душу усопшаго раба твоего N. на месте светле, на месте злачне, на месте покойне. отнюдуже отбеже болезнь, печаль и воздыхание. Всякое прегрешение содеянное им, словом или делом или помышлением, яко благ и человеколюбец Бог прости. Яко несть человека иже жив будет и не согрешит. Ты бо един кроме греха еси, правда твоя, правда во веки, и слово твое истина.

Возглас. Яко ты еси живот, покой, и воскресение преждепочившому и ныне поминаемому рабу твоему N. Христе Боже наш и тебе славу возсылаем со безначальным ти Отцем, и всесвятым благим и животворящим ти Духом. ныне. — Аминь.

Chrysostomus

Celebrantes		Chorus.
Pontifex altâ voce:	Quoniam misericors et Clemens Deus es, et tibi gloriam damus, Patri et Filio et Sancto Spiritui nunc et semper et in secula seculorum	Amen.
	Quodsi est sacrificium Divinum pro defunctis,	
Archidiaconus: Pontificale Ruthenum	Miserere nostri Deus, secundum magnam misericordiam tuam, quæsumus Dne exaudi et miserere.	Kyrie eleyson. ter. R. Ruthenum
	Etiam quæsumus pro requie beatæ memoriæ, et remissione peccatorum, præmortui, cuius nunc memoriam agimus servi Dei N. et ut dimittantur illi omnia delicta voluntaria et involuntaria, dicamus omnes	Kyrie eleyson. ter.
	Ut Dominus Deus collocet spiritum illius, ubi omnes Iusti quiescunt Dm deprecemur	Kyrie eleyson. ter.
	Pro misericordia Divina, et Regno Cælorum et remissione peccatorum illius supplicantes nosmetipsos et invicem, et totam vitam nostram Deo committamus.	Tibi Domine.
	Dominum deprecemur.	Kyrie Eleyson 12
Pontifex secreto orat:	Deus spirituum et omnis carnis, qui mortem vicisti, diabolum sustulisti, et vitam orbi tuo donasti. Tu Domine colloca animam demortui servi tui N. in loco lucido, in loco ameno, in loco quieto, unde fugit dolor, labor, et gemitus. Omnia delicta commissa per illum, verbo aut opere, aut cogitatione, ut bonus et Clemens Deus dimitte. Quia non est homo qui vixit et tibi non peccavit. Tu enim solus nullius es conscius peccati; Iustitia tua Iustitia in æternum, et verbum tuum veritas.	
Altâ voce.	Quoniam tu es vita, Requies et Resurrectio præmortui, cuius nunc memoriam agimus servi tui N. Christe Deus noster, et tibi gloriam damus cum æterno tuo Patre, et cum Sanctissimo, optimo et vivificante tuo Spiritu, nunc.	Amen.

Служители. Архидиакон возглашает. — Во блаженное успение, во вечный покой преставльшимся ... рабом Божиим N. вечная память. — Лик: Вечная память.

Таже глаголет на ексапостиларий ... по первом оглашении возглас.

Помолитеся оглашеннии Господеви. — Господи помилуй.

Вернии за оглашенных помолимся, яко да Господь помилует их. — Госп. пом.

Огласит их словом истины. — Госп. пом.

Открыет им евангелие правды. — Госп. пом.

Соединит их святей своей соборней и апостольстей церкви. — Госп. пом.

Спаси, помилуй, заступи и сохрани их Боже твоею благодатию. — Госп. пом.

Оглашеннии главы ваша Господеви приклоните. — Тебе Господи.

Архиерей тайно. Господи Боже наш, иже на высоких живый и на смиренныя призираяй, иже спасение роду человеческому ниспославый единороднаго твоего Сына и Бога, Господа нашего Иисуса Христа, призри на рабы своя оглашенныя, приклонившыя тебе своя выя, и сподоби их во время благополучно бани пакибытия, оставления грехов, и одежды нетления. Соедини их святей твоей соборней и апостольстей церкви, и сопричти их избранному твоему стаду.

Архиерей возглашает. Да и тии с нами славят пречестное и великолепое имя твое, Отца и Сына и Святаго Духа ныне. — Аминь.

Таже иереи простирают антимин на престоле.

Архидиакон. Елицы оглашеннии изыдите.

Диакон: Оглашеннии изыдите. Елицы оглашеннии изыдите.

Celebrantes.		Chorus.
Archidiaconus altâ voce:	Beatæ obdormitionis in æterna requie defunctorum, cuius nunc memoriam agimus Servi Dei N. æterna memoria.	Æterna memoria. ter.
	Hæc autem dicit in quolibet Sacro post primam Pontificis altâ voce pronunciationem.	
Chrysost.	Deprecemini Catechumeni Dominum.	S. Chrysost. Kyrie eleyson
	Fideles pro Catechumenis deprecemini ut Dominus misereatur ipsorum.	K. E.
	Infundat ipsis Verbum Veritatis.	K. E.
	Aperiat ipsis Evangelium Iustitiæ.	K. E.
	Vniat ipsos Sanctæ Suæ Catholicæ et Apostolicæ Ecclesiæ.	K. E.
	Salva, miserere, adiuva et conserva ipsos Deus tua gratia.	K. E.
	Cathechumeni capita vestra Dño humiliate.	Tibi Domine.
Pontifex Secreto:	Domine Deus noster, qui in altis habitas, et humilia respicis, qui Salutem generi humano misisti Vnigenitum Filium tuum, et Deum Dnum nrum Iesum Christum. Respice Servos tuos Catechumenos, inclinantes tibi suam cervicem, et dignos facias ipsos in tempore opportuno lavacro Regenerationis, remissionis peccatorum, et indumenti Incorruptionis. Vnias ipsos Sanctæ tuæ et Apostolicæ Ecclesiæ, et adnumeres illos electo tuo gregi.	
Archipræsbyter altâ voce:	Vt et ipsi nobiscum glorificent venerabile et magnificum Nomen tuum, Patris et Filij et Spiritus Sancti nunc.	Amen.
	Hic Sacerdotes extendunt Corporale supra Sacram Mensam.	
Archidiaconus:	Quicunq́ estis Catechumeni, exite.	
Diaconus:	Catechumeni exite, quicunq́ estis Catechumeni, exite.	

Служители

Архидиаконъ. Да ни что сотъ соглашенныхъ, Лицы обрьвнши

Паки и паки миромъ Господу помолимся. — Мирь

О свышнемъ мирѣ и спасении душъ нашихъ — Господи по[милуй]

Господу помолимся. — Госп. Пом.

О мирѣ всего мира, благостояніи святыхъ

Божіихъ церквей и соединеніи всѣхъ, Господу пом. — Госп. Пом.

О святѣмъ храмѣ семъ, и со вѣрою, благого:

вѣніемъ и страхомъ Божіимъ входящихъ въ онь

Господу помолимся. — Госп. Пом.

Заступи спаси помилуй и сохрани насъ Боже,

твоею благодатію. — Госп. Пом.

Премудрость.

Архиерей тай молитв:

Благодаримъ тя Господи Боже силъ сподобль:
шаго насъ предстати нынѣ святому твоему жер:
твеннику, и припасти ко щедротамъ твоимъ, о
нашихъ согрѣшенияхъ и о людскихъ невѣдѣ:
ніяхъ. Пріими Боже молитву нашу, и со:
твори насъ достойныхъ быти. Еже приносити тѣ:
бѣ моления и молитвы, и жертвы безкровныя,
за вся люди твоя. И удовли насъ ихже по:
ставилъ еси на служение твое сие, силою Ду:
ха твоего Святаго, неосужденно, и непреткно:
венно въ чистѣмъ свидѣтелствѣ совѣсти
нашея, призывати тебе на всякое время, и
на всякомъ мѣстѣ да послушавъ насъ милос:
тивъ намъ будеши во множествѣ твоея благости.

Презвитеръ возглашаетъ;

Яко подобаетъ ти всякая слава, честь и по:
клоненіе Отцу и Сыну и Святому Духу, нынѣ — Аминь

Ар

Chrysostomus

Celebrantes		Chorus. Chrysostomus
Archidiaconus.	Nullus Catechumenorum, quicunq estis fideles, iterum atq iterum in pace Dm deprecemur.	Kyrie eleyson
Iude de Basm	Pro pace quae sursum est, et Salute animaru nostrarum Dominum deprecemur.	K. E.
Pro pace totius mundi stabilitate Sanctarum Dei Ecclesiarum et vnione omnium Dm deprec.	K. E.
Pro Sancta domo ista, et cum fide, innocentia, ac timore Dei intrantibus in ipsam, Dm deprec.	K. E.
Adiuua, Salua, miserere et conserua nos Deus tuâ gratiâ.	K. E.
Sapientia.
Pontifex secreto orat: Chrysostomus	Gratias agimus tibi Domine Deus Virtutum, qui dignos nos fecisti assistere nunc quoq Sancto tuo Altari, et procidere ante miserationes tuas pro nostris reatibus et populi ignorantijs. Suscipe Deus, preces nostras, fac nos dignos fieri, ut offeramus tibi Supplicationes et preces, et Sacrificia incruenta pro cuncto populo tuo, et fac nos sufficere, quos posuisti in ministerio tuo hoc virtute Spiritus tui Sancti irreprobabile et inoffense, in puro testimonio Conscientiae nostrae, inuocare te in omni tempore, et in omni loco, Vt exaudiens nos, benignus nobis adsis in multitudine tuae bonitatis:
Sacerdos altâ voce:	Quoniam decet te omnis gloria, honor et veneratio, Patrem, et Filium et Spiritum S. nunc &c.	Amen.

Сослужители

Архидиаконъ. Паки и паки миромъ Господу помолимся. — Ликъ. Господи помилуй.

О Святѣмъ обители сей, со всяком градѣ и странѣ и вѣрою живущихъ в нихъ Господу помолимся. — Госп. пом.

О благорастворении воздуха, изобилии плодовъ земныхъ и временѣхъ мирныхъ Госп. пом. — Госп. пом.

О плавающихъ, путешествующихъ, недугующихъ, труждающихся, плѣненныхъ и спасении ихъ Господу помолимся. — Госп. пом.

О избавитися намъ отъ всякия скорби, гнѣва и нужды Господу помолимся. — Госп. пом.

Заступи, спаси, помилуй и сохрани насъ Бже [...] — Госп. пом.

Премудрость.

Архиерей молитва: Паки и многажды Тебѣ припадаемъ и Тебѣ ся молимъ, Благий и Человѣколюбче, яко призрѣвъ на моления наша очистиши наша души и тѣлеса отъ всякия скверны плоти и духа и подаси намъ неповинно, и неосужденно предстояние святаго Твоего жертвенника. Даруй же, Боже, и молящимся с нами преспѣяние жития, и вѣры и разума духовнаго. Даруй имъ всегда со страхомъ и любовию служащимъ Тебѣ неповинно и неосужденно причаститися святымъ Твоимъ таинамъ и небеснаго Твоего царствия сподобитися.

Возглашаетъ обращся ко святымъ вратамъ: Яко да подъ державою Твоею всегда хранимии, Тебѣ славу возсылаемъ Отцу и Сыну и Святому Духу, нынѣ и [...] — Аминь.

Пѣние. Поется: Иже херувимы тайно образующе, и животворящей Троице трисвятую пѣснь приносяще, всякое нынѣ житейское отложимъ печаль.

[...]transformas
Celebrantes. | Chorus.
[...]chidiacono:

Iterum atq iterum in pace Dm deprecemur. — Kyrie Eleyson
Pro Sancto hoc Habitaculo, omni Urbe et Regione, et cum fide habitantibus in ipsis, Dm deprecemur. — Kyrie Eleyson
Pro Salubritate aeris, fertilitate fructuum terrae, et temporibus pacificis Dm deprecemur. — K. E.
Pro navigantibus, itinerantibus, aegrotantibus, laborantibus, Captivis, et Salute ipsorum Dm deprec. — K. E.

Ut liberet nos ab omni tribulatione, ira periculo et necessitate Dm deprecemur. — K. E.
Adiuva, Salva, miserere, et conserva nos Deus tua gratia. — K. E.
Sapientia

[...]lifex orat secreto: Iterum et Saepius tibi procumbimus, et te rogamus bone et clemens. ut respiciens ad preces nostras, purges nostras animas et corpora ab omni inquinatione Carnis, et Spiritus, et indulgeas nobis, ut absq reatu, et reprobatione adsistamus Sancto tuo Altari. Concede Deus et orantibus nobiscum profectum vitae, ac fidei, ac intelligentiae Spiritualis. Tribue et qui ubiq cum timore et amore Servientium tibi absq reatu et reprobatione participes fiant Sanctorum tuorum mysteriorum, et Supercaeleti tuo Regno digni efficiantur.

[...]ta voce[...] S. Porlam. — Ut a potentia tua ubiq custoditi tibi gloriam [...]lemus Patri et Filio et Spiritui Sancto. nunc. — Amen.

Cant[...] [...]transformas — Nos qui Cherubim mystice exprimimus et Vivificae Trinitati ter Sanctum Hymnum afferimus omnimodam hodie temporalem abjiciamus Sollicitudinem.

Служитель

Архиерей ѿвратъся ко престолу молитвою сїю.

Лист

Никтоже достоинъ ѿ связавшихся плот-
скими желанми, и сластми, приходити или при-
ближитися, или служити тебѣ царю славы. Еже
бо служити тебѣ велико и страшно, и самѣмъ
небеснымъ силамъ. Но обаче неизреченнаго ради
и безмѣрнаго твоего человѣколюбїя, непреложно и неизмѣнно былъ еси человѣкъ и архиерей
намъ нарекъся, и служебныя сея и безкровныя
жертвы священнодѣйствие предалъ еси намъ, яко
владыка всѣхъ. Ты бо единъ Господи Боже
нашъ владычествуеши небесными и земными,
иже на престолѣ херувимстѣмъ носимъ, иже
серафимомъ Господь и царь израилевъ, иже единъ святъ и на святыхъ почиваяй. Тебе бо молю единаго благаго, и благопо-
слушливаго, призри на мя грѣшнаго, и непо-
требнаго раба твоего, и очисти мою душу и
сердце ѿ совѣсти лукавыя, и удовли мя
силою святаго твоего духа, облеченна благодатию священства предстати святѣй
твоей сей трапезѣ, и священнодѣйствовати святое и пречистое тѣло твое, и честную кровь.
Къ тебѣ бо прихожду приклонь мою выю, и молю тя, да не отвратиши лица твоего
ѿ мене, ниже да отриниши мя ѿ отро-
къ твоихъ: но сподоби принесеннымъ быти
тебѣ мною грѣшнымъ и недостойнымъ рабомъ
твоимъ даромъ симъ. Ты бо еси приносяй и
приносимый, и приемляй и раздаваемый Христе
Боже нашъ, и тебѣ славу возсылаемъ со безна-
чалнымъ твоимъ ѿцемъ, и пресвятымъ и благимъ
и животворящимъ твоимъ духомъ нынѣ и присно
и во вѣки вѣкомъ. Аминь.

Celebrantes.

[...]thica conuersus [ad] Altare orat se-creto:

Nemo dignus est eorum, qui illigati sunt carnalibus desiderijs, ac voluptatibus, accedere, aut appropinquare, aut ministrare tibi Rex gloriæ, nam inseruire tibi magnum, et tremendum est et ipsis Cælestibus Potestatibus. Sed tamen propter ineffabilem, immensamq. tuam clementiam, sine mutatione, aut variatione factus es homo, et summus Sacerdos noster esse statuisti, et ministerij huius ac incruenti sacrificij celebrationem tradidisti nobis ut Dominus omnium. Tu enim solus, Domine Deus noster imperas Cælestibus et terrestribus, qui super throno Cherubico insides qui Seraphim dominaris, et es Rex Israel, qui solus Sanctus es, et in Sanctis requiescis. Te igitur exoro solum bonum et facilem ad audiendum, respice super me peccatorem, et inutilem seruum tuum, et munda animam meam, et cor a conscientia praua, et fac idoneum me virtute Sancti tui Spiritus, indutum Sacerdotij gratia, assistere Sanctæ tuæ huic mensæ, et consecrare sanctum et immaculatum tuum corpus, et pretiosum sanguinem, ad te enim accedo inclinans meam ceruicem, et deprecor te ne auertas faciem tuam a me, ne reijcias me à filijs tuis, sed fac dignum offerri tibi à me peccatore, et indigno seruo tuo hæc munera, Tu enim es offerens et oblatus, et suscipiens, et distributus Christe Deus noster et tibi gloriam damus, cum carente principio tuo Patre, et Sanctissimo, ac optimo et viuificante tuo Spiritu, nunc et semper, et in secula seculorum. Amen.

Егда же Святитель совершаетъ молитву, Архидиаконъ возметъ блюдалницу; даетъ ю мирянo
презвитерствующимъ, иже станутъ передъ Святыми
вратми. По совершеніи же молитвы, обратив-
ся ко Святителю держитъ. Благословляетъ воду

Архиерей: Господи Боже нашъ, освятившій струи Иор-
данскія спасителнымъ явленіемъ своимъ.
Самъ нынѣ нисъпосли благодать Святаго твоего духа, и благослови + воду сию ко освя-
щенію людій твоихъ, яко благословенъ еси во
вѣки Аминь. Посемъ блюдо вынесши наверхъ.
По блюдничѣ верхъ Архидиаконъ паки блюдалницу пріемлетъ отъ мирянъ: Архиерей же
развязуетъ на шию Архидиаконову. Яко и
взявъ Крестъ отъ диакона, даетъ и целовати
первее же Архидиакону: иже целовавъ
отходитъ со блюдалницею во олтарь, и отъ-
даетъ ю паламареви) потомъ же мирянотъ по-
слѣдовавшимъ на блюдѣ ини. И тако паки отъ-
даетъ крестъ диакону. Самъ же отходитъ ко
жертвенику. А тамо взявъ копію и просфору
глаголетъ воспоминаніе, изъемлетъ части и
полагаетъ е по ряду по предъписанъному.

Взявъ первую часть полагаетъ ю со десную страны ка глаголя.

Во честь и память преблагословенныя
славныя владычица нашея Богородица и
присно дѣвы Марія. Ея же молитвами прими Господи жертву сію во пренебесный твой
жертовникъ. Та же: Предста царица
одесную тебе в ризахъ позлащенныхъ
одѣянна и преиспещренна.

Celebrantes. | Chorus.

[...]tificale [...]

℟. Autem.

Absoluente vero Pontifice orationem, Archidiaconus accepto lavacro, dat illud Secularibus praecipuis: qui consistunt ad [...] Portam. Finita itaque oratione, conversus versus [...] Portam benedicit aquam.

Pontifex:

Domine Deus noster, qui Sanctificasti aquas Jordanis Salutifera apparitione tua. Ipse nunc demittas gratiam Sancti tui Spiritus, et bene✠dic aquam istam ad Sanctificandum populum tuum. Quoniam benedictus es in secula. Amen.

Postea: Lavabo inter innocentes manus &c.

Ablutis vero manibus Archidiaconus rursus lavacrum recipit à Secularibus. Pontifex autem Tobaleam superponit collo Archidiacono. Sed et accepta Cruce à Diacono, dat illam ad osculandum primo quidem Archidiacono, qui osculatus recipit sese cum lavacro intra Sacrarium, et reddit illud Sacristae. Postea vero Secularibus, qui manuum ablutioni inservierunt; Atque ita rursus reddit Crucem Diacono. Ipse vero recedit ad Altare Propositionis. Hic accepta lancea et Hostia, dicit commemorationem, eximens particulas, et ex ordine collocans, secundum quod infra scriptum est.

[...] eximens primam [...]ticulam, ponit illam [...] Agni, dicens:

[...] Chrysostomus

In honorem et memoriam plusquam benedictae, gloriosae Reginae nostrae Deiparae et Semper Virginis Mariae: Cuius precibus accipe Domine Sacrificium istud ad Supercaeleste tuum Altare. Ejusdem: Astitit Regina à dextris tuis, in vestitu deaurato, circumdata varietate.

+

Слѣдуетъ ли архиерей взятъ вторую часть полагаетъ ю ошуюю агнца и глаголя; — литъ

Силою честнаго и животворящаго креста
заступлениемъ честныхъ, небесныхъ силъ безплотныхъ. Честнаго, славнаго, пророка пред-
теча, и крестителя. Господня Иоанна, и
всехъ святыхъ пророкъ. Святыхъ, славныхъ и
всехвалныхъ апостолъ. Иже во святыхъ о-
тецъ нашихъ иерархъ, Василия великаго,
Григория Богослова, Иоанна Златоустаго,
Афанасия, Кирилла, и Николая. и всехъ святыхъ иерархъ. Святаго апостола, первому-
ченника и архидиакона Стефана. Святыхъ ве-
ликомученникъ Георгия, Димитрия, Феодора
и всехъ святыхъ мученикъ, преподобныхъ и
богоносныхъ отецъ нашихъ, Антония, Феодосия,
Савы, Онуфрия, Арсения, и всехъ преподобныхъ.
Святыхъ врачев безсребреникъ Козмы и
Дамиана, Кира и Иоанна, Пантелеимона и Ер-
молая, Самсона и Диомида, Фалалея и Три-
фона и всехъ святыхъ безсребреникъ. Святыхъ
праведныхъ богоотецъ Иоакима и Анны, и
святаго [егоже есть день] N. N. и всехъ святыхъ
ихже молитвами посети насъ Боже

Взявъ третю полагаетъ подъ агнцемъ.

О всечестномъ епископстве православномъ.
О вселенскомъ архиерею святейшомъ N.
о ~~[illegible]~~ митрополите нашомъ N.
[аще служба самъ есть митрополита]
честнемъ презвитерстве, еже о Христе диаконъ-
стве и о всемъ священническомъ и иноческомъ
чинѣ.

Взявъ четвертую полагаетъ тамо же.

О благоверномъ государе нашомъ великомъ
короли N. о всей палате и воехъ его.

Взявъ пятую полагаетъ тамо же.

О братии нашой сослужебникехъ презвите-
рехъ и диаконехъ, и всей еже о Христе братии нашой,
ихже призвалъ еси во твое преблагоутробие
за твое благоутробие всеблагий владыко.

+

Celebrantes. Virtute pretiosæ et vivificæ Crucis; protectione gloriosarum Cælestium virtutum Incorporearum. Honorandi gloriosi Prophetæ præcursoris, et Baptistæ Joannis. Sanctorum gloriosorum et perquam benedictorum Apostolorum. Sanctorum Patrum nostrorum, Pontificum, Basilij Magni, Gregorij Theologi Joannis Chrysostomi, Athanasij, Cyrilli, Nicolai, et omnium Sanctorum Pontificum. Sancti Apostoli, primi Martyris et Archidiaconi Stephani. Sanctorum magnorum Martyrum, Georgij, Demetrij Theodori, et omnium Sanctorum Martyrum. Sanctorum Deiferorum Patrum nostrorum, Antonij, Euthymij, Sabbæ, Onuphrij. Arsenij, et omnium patrum; Sanctorum medentium absq argento, Cosmæ et Damiani, Cyri et Joannis, Pantaleonis et Hermolai, Samsonis et Diomedis, Thallalei et Tryphonis et reliquorum. Sanctorum Justorum Dei parentum Joachim et Annæ Sancti [illius diei] et omnium SS. quorum precibus protege nos Deus.

Chorus

+ et omnis SS. Prophetarum.

P. But.

3°

Pontifex accipiens secundam particulam ponit illam sinistris agni.

Chrysostomus ... in principio ... Alab ... loco ... Pontificale ... Pontifex. quod idem servant Eppi Græci.

Accipiens tertiam, ponit sub agno

Pro omnibus Episcopatibus orthodoxis: Pro Oecumenico Pontifice Sanctissimo N. Pro Metropolita nostro [Si celebrans ipse non est Metropolita] N. Venerandis Presbyteris in Christo Diaconis et omni Sacerdotali et Religioso ordine.

Accipiens quartam ponit ibidem:

Pro orthodoxo Domino nostro magno Rege N. pro toto Senatu et exercitu ipsius.

Accipiens quintam ponit ibidem.

Pro Fratribus nostris Concelebrantibus, Presbyteris et Diaconis, et omnibus in Christo fratribus nostris quos vocasti in tuam communitatem tua misericordia optime Domine.

+

Лит

Святители. Архиерей взем шестую часть полагает ю тамо ж глаголя.

Во благочестивейших архиереях святыя обители сия, и во творящих нам милостыню, и заповедавших нам недостойным молитися о них, за вся православныя христианы.

Взем седмую полагает тамо ж.

Господи Ис Хе прием жертву сию во оставление грехов рабом твоим NN. зде и поминает и изъемлет части елико хощет.

Взем часть иконную полагает под перстом

Помяни Господи души усопших раб твоих всех блаженных архиереев патриархов, архиепископов, епископов, королей, князей, иных, и всех в надежди воскресения и вечныя жизни опочивших во твоем прибежищи усопших, отец и братий наших человеколюбче Господи прости.

Взем еще часть полагает тамо ж.

Помяни Господи души усопших раб твоих NN. зде и поминает и части изъемлет елико хощет.

Взем же часть полагает —

Помяни Господи по множеству щедрот твоих и мое недостоинство, и прости ми всякое прегрешение вольное же и невольное.

Известно же буди яко агнец и вся части на дискос полагаются сицевым образом.

IC XC
NI KA

Живым
Усопшим

elebrantes.

ntifex accipiens sex particulam ponit in ibidem.

ipiens Septimam nit ibidem.

Pontificale Aut

ipiens particulam alia illa sub primis

ccipiens nonam ponit ibidem.

ipiens particulam ponit illa ibidem.

Chorus.

Pro orthodoxis Fundatoribus S. Habitaculi huius, et benefactoribus nostris: pro illis qui à nobis indignis oratio, nes postularunt, pro omnibus orthodoxis Christianis.

Domine Iesu Christe, Suscipe Sacrificium hoc pro remissione peccatorum Seruis tuis, qui mandaue, runt mihi indigno Famulo tuo, ut orarem pro illis N. N. Hic et comemorat et eximet particulas quot vo, luerit.

P. Aut.

Memento Domine animarum Seruorum tuorum, qui obdormierunt, Oecumenicorum Pontificum, Patriarcharum Metropolitarum Archiepiscoporum, Episcoporum, Regum, Sacerdotum et Religiosorum. Et omnibus in spe Resurrectionis, et vitæ æter, næ in tua comunione defunctis Patribus et Fra, tribus nostris Clementissime Dñe veniam indulge.

Memento Domine animarum defunctorum Ser, uorum tuorum N. N. [Hic et comemorat et eximit par, ticulas, quot placet.]

Memento Domine secundum multitudinem miserationum tuarum, et meæ indignitatis ac dimitte mihi omnia delicta voluntaria et in, uoluntaria.

Sciendum uero quod Agnus et omnes Particulæ in patena col, locantur in hunc modum

BV IS XC NI KA SS

Viui

Mortui

Сослужители Егдаже Святитель Проскомидию соверша- Литу.
етъ, надилницу и фимиама принесшимъ.

Архидиаконъ; Благослови Владыко кадило

Архиерей Кадило ти + приносимъ ...

Взявже кадилницу от Архидиакона. Начинаетъ псаломъ Н. помилуй мя Боже. и глаголетъ весь. И тако предъ кадящима ему диаконома со свещами кадитъ престолъ крестообразъ-
но (начинаетъ от царьскихъ вратъ) жертовникъ,
сослужители, весь олтарь, и люди, стояще
во святыхъ вратехъ. Потомже обращся
кадитъ престолъ, и отдаетъ кадилницу Ар-
хидиаконови. Самъже со сослужители и кланя-
ющеся трижды глаголетъ: Иже херувимы.
Тамже отшед паки святей, и целовавъ самъ
... на престоле.
Иереи порядку престолъ ... целуютъже престолъ, ... Поклонъже сотворша
отходятъ к жертовнику. Архиерейже
отдавъ третьему иерееви ... а ...
... Митру, станетъ самъ у престола
посреди прочихъ Священниковъ. И егда
целуютъ руку его.

Архиерей Благодатию всяку и твари всякои сотворилъ, приими сихъ иереовъ входящихъ в церковь
твою, и служащихъ тебе: даждьже ...
нихъ ... на пользу, и ... на соверъ-
шение, и ... сотвори царьствию твоему. Благодатию и щедротами Единороднаго
Сына твоего, с нимже благословенъ еси во
веки Аминь.

Celebrantes. | Cum vero Pontifex oblationem finit, afferens Thuribulum | Chorus. 32

Archidiaconus: ~~Thus afferens~~ : Benedic Domine Thymiama.

Pontifex: Incensum tibi offerimus &c. Et accepto Thuribulo apud Diaconum Incipit Psalmum 50 Miserere mei Deus. | P. Aut.

Pontificale Antonii: Et dicit totum. Atq. ita praecedentibus illum Diaconis cum Candelis, incensat Sacram mensam in modum Crucis [Incipiens à porta Regia] Altare Propositionis, Concelebrantes, totum Altare et populum, consistens in Sancta Porta. Postea conuersus incensat Sacram Mensam, et reddit Thuribulum Archidiacono. Ipse vero cum Concelebrantibus ter faciens adorationem dicit

Pontifex: Nos qui Cherubim &c. Postmodum accipiens Pontifex Sanctam Crucem, et osculatus eam, tenet illam directe manu dextera, supra sacram mensam.

Sacerdotes ex ordine accedunt, osculanturq. sacram mensam, manum et Crucem, facta vero reuerentia recedunt ad Altare Propositionis. Et Pontifex quidem reddita Cruce tertio Sacerdoti quarto vero Infula, consistit ante sacram mensam inter Sacerdotes residuos. Sed dum osculant. manu illi

Pontifex: Benefactor omnium et omnis Creaturae ~~Iudex~~ conditor, suscipe nos sacerdotes, ingredientes Ecclesiam tuam, et seruientes tibi. Da quoq. cuilibet illorum quae sunt vtilia, et promoue omnes in perfectionem, et dignos facias Regno tuo. Gratia et misericordia Vnigeniti Filij tui, cum quo benedictus es in secula. Amen.

Служители И тако архипрезвитеръ возметъ надилницу и архидиакона попадитъ предсловение. Архидиаконъ абие снемъ з себе омофоръ полагаетъ и на обѣихъ двухъ диакона простерше. И возвращается ко архипрезвитеру. Митр

Архидиаконъ. Возгласи владыко.

Архипрезвитеръ. Во миръ возвеличите руки ваша во святая и благословите Господа. Благословитъ тя Господь отъ Сиона, сотворивый небо и землю всегда нинѣ.

И возметъ покровъ полагаетъ на рамѣхъ обѣхъ втораго иерея: дискосъ же даетъ архидиаконъ: самъ обѣма руками приимаетъ потиръ. И тако исходитъ с сокровенными враты сицевымъ образомъ. Предходятъ свѣщеносцы: послѣдъ стоятъ имъ диаконъ со омофоромъ: таже архидиаконъ з дискосомъ: послѣ архипрезвитеръ с потиромъ: вторый иерей с покровомъ: третий с крестомъ: четвертый же с митрою

Архидиаконъ изшедъ возглашаетъ Всѣхъ насъ православныхъ христианъ да помянетъ Господь Богъ во царствии своемъ живоносномъ, всегда нинѣ и присно и во вѣки вѣкомъ.

Архипрезвитеръ возглас. ~~[illegible]~~ Митрополита или Архиепископа или Епископа нашего N. [что есть сл [~~[illegible]~~ ~~Архиепископа~~: ~~[illegible]~~] ~~[illegible] нашего N.~~ И весь чинъ иерейский иноческий и диаконский да помянетъ Господь Богъ во царствии своемъ, всегда нинѣ

Архиерей абие исходитъ во срѣтение, и станетъ во святыхъ вратахъ. Два диакона возлагаютъ на выю его омофоръ. Потомъ приемъ надилницу со архидиакономъ надитъ дискосъ. и отдавъ его диакону приимаетъ дискосъ отъ архидиакона: и возметъ [illegible]

Atq. ita Archipraesbyter, accepto Thuribulo apud Archidiaconum, incensat Propositionem. Archidiaconus autem Pallium deponens, ponit illud supra vtramq. manum Diaconi expansum: et conuertitur ad Archipraesbyterum:

Archidiaconus: Eleua Domine.

Archipraesbyter: In pace extollite manus vestras in Sancta et benedicite Dominum. Benedicat te Dominus ex Sion, qui fecit Caelum et terram, vbiq. nunc. Et accepto velo ponit illud super humeros Secundi Sacerdotis. Patinam vero dat Archidiacono. Ipse vero vtraq. manu accipit Calicem. Et ita progrediuntur Porta Septentrionali, hoc modo. Praecedunt Ceroferarij: sequitur Diaconus cum Pallio: Postea Archidiaconus cum Patina: Tandem Archipraesbyter cum Calice: Secundus Sacerdos cum velo: tertius cum Cruce: quartus cum Infula.

Archidiaconus egressus alta voce: Omnium nostrum Orthodoxorum Christianorum, recordetur Dominus Deus in Regno suo Caelesti, vbiq. nunc et semper et in secula seculorum.

Archipraesbyter alta voce: Pontificale Antimi: Metropolitae [illegible] Archiepiscopi nostri N. [illegible] quis celebret [illegible] et totius ordinis Sacerdotalis, Monastici et Diaconalis, recordetur Dominus Deus in Regno suo. secundum quod S. Anthem.

Pontifex autem egreditur in occursum et consistit in S. Porta. Archidiaconus imponit collo illius Pallium. Ille vero accepto Thuribulo cum Thymiamate incensat Patinam: et reddit illud Diacono, accipit quoq. Patinam apud Archidiaconum, et eleuans tenet illam manu dextera versus populum.

Сослужители. Литургия.

Архиерей велегласно. Благочестивейшаго Великаго Государя нашего Короля N. и всех вас православных христиан, да помянет Господь Бог во царствии своем всегда, ныне и присно и во веки веков. Аминь.

Пение. Яко да царя всех подъемлюще, ангельскими невидимо дориносима чинми. Аллилуиа, аллилуиа, аллилуиа.

Архиерей дискос поставляет на престоле. Возвращшеся ко святителю братия, и взем кадильницу от архидиакона кадит трижды потира. И взяв и от архипресвитера ставляет на престоле со дискосом.

Архиерей вслух. Возмите врата князи ваша, и возмитеся врата вечная, и внидет царь славы.

Архидиакон вслух. Благословен грядый во имя Господне, Бог Господь, и явися нам.

Таже исходят вси сослужители. ~~Святители~~ Архипресвитер первее со иереем взявше покров возносят и над главою святителевою, и пренесше оттуду чрез главу покрывают им потир и дискос: и вступят на место свое.

Архиерей вслух. Благообразный Иосиф со древа снем пречистое тело твое, плащаницею чистою обвив, и вонями во гробе нове закрыв положи. Затем третий пресвитер полагает крест на престоле: четвертый же митру. Святитель кадит предложенная.

Архиерей ~~—~~ тайно. Ублажи Господи благоволением твоим Сиона и да созиждутся стены Иерусалимския. Тогда благоволиши жертву правды возношения и всесожегаемая, тогда возложат на олтарь твой тельцы.

Celebrantes		Chorus
Pontifex alta voce. Pontificale Part.	Orthodoxi, Magni Domini nostri Regis N. et omnium vestrum Orthodoxorum Christianorum recordetur Dnus Deus in Regno Suo Cœlesti; ubiq nunc &c.	P. Ryten. Amen
Cantus: Chrysost.	Canitur: Ut Regem omnium Suscipientes Angelicis inuisibiliter Stipatum agminibus. Alleluia, Alleluia, Alleluia.	S. Chrys.
	Pontifex Patinam reponit in S. Mensa, Iterum quoq reuersus ad S. Portam, et accipiens Thuribulum ab Archediacono incensat versus Calicem. Quem recipiens ab Archipræsbytero collocat in S. Mensa, ex parte dextra patinæ.	
Pontifex secreto: Pontificale Part.	Attollite portas Principes vestras, et eleuamini portæ æternales, et introibit Rex Gloriæ.	P. Part. Stiæ.
Archidiaconus secreto.	Benedictus qui venit in nomine Dni, Deus Dnus et illuxit nobis.	
	Tum ingrediuntur omnes concelebrantes. Archipræsbyter autem cum Sacerdote accepto velo leuant illud supra caput Pontificis, et transferentes dextre per caput, cooperiunt illo Calicem, et Patinam, et recedunt ad locum suum.	
Pontifex secreto: Chrysost.	Spectatissimus Joseph de ligno deponens intemeratum Corpus tuum, syndone munda inuoluens et aromatibus, in monumento nouo sepeliens deposuit.	S. Chrysost.
	Tunc tertius Presbyter ponit Crucem in S. Mensa: Quartus vero Mitram. Pontifex incensat Proposita.	
Pontifex incensans:	Benigne fac Domine in bona voluntate tua Syon, ut ædificentur muri Jerusalem. Tunc acceptabis Sacrificium Justitiæ, oblationes et holocausta, Tunc imponent super Altare tuum Vitulos.	

Слѹжители

Архиерей ѿтдавъ Кадилницѹ мо- литвѹ чтѧ. Владыко Господи Животворче, благихъ дателю, давый намъ наслаждение вѣчныя жизни, человѣкомъ и Богомъ нашимъ Iис Хмъ. Сподоби насъ во священии семъ сконьчати сию Божественную службѹ, в наслѣдие будущаго блаженства. Яко благословенъ еси всегда, нынѣ &. Лит.

Поклонъ творитъ. Боже: милосердни бѹди мнѣ грѣшному. Таже: Просвѣтите мя и помяните мя честнии ѿтцы и братия Сослужители.

Сослужители. Благодатию Своего Господь Богъ да просвѣтитъ и помянетъ Архиерейство твое во царствии Своемъ. Помолися ѡ насъ Владыко Святый.

Архиерей. Духъ Святый найдетъ на вы, и сила Вышняго осѣнитъ вы.

Сослужители. Самъ тои Святый Духъ да будетъ с вами и с нами во вся дни живота нашего. Помяни насъ Владыко Святый.

Архиерей. Да помянетъ васъ Господь Богъ во царствии Своемъ нынѣ &.

Сослужители. Аминь. Здѣ Святитель приемлетъ Митрѹ ѿ [illegible]

Тогда Архидиаконъ даетъ Архиерею трисвѣщникъ возжегши три свѣщи. Архиерей абие ѡбращься ко людемъ и ставъ во святыхъ вратѣхъ, держаще лѣвою посохъ трижды знаменуетъ трисвѣщникомъ народъ. Глаголя молитву вышеписанную.

Архиерей. Господи Господи призри с небесе &. Ис полла деспота

ѿтдавъ же трисвѣщникъ Архидиакону, и приемлетъ ѿтъ него Крестъ, благословляетъ имъ людъ трижды.

Архиерей. Спаси Боже люди Своя, и благослови достояние твое.

Абие Архиерей ѡбращься Крестъ полагаетъ на престолѣ, и самъ тамо же стоитъ.

Здѣ аще будетъ становленникъ посвящаетъ во Презвитеры.

Посемъ диаконъ исходитъ северными враты и ставъ предъ царскими творитъ поклонъ

35

[Conce]lebrantes	Domine Dñe, viuificans, benefaciens, dans	Chorus.
[Pon]tifex reddito Thu[ribu]lo orat secreto:	nobis Satietatem vitæ æternæ, per hominem	
[Pon]tificale Ruth.	et Deum nostrum Jesum Christum. Dignos	S. Rut.
	nos facias, vt in Sacrificio hoc perficiamus hanc	
	Diuinam Lithurgiam, ad consequendam futuram	
	Beatitudinem. Quoniam benedictus es nunc &c.	
Caput inclinat:	Deus propitius esto mihi peccatori. Item:	
	Veniam indulgete mihi, et recordemini mei	
	venerabiles Patres et Fratres conseruientes.	
Concelebrantes:	Gratiâ suâ Dnus Deus veniam indulgeat,	
	et recordetur Pontificatus tui in Regno suo.	
	Deprecieris pro nobis Episcope Sancte.	
Pontifex: [S.] Chrysost.	Spiritus Sanctus descendat super vos, et vir-	S. Chrysost.
	tus altissimi obumbret vos.	
[Co]ncelebrantes:	Idem ipse Sanctus Spiritus sit vobiscum et	
	nobiscum omnibus diebus vitæ nostræ. Re-	
	corderis nostri Episcope Sancte.	
Pontifex:	Recordetur[?] vestri Dominus Deus, nunc &c.	
[Co]ncelebrantes:	Amen.	
	Hic Pontifex suscipit Mitram per Archipræsbyterum. Archidiaconus dat Pontifici Tricerium, accensis tribus candelis. Pontifex vero conuersus ad Populum, et consistens in Sancta Porta, ac tenens manu sinistra Pedum, cum benedicit Tricerio populum, dicens orationem supra scriptam.	
Pontifex: [Pon]tificale Ruth.	Dñe Dñe, respice de Cœlis &c. In multos annos Dñe	In multos an-nos Domine. S. Ruth.
	Sed et reddens Tricerium Archidiacono, ab eodem accipit Crucem et benedicit per populum: Saluum fac Deus	
Pontifex:	populum tuum, et benedic hæreditati tuæ.	In multos an-nos Dñe.
	Postmodum Pontifex reuersus Crucem ponit in Altari et ipse ibidem consistit.	
[Pon]tificale Ruthenum	Hic si adest Consecrandus, conferat in Presbyterum.	S. Rut.
	His finitis Diaconus egreditur Porta Septentrionali et consistens ante Regiam Portam, facit adorationem.	

Служители диаконъ.

Исполнимъ молитву нашу Господеви. — Литъ. Господи по[милуй]

О предложенныхъ честныхъ дарѣхъ Господу помолимся. — Гос.

О святѣмъ храмѣ семъ, и со вѣрою, благоговѣниемъ, и страхомъ Божиемъ входящихъ въ онь Господу помо. — Госп.

О избавитися намъ отъ всякия скорби, гнѣва, бѣды и нужды Господу помолимся. — Госп.

Заступи, спаси, помилуй и сохрани насъ Боже твоею благодатию. — Госп.

Дне всего совершенна, свята, мирна, и безгрѣшна у Господа просимъ. — Подай Госп.

Ангела мирна, вѣрна наставника, хранителя душамъ и тѣломъ нашимъ у Господа просимъ. — Под. Госп.

Милости и оставления грѣховъ и прегрѣшений нашихъ у Господа просимъ. — Под. Госп.

Добрыхъ и полезныхъ душамъ нашимъ, и мира мiру у Господа просимъ. — Под. Го.

Прочее время живота нашего въ мирѣ и покаянии скончати у Господа просимъ. — Под. Госп.

Христианския кончины живота нашего безболѣзненны, непостыдны, мирны, и добраго отвѣта иже на страшнѣмъ судѣ Христовѣ у Господа просимъ. — Под. Госп.

Пресвятыя честныя, и преблагословенныя Б. — Тебѣ Го.

Архиерѣй. Молит. Свята.

Господи Боже Вседержителю, единъ святъ, приемляй жертву хваления отъ призывающихъ тя всѣмъ сердцемъ, приими и отъ насъ грѣшныхъ моление и принеси ко святому твоему жертвеннику, и удовли насъ принести тебѣ дары же и жертвы духовныя, о нашихъ согрѣшенияхъ, и о людскихъ невѣдѣнияхъ, и сподоби насъ обрѣсти благодать предъ тобою. Еже быти тебѣ благоприятнѣй жертвѣ нашей и вселитися духу благодати твоея благому в насъ, и во предлежащихъ дарѣхъ сихъ и во всѣхъ людехъ твоихъ.

Chrysostomus Celebrantes		Chorus S. Chrysostomus
Diaconus:	Expleamus Supplicationem nostram coram Domino	Kyrie Eleyson
	Pro propositis honorabilibus muneribus Dm̃ deprecemur,	Kyr. El.
	Pro Sanctâ domo ista, et cum fide innolentia, et timore Dei ingredientibus in ipsam Dominum deprecemur.	Kyr. El.
	Vt liberet nos ab omni tribulatione, ira, periculo et necessitate, Dm̃ deprecemur.	K. E.
	Adiuua, Salua, miserere et conserua nos Deus tua gratia.	K. E.
	Diem totum perfectum, Sanctum, pacificum, et absq peccatu à Dño rogemus.	Concede Domine.
	Angelum pacis, fidelem ductorem, custodem animarum et corporum nostrorum à Dño rogemus.	Conc. Dñe
	Indulgentiam et remissionem peccatorum et delictorum nostrorum à Dño rogemus.	Conc. Dñe
	Bona et conferentia animabus nostris, et pacem mundo à Dño rogemus:	Concede Dñe.
	Vt residuum tempus vitæ nostræ, absq dolore, in pace ac pænitentia perficiamus, à Dño rogemus.	Conc. Dñe
	Christianum finem vitæ nostræ, absq dolore, improperio pacificum, et bonam responsionem ante tremendum Judicium à Dño rogemus.	Conc. Dñe
	Sanctissimæ, intemeratæ, Superbenedictæ &c.	Tibi Domine
Pontifex orat secreto:	Domine Deus omnipotens, Solus Sanctus qui suscipis Sacrificium laudis ab inuocantibus te, in toto corde, Suscipe etiam nostri peccatorum preces, et admoueas Sancto tuo Altari, et idoneos facias nos ad offerendum tibi munera ac Sacrificia Spiritualia, pro peccatis nostris et populi ignorantia, et dignos facias nos inuenire gratiam in conspectu tuo, ut fiat acceptum Sacrificium nostrum, et inhabitet Spiritus gratiæ tuæ optimus Super nos et super apposita munera ista et Super omnem populum tuum.	

Служители Архиерей возглашает.	Щедротами Единороднаго Сына твоего, с ним же благословен еси, со пресвятым, благим, и животворящим твоим Духом, ныне и присно, и во веки веков.	Лик. Аминь
Обращшеся благословит люди.	Мир всем.	И со духом твоим.
	Архидиакон затворяет святые врата. Потом взяв литер со святителя полагает его на престоле.	
Диакон	Возлюбим друг друга, да единомыслием исповемы.	
Пение	Поется. Отца, Сына, и Святаго Духа, Троицу единосущную и нераздельную.	
Архиерей тайно	Господи Иисусе Христе любви творче, делателю благих, давый нам даром твоим любити друг друга, яко ты возлюби нас, да верою и любовию единомысленно и единодушно к тебе Богу приближившеся, и причастившеся святых твоих таин, и царствию твоему достойни будем и тебе славу возсылаем, Отцу, и Сыну и Святому Духу ныне и присно. Таже иереи сослужители вси приступают ко архиерею, целующе престол десницу, и ланиту десную его.	
Архиерей	Христос посреде нас.	
Сослужители	Есть и будет.	
Архиерей поклонися трижды	Возлюблю тя Господи, крепосте моя, Господь утверждение мое и прибежище мое. Посем сам архиерей целует покров иже на дарех суть покровены, над святыя трапезы перед собою, верхи дискоса и святыя чаши. И абие взяв со сослужители разширяют над чашею и дискосом держат.	
Диакон	Двери двери премудростию вонмем.	
Стих глаголют всесвятейшим	Верую во единаго Бога О(тца).	

Celebrantes.		Chorus.
Chrysostomus Pontifex alta voce:	Per miserationes Unigeniti tui Filij, cum quo benedictus es, cum Sanctissimo et optimo, et viuificante tuo Spiritu nunc et semper et in secula seculorum.	S. Chrysost. Amen.
Conuersus recitat …	Pax omnibus.	Et cum spiritu tuo.
	Archidiaconus claudit S. Portam: accipiens etiam Mitram ex Pontifice reponit illam in Altari.	
Diaconus:	Diligamus nos inuicem, ut in concordia confitemur.	
Cantus:	Canitur: Patrem Filium et Sanctum Spiritum Trinitatem consubstantialem et indivisibilem.	
Pontifex secreto: Pontificale Rutenum	Domine Jesu Christe Charitatis Creator, bonorum operator, concede nobis famulis, ut diligamus nos inuicem, prout tu dilexisti nos, ut per fidem et Charitatem ad te Deum approximemus, et participes fiamus SS. tuorum Sacramentorum, et Regno tuo digni efficiamur. Et tibi gloriam damus, Patri et Filio et Spiritui Sancto nunc &c.	P. Rutenum
	Tum Sacerdotes Concelebrantes omnes accedunt ad Pontificem osculantes Sacram Mensam, manum dextram, et genam illius dextram.	
Pontifex:	Christus in medio nostrum.	
Concelebrantes	Est et erit.	
Pontifex ter facit ad …	Diligam te Domine fortitudo mea, Dominus firmamentum meum, et refugium meum. ter.	
	Postea solus Pontifex osculatur Velum, quo Propositia … cooperta, supra S. Mensam, supra Patinam et Calicem. Cum Concelebrantibus autem flexans illud … extensum supra Calicem et Patinam.	
Chrysostomus Diaconus: … voce alta.	Januas, Januas in Sapientia attendamus.	S. Chrysost.
	Credo in unum Deum &c.	

Служители

Сиеже веры исповедание глаголеть отаи, Архиерей со сослужителями. Еще же дважде реши наъ лице. Подвевають мало покров трижды. — Лик

Архиерей отаи — Святый Боже, Святый Крепкий, Святый Безсмертный помилуй нас.

И отвлачают покров. Архидиакон двери отверзает.

Диакон. — Станем добре, станем со страхом, вонмем святое возношение с миром приносити.

— Милость мира, жертву хваления.

Зде отходит диакон внутрь олтаря, и стает ошуюю Архиерея.

Архиерей возглас. — Благодать Господа нашего Ис Ха, и любовь Бога Отца и причастие Святаго Духа буди со всеми вами.

— И со духом твоим.

Горе имеем сердца.

— Имамы ко Господу.

Благодарим Господа.

— Достойно и праведно.

Зде аще есть презвитер новопоставленный, Архиерей дает ему десницею от части на дискосе лежащих.

Архиерей отаи. — Восприими иерею часть сию, и соблюди ю чисту и непорочну, понеже имаши воздати ответ на страшном суде.

Иерейже дав целуя святителю десницу и руце держит на престоле: Молитвы же отаи читает со Архиереем.

Архиерей молитву. — Достойно и праведно тебе пети, тебе благословити, тебе благодарити, тебе покланятися, на всяком месте владычествия твоего. Ты бо еси Бог неизреченен, недоведом, невидим, непостижим, присно сый, такожде сый. Ты и единородный твой Сын, и Дух твой Святый. Ты от небытия во бытие нас привел еси, и отпадшихся возставил еси паки, и не отступил еси вся творя, дондеже нас на небеса возвел еси, и царство твое даровал еси будущее.

Celebrantes. | Chorus.

Pontificale Ant. | P. Ant.

Hoc vero fidei Symbolum dicit Secreto Pontifex cum Concelebrantibus. Postquam vero dixerint, Amen, elevant parum Velum ter

Pontifex secreto: Sancte Deus, Sancte fortis, Sancte immortalis miserere nobis. Et reponunt Velum. Archidiaconus Portam aperit

Diaconus: S. Chrysost. Stemus honestè stemus cum timore, attendamus ut Sanctam oblationem in pace offeramus. Hic Diaconus recipit sese intra Altare, et consistit à sinistra Pontificis.

Misericordiam pacis, nostram laudis.

NB. Ἔλεος apud Graecos sive duplicē ethimologiā. nempe Oleū, & misericordiam. hinc hic vertit: Oleū pacis. hi missa S. Jacobi [illegible] vero, mi[illegible]sericordiam [illegible] S. Chrysost.

Pontifex altâ voce: Gratia Domini nostri Jesu Christi, et amor Dei Patris, et communicatio Sancti Spiritus sit cum omnibus Vobis.

Et cum Spiritu tuo.

Sursum habeamus corda.

Habemus ad Dnm.

Gratias agamus Domino.

Dignum et Justum est.

Coetique verba plus habent in Graeco sed recipit Graeci cantant, nec [illegible]

Pontifi. Antent. Hic si est Presbyter novus consecratus, Pontifex dat in manum ejus dexteram, unam ex particulis in Latina collocatis

P. Ant.

Pontifex Secreto. Accipe Presbyter, particulam hanc, et conserva illam Castam et immaculatam, de qua rationem reddes in terribili Judicio

Sacerdos vero manum osculatus Pontificis, recedit et dextram tenet supra Altare. Orationes vero Secreto recitat cum Pontifice:

Pontifex Secreto: S. Chrysost. Dignum et Justum est te canere, te benedicere, te laudare, tibi gratias agere, te adorare in omni loco Dominatus tui. Tu enim es Deus inexplicabilis, imperceptibilis, invisibilis incomprehensibilis, semper existens eodem modo existens, Tu et Unigenitus tuus Filius, et Spiritus tuus Sanctus tu ex non esse ad esse nos produxisti, et prostratos erexisti denuo, nec desististi omnia agens donec nos in Coelum perduceres et regnum tuum donares Futurum.

S. Chrysost.

Служители — О сихъ всѣхъ благодаримъ тя, и единороднаго твоего Сына, и духа твоего святаго, о всѣхъ ихже вѣмы, и ихже не вѣмы, явленныхъ и не явленныхъ благодѣяниихъ бывшихъ на насъ. Благодаримъ тя и о службѣ сей, юже от руку нашихъ прияти сподобилъ еси, аще и предстоятъ тебѣ тысящами архангеловъ, и тмами ангеловъ, херувими и серафими, шестокрилатая, многоочитая, возвышающаяся, пернатая. — Лит.

Архиерей возглас. — Побѣдную пѣснь поюща, вопиюща, взывающа и глаголюща.

Пѣвцы. — Поютъ. Святъ, святъ, святъ Господь Саваофъ. исполнь небо и земля славы его, осанна во вышнихъ. Благословенъ грядый во имя Господне. Осанна во вышнихъ.

Егда же чтетъ молитву святитель, совершающии со служащими исходятъ с оружиемъ [illegible] и преклонивше колѣна во царскихъ вратѣхъ на святое освящение.

Егда возглашаетъ: Побѣдную: и архидиаконъ звѣздою со дискоса творитъ крестъ вверху дискоса, и цѣлование благословение странъ. Пришедъ со дигнитарии, или со бояры, держатъ гострупъ предвовечными.

Архиерей тайно. — Съ сими и мы, Владыко, блаженными силами, Владыко человѣколюбче, вопиемъ, и глаголемъ. Святъ еси и пресвятъ, ты и единородный твой Сынъ, и Духъ твой Святый. Святъ еси и пресвятъ, и великолѣпна слава твоя. Иже миръ твой тако возлюбилъ еси, яко и Сына твоего единороднаго дати, да всякъ вѣруяй в него не погибнетъ, но да иматъ животъ вѣчный. Иже пришедъ и все еже о насъ смотрѣние исполнивъ, в нощь в нюже предаяшеся, паче же самъ себе предаяше за мирский животъ, приемъ хлѣбъ во святыя своя, и пречистыя и непорочныя руки, благодаривъ, и благословивъ, освятивъ, преломивъ, даяше святымъ своимъ ученикомъ и апостоломъ

Celebrantes. Pro his omnibus gratias agimus tibi, et Unigenito tuo Filio, et Spiritui tuo Sancto, pro omnibus quæ novimus et quæ ignoramus, manifestis et latentibus beneficiis quæ in nos contuleras, gratias agimus tibi, et pro hoc Sacrificio, quod ex manibus nostris suscipere dignatus es, quamuis tibi adsistant millia Archangelorum, et decem millia Angelorum, Cherubim et Seraphim, sex alas habentia, multis oculis prædita, sublimia, alata. — Chorus. S. Chrys.

Pontifex alta voce: Victorialem hymnum canentia, clamantia, inuocantia, et dicentia.

Cantus. Canitur: Sanctus, Sanctus, Sanctus Dominus Sabaoth; Pleni sunt Cœli et terra gloria tua Osanna in excelsis. Benedictus qui venit in nomine Domini, Osanna in excelsis.

Cum vero Pontifex legit orationem, Ceroferarij cum candelis exeunt per Septentrionalem Portam, et flexis genibus in Regia expectant S.ᵐ Consecrationem.

Cum dicit Victorialem &c. Archidiaconus tollens Stellam ex Patina exprimit Crucis Signum supra Patinam, et osculatus illam reponit ad partem; accipiens cum Diacono flabella, uel suas stolas tenent alte supra Apostola.

Pontifex Secreto: Cum his et nos beatis Potestatibus Domine clementissime clamamus, et dicimus, Sanctus es, et Sanctissimus, tu, et Unigenitus tuus filius, et Spiritus tuus Sanctus. Sanctus es et Sanctissimus, et magnifica gloria tua, qui mundum tuum sic dilexisti, ut Unigenitum tuum filium dares, ut omnis qui credit in illum non pereat, sed habeat vitam æternam, qui cum venisset, et omne super nos Regimen complesset, nocte qua tradebatur, uel potius se tradens pro mundi vita, accipiens panem in Sanctas et intemeratas ac immaculatas manus suas gratias agens et benedixit, Sanctificauit fregit dedit S.ᵗⁱˢ suis Discipulis, et Apostolis dicens.

+

Служители. Таже святитель возвращает звездицу свою благо- Аминь
лагая, и посвящая звездицу и вся части хлеба и чашу
глаголет велегласно. Глаголют же тогда втай
вси иереи сослужители вслух со святителем.
Аще ли есть презвитер же во станоотвентный глаголет тогда, и на участие его же аще предвар-
дал есть святитель.

Архиерей возглашает. Приимите и ядите. Се есть тело мое еже
за вы ломимое во оставление грехов. Аминь.

Поклоняется и глаголет втай. Также и чашу по вечери глаголя.

Возглашает. Пийте от нея вси, сия есть кровь моя
нового завета, яже за вы и за многих изли-
ваемая во оставление грехов. Аминь.

Поклоняется и глаголет втай. Поминающе убо спасительную сию заповедь
и всех яже о нас бывших, креста, гроба,
тридневнаго воскресения, яже на небеса возшествия,
одесную седения, втораго и
славнаго паки пришествия.
И абие приемлет святая крестообразно:
десною убо рукою святый дискос, левою же
святую чашу, и возвышает я.

Архиерей возглашает. Твоя от твоих тебе приносяще о всех и
за вся.

Пение. Поют же вся. Тебе поем, тебе благословим,
тебе благодарим Господи и молимтися
Боже наш.

Поклоняется и глаголет втай. Еще приносим тебе словесную сию и безкровную службу, и просим и молимся и
милися деем, посли Духа твоего Святаго на ны
и на предлежащия дары сия.
Зде диакони отлагают рипиды, священнодейцы же
оставльше и поклон сотворше от-
ходят паки во олтарь с совершенными братие.

Celebrantes | Chorus. | 48

S. Chrysost.

Tum Pontifex eleuans dextram suam benedicens, et consecrans Agnum et omnes particulas Panis et Calicem dicit alta voce. Sed et idem secreto Sacerdotes Concelebrantes simul cum Pontifice dicunt: Quodsi est Praesbyter recens creatus dicit idem super Particulam quam illi antea dederat Pontifex.

Sacerdos alta voce: Accipite et manducate, hoc est corpus meum, quod pro vobis frangitur in remissionem peccatorum. — Amen.

Caput demisse inclinat et dicit secreto: Similiter et Calicem postquam cœnauit dicens.

Alta voce: Bibite ex hoc omnes, hic est Sanguis meus noui Testamenti, qui pro vobis et pro multis effunditur in remissionem peccatorum. — Amen.

Adorat et dicit secreto: Memores itaq. Saluliferi huius mandati et omnium quæ pro nobis facta sunt, Crucis Sepulchri, triduanæ Resurrectionis, in cœlos ascensionis ad dexteram Sessionis, Secundi et gloriosi iterum aduentus.

Et tunc accipit Sancta in modum Crucis: dextera quidem manu Sanctam Patinam, sinistra vero Sanctum Calicem, et eleuat illa.

Pontifex alta voce: Tua ex tuis tibi offerimus pro omnibus et per omnia.

Cantus: Canitur: Te canimus te benedicimus, tibi gratias agimus Dñe, et supplicamus tibi Deus nr.

Pontifex adorat et dicit secreto: Præterea offerimus tibi rationabile hoc et Incruentum Sacrificium, et rogamus et supplicamus, et deprecamur demittas Spiritum tuum Sanctum super nos et super Proposita dona hæc.

Hic Diaconi reponunt flabella. Ceroferarij vero surgentes et adoratione facta recedunt iterum ad Altare per Septentrionalem Portam.

Священницы

Архиерей поклоня[ется]: Боже милостив буди мне грешному.

Трижды глаголя: Господи иже пресвятаго Духа в третий час апостолом послав, того благий не отыми от нас, но обнови нас молящихтися.

Архидиакон: Не отвержи мене от лица твоего, и Духа Святаго твоего не отыми от мене.

Архиерей: Господи иже пресвятаго Духа и пр.

Архидиакон: Сердце чисто созижди во мне Боже, и дух прав обнови во утробе моей.

Архиерей: Господи иже пресвятаго Духа и пр.

Архидиакон: Благослови владыко святый хлеб.

Архиерей благословляет тело Хво: Сотвори убо хлеб сей честное тело Христа твоего.

Архидиакон: Благослови владыко святую чашу.

Архиерей. Благослов. кровь Хву: А иже в чаши сей честную кровь Христа твоего.

Архидиакон: Благослови владыко обоя.

Архиерей: Преложив Духом твоим Святым.

Яко быти причащающимся во трезвение души, во оставление грехов, во общение Святаго Духа, во исполнение царствия небеснаго, во дерзновение еже к тебе, не во суд или во осуждение. Еще приносим тебе словесную сию службу, о иже в вере почивших, праотцех, отцех, патриарсех, пророцех, апостолех, проповедницех, евангелистех, мученицех, исповедницех, постницех, и о всяком дусе во вере скончавшемся.

Celebrantes.		Chorus.
[Pon]tifex adorat ter dicens:	Deus propitius esto mihi peccatori.	S. Chrysostomus
	Domine qui Sanctissimum Spiritum tertia ho[ra] in Apostolis misisti, hunc optime, ne auferas a nobis, sed innoves nos supplicantes tibi.	
[A]rchidiaconus:	Cor mundum crea in me Deus, et Spiritum rectum innova in visceribus meis.	
Pontifex:	Domine qui Sanctissimum Spiritum etc.	
Archidiaconus:	Ne projicias me a facie tua, et Spiritum San[c]tum tuum ne auferas a me.	
Pontifex:	Domine qui Sanctissimum Spiritum etc.	
Archidiacon.	Benedic Domine Sanctum panem.	
Pontifex benedi[cit] Corpus Christi:	Fac panem quidem hunc pretiosum corpus Christi tui.	
Archidiacon:	Benedic Domine Sanctum Calicem	
Pontifex benedicit [S]anguinem Chri[sti]:	Qui autem est in Calice pretiosum Sanguinem Filii tui.	
Archidiacon:	Benedic Domine Utrumq[ue]	
Pontifex:	Permutans Spiritu tuo Sancto.	
	Ut fiat accipientibus in sobrietatem animae, in remissionem peccatorum, in communicationem San[c]ti Spiritus, in regni Caelorum plenitudinem, in fiduciam erga te, non in Judicium aut da[m]mnationem, Item offerimus tibi rationabile hoc obsequium, pro his, qui in fide requiescunt Propatribus, Patribus, Patriarchis, Prophetis, Apostolis, Praeconibus, Evangelistis, Martyribus, Confessoribus, continentibus, et omni Spiritu in fide decedente.	

Служители

Лист

Посем Архидиакон дает Кадилницу Святителю: Который кадит Святая.

Архиерей возглашает. Изрядно Пресвятое, чистое, преблагосла-
венное, Славное, Владычице нашее, Богоро-
дице, приснодевы Марии.

Пение. Поют вси. Достойно есть яко воистинну
блажити тя Богородицу, присноблажен-
ную и пренепорочную, и матерь Бога нашего.
Честнейшую херувим, и Славнейшую без сравне-
ния Серафим, без истления Бога Слова
родшую, сущую Богородицу тя величаем.

Но Архидиакон по возгласе Святите-
леве, взяв кадилницу кадит престол.
Пресвятаго образно, и весь олтарь, отдав же
Кадилницу Панамарю, станет на месте своем.

Архиерей гл. Святаго честнаго и всеславнаго Пресвятаго Господина. Заступлениям честных Небесных сил безплотных. Честнаго и славнаго пророка, предтечи и крестителя Господина Иоанна. Святых славных и все-
хвалных Апостол. Святаго N. и всех

Х Святаго На-стоящаго.

Святых твоих, ихже молитвами посети
нас Боже, и помяни всех прежде усопших
о надежди воскресения живота вечнаго.

Воспоминает живых. Усопших.

О спасении, посещении и оставлении грехов раба божия N.N.
О покои и оставлении грехов души раба твоего N.N.
Бывшим во Боже наш На месте светле, идеже
отбеже печаль и воздыхания, и покой во
идеже присещает свет лица твоего. Еще молимтися помяни Господи всякое епископ-
ство православных право правящих Слово
твоея истинны, всякое пресвитерство,
еже о Христе диаконство и всякий Священнический
чин. Еще при-

Postea Archidiaconus dat Thuribulum Pontifici, ille vero incensat Sancta.

Pontifex alta voce: Præsertim Sanctissimæ, et intemeratæ plus quam benedictæ Reginæ nostræ Deiparæ et semper Virginis MARIÆ.

Cantus: Canitur: Dignum est, ut vere beatificemus te Deiparam semper beatissimam et penitus irreprehensibilem et Matrem Dei nostri: Venerabiliorem Cherubim, et gloriosiorem absque comparatione Seraphim, incorruptibiliter Deum verbum parientem, vere Deiparam te magnificamus.

Sed Archidiaconus post Pronunciationem Pontificis, accipiens Thuribulum incensat Sanctam Mensam in modum Crucis, et totum Altare et reddens Thuribulum Sacerdoti consistit in loco suo.

Pontifex secreto: Pontificale Myster. Virtute pretiosæ et Vivificantis Crucis Domini, Protectione Gloriosarum, Cœlestium Virtutum, Incorporearum, Honorabilis et Gloriosi Prophetæ, Præcursoris ac Baptistæ Domini, Joannis, SS. gloriosorum et laudabilissimorum Apostolorum Sancti N. N. et omnium SS. tuorum

S. Chrysostomus

... commemorat viventis

quorum precibus protege nos Deus et memento omnium defunctorum in spe Resurrectionis vitæ æternæ.

Commemorat vivos: Pro salute, Protectione, remissione peccatorum servi Dei N. N.

Mortuos: Pro requie et remissione peccatorum animæ famuli tui N. N. in loco luminoso, ubi non est dolor, gemitus, colloces ipsam Deus noster et requiescere facias ipsam ubi visitat lumen vultus tui. Item precamur te memento Dñe omnium Episcoporum orthodoxorum rite dicentium verbum tuæ veritatis, omnis Presbyteratus in Christo Diaconatus, et totius Sacerdotalis Ordinis.

+

Служители — *Лит*

Еще приносим тебе словесное сие служение, о вселенней, о святей Кафолическей и Апостольстей церкви, и о иже в чистоте и честнем жительстве пребывающих. О благоверном и Христолюбивом Короли нашем N. о всей палате и воех его. Даждь ему Господи мирно царствовати, да и мы в тишине его, тихое и безмолвное житие поживем, во всяком благочестии и чистоте.

Архиерей аще есть Митрополита возглашает.

Во первых помяни Господи Вселенскаго Архиерея Нашего, Святейшаго N. егоже даруй святым твоим церквам во мире, цела, честна, здрава, долгоденствующа право правяща слово твоея истины.

Архипресвитер.

Во первых помяни Господи Митрополита Нашего N. егоже даруй. и.

Архиерей аще несть Митрополита возглашает.

Во первых помяни Господи Митрополита нашего N. и.

Архипресвитер.

Во первых помяни Господи Архиепископа, или Епископа Нашего N. и.

Архиерей втай

Помяни Господи града сего в немже живем, и всякаго града и страны, и иже верою живущих в них. Помяни Господи плавающих, путешествующих, недугующих, страждущих, плененных и спасение их. Помяни Господи плодоносящих, и добродеющих, во святых твоих церквах, и поминающих нищая, и на вся нас милости твоя низпосли.

Возглашает.

И даждь нам Господи, единеми усты, и единем сердцем славити и воспевати пречестное и великолепное имя твое, Отца и Сына и Святаго духа, ныне и присно и во веки веков. Аминь

И да будут милости великаго Бога, и Спаса нашего Иисуса Христа со всеми вами.

И со духом тво

Chrysostomi

Celebrantes.		Chorus.
	Etiam offerimus tibi rationabile hoc obsequium pro orbe Terrarum, pro Sancta Catholica et Apostolica Ecclesia, pro his qui in Sanctitate et venerabili [illegible] vitam degunt. Pro fidelissimo et Christianissimo nostro Rege, cuncto palatio et exercitu ipsius, tribue illi Domine pacificum Regnum, ut et nos in tranquillitate ipsius quietam et pacificam vitam peragamus in omni pietate et honestate.	S. Chrysostomi
[illegible]tifex est Metropo. altâ voce dicit:	Inprimis memento Domine Oecumenici Pontificis nostri Sanctissimi N. quem dones Sanctis tuis Ecclesijs in pace, sospitem, honorabilem, incolumem, longaevum, recte dirigentem Verbum tuae Veritatis.	
[illegible]int. Rur.		P. Ruten.
[illegible]tificale Rut. [illegible]rchipresbyter:	Inprimis memento Domine Metropolitae nri N. quem dona &c.	
[illegible] Pontifex n' est Metro. [illegible] altâ voce dicit:	Inprimis memento Dñe Metropolitae nri N. quem dones &c.	
[illegible]presbyter:	Inprimis memento Dñe Archiepiscopi [uel Episcopi] nostri N. quem dones &c.	
[illegible]tifex secreto: Chrysostomus.	Memento Dñe Urbis in qua habitamus, et omnis Civitatis, et Regionis, et cum fide habitantium in ipsis: Memento Dñe nauigantium, peregrinantium, aegrotantium, laborantium, captiuorum, et salutis ipsorum. Memento Dñe fructus et bona opera exhibentium in Sanctis tuis Ecclesijs et qui recordantur pauperum, et super omnes nos miserationes tuas demitte.	S. Chrys.
Altâ voce:	Et tribue nobis in uno ore et uno corde laudare et glorificare valde honorabile et magnificum nomen tuum Patris et Filij et Spiritus Sancti, nunc et semper, et in secula seculorum.	Amen.
	Et sint misericordiae magni Dei et saluatoris nostri Jesu Christi cum omnibus vobis.	Et cum Spiritu tuo.

Святителли — Заде аще есть нарочитый празвитер: диаконъ приносит евангелие и поставляет е пред святою трапезою. Архипрезвитер же дает митру святителеви. Се же поклон святитель сотворивше и митру приимут глаголет ли: цем по молитве. И архидиаконъ станет в царских дверех. — Лит.

Архидиаконъ велегласно. — О себе и всякой семьи помышлении, со своих сослужителех, и о всех и за вся.

Архиерей стат. — Всечестнейшом Архиереом, Святейшом N. приносящом честныя и святыя дары Господу Богу нашему.

Митрополита глаголет. — Преосвященном Митрополите нашем кир N. Архиепископе Киевском, Галицком и всея Россіи приносящом честныя и святыя дары Господеви Богу нашему.

Аще нест Митрополита глаголет. — О освященном Деспоте нашем кир N. Архиепископе или епископе N. приносящем честныя и святыя дары Господеви Богу нашему.

Архиерей глаголет. — Честном их пресвитерстве, еже о Христе диаконстве и всем освященническом чине.

Архиерей стоит. — О державе, победе, пребывании, во мире, здравии, и спасении Благоверному Господарю нашему Королю N. и всей полати его, и всем православным Князем и паном нашым.

Глаголет. — О мире всего мира, благостоянии, и соединении святых Божиих церквей. О епархиях и утвержении, и утешении Христолюбиваго воинства.

О спасении людей предстоящих во святем церкви сей и помышляющих и молящихся кождо их со своих сослужителех, и со всех и за вся. — И о всех и за вся

Заде аще будет становление, посвящает в диаконы. Святитель остав митру злову станет в престоли. Архидиаконъ же исходит царскими враты и станет на амвоне.

lebrantes. Chorus. 44

ontificale Rituum.

Hic si est solennissimum festum Diaconus adfert sedem, et collocat eam ante Sacram Mensam. Archipresbyter vero imponit Mitram Pontificii. Hic autem facta Sanctis adoratione et Mitra suscepta consistet facie versus Populum, tenens manu dextera sedem Episcopale. Et Archidiaconus consistit in Sacra Porta.

J. Rituum.

Pro omnibus, quaecunque quis cogitat, pro proprijs peccatis et pro vniuersis et singulis.

Oecumenico Pontifici Sanctissimo N. offerenti pretiosa et Sancta dona Domino Deo nostro.

Illustrissimo Metropolitae nostro Dno N. Archiepiscopo Chiouiensi, Haliciensi, et totius Russiae offerenti pretiosa et Sancta dona Dno Deo.

Pontifex non est Metropolita, additur:

Reuerendissimo Domino nostro Domino N. Archiepiscopo vel Episcopo offerenti &c.

Pontifex sedet

Venerabilibus illorum Praesbyteris, in Christo Diaconis, et vniuerso Sacerdotali ordini.

Pontifex stat.

Pro Dominio Victoria, permanentia in pace, Sanitate et Salute, orthodoxo Dno nostro Regi N. et toti Senatui ipsius et omnibus orthodoxis Ducibus et Dominis nostris.

Sedet.

Pro pace totius Mundi, Stabilitate et vnione Sanctarum Dei Ecclesiarum. Pro confortatione et corroboratione et consolatione Exercitus Christiani. Pro Salute populi praesentis in Sancta Ecclesia hac, et cogitantibus singulis illorum, pro proprijs peccatis et pro vniuersis et pro singulis.

Et pro vniuersis et singulis.

Pontificale Rituum. Hic si adest Consecrandus, consecratur in Diaconum. Pontifex consurgens Mitra deposita consistit ante Altare. Archidiaconus vero egressus ex Altari Porta Regia consistit in Ambona.

Pontific. Rit.

Священ. Архидиакон:

Вся святыя помянувше паки и паки миром Господу помолимся. — Лик. Господи пом.

О принесенных и освященных честных дарех Господу помолимся. — Госп. пом.

Яко да человеколюбец Бог наш приемь их во святый и пренебесный и мысленный свой жертвенник, во воню благоухания духовнаго, возниспослет нам божественную благодать и дар святаго духа Господу помолимся. — Госп. пом.

О избавитися нам от всякия скорби гнева беды и нужды Господу помолимся. — Госп. пом.

Заступи, спаси и(.) — Госп. пом.

День весь совершенна(.) — Подай Господи.

Ангела мирна(.) — Под. Госп.

Милости и прощения(.) — Под. Госп.

Добрых и полезных(.) — Под. Госп.

Прочее время(.) — Под. Госп.

Христианския кончины(.) — Под. Госп.

Соединение веры и причастие святаго духа испросивше, сами себе, и друг друга, и весь живот наш Христу Богу предадим. — Тебе Господи.

Архиерей молитву тай.

Тебе предлагаем живот наш весь и надежду, владыко человеколюбче, и просим и молим и милися деем, сподоби нас причаститися небесных твоих и страшных таин, сея священныя и духовныя трапезы, с чистою совестию, во оставление грехов, во прощение прегрешений, во общение духа святаго, в наследие царствия небеснаго, в дерзновение еже к тебе, не в суд или во осуждение.

[Chrysostomus] | + | 45
[Ce]lebrantes. | | Chorus.
[...]hidiacon[us]

Omnium Sanctorum mentione facta, iterum atque iterum Dnm deprecemur. — S. Chrysost. Kyrie Eleyson.

Pro oblatis et consecratis pretiosis donis Dnm deprecem. — Kyr. El.

Vt amator hominum Deus noster suscipiens ipsa in Sanctum, et Supercœleste, ac Intellectuale Suum Altare, in odorem Suauitatis Spiritualis, uice uersa demittat nobis Diuinam gratiam et donum Sancti Spiritus, Dnm deprecemur. — K. E.

Vt eripiat nos ab omni Tribulatione &c. — K. E.

Adiuua salua, miserere et custodi nos &c. — K. E.

Diem totum, perfectum, Sanctum, pacificum &c. — Concede Dne.

Angelum pacis fidelem Ductorem. &c. — Conc. Dne.

Indulgentiam et remissionem peccatorum &c — Conc. Dne.

Bona et vtilia animabus nostris &c. — Conc. Dne.

Vt residuum tempus vitæ nostræ &c. — Conc. Dne.

Christianum finem vitæ nostræ &c. — Conc. Dne.

Vnionem fidei et Comunicationem Sancti Spiritus postulantes, nosmetipsos et inuicem et totam vitam nostram Chro Deo comittamus. — Tibi Domine

[P]ontifex secreto

Tibi committimus vitam nostram totam et spem Dne Clementissime, et rogamus, et deprecamur, ac Supplicamus: dignos fac nos participes esse Supercœlestium tuorum, et tremendorum mysteriorum huius Sacræ, et Spiritualis mensæ cum pura conscientia, in remissionem peccatorum, in veniam delictorum, in Spiritus Sancti comunicationem, in Regni Cœlorum hæreditatem, in fiduciam erga te, non in reatum, aut in damnationem.

Служители.		
Архиерей возглашает.	И сподоби нас Владыко со дерзновением неосужденно смети призывати Тебе пренебеснаго Бога Отца и глаголати.	Лик. Отче наш.
~~Глаголашате~~	Яко Твое есть царство, и сила, и слава, Отца и Сына, и Святаго Духа, ныне и присно и во веки веком.	Аминь.
Обращся благославит.	Мир всем.	И со духом твоим.
	Диакон врата святыя затворяет.	
Архидиакон	Главы ваша Господеви преклоните.	Тебе Господи.
Архиерей главу преклонше отай молит.	Благодарим Тя Царю невидимый иже неисчетною Твоею силою вся содетельствовал еси, и множеством милости Твоея от не сущих во бытие вся привел. Сам Владыко свыше призри на преклоншая Тебе главы своя, не бо преклониша плоти и крови, но Тебе страшному Богу. Ты убо Владыко предлежащая всем нам во благое изравняй по коегождо своей потребе, плавающим сплавай, путешествующим спутешествуй, болящих исцели, Врачу душ и телес.	
Возглашает.	Благодатию и щедротами и человеколюбием единороднаго Твоего Сына с нимже благословен еси со пресвятым, и благим и животворящим Твоим Духом, ныне и присно и во веки веком.	Аминь.
Паки отай. Главу преклонше	Вонми Господи Иисусе Христе Боже наш от святаго жилища Твоего, и от престола славы царствия Твоего, и прииди во еже освятити нас, иже горе со Отцем седяй, и зде нам невидимо спребываяй. И сподоби державною Твоею рукою преподати нам пречистаго тела Твоего, и честныя крове, и нами всем людем.	

Chrysostomus.

Celebrantes. | Chorus. 46

S. Chrysostomus

Alta voce: Et dignos facias nos Dñe cum fiducia irreprobatos audere inuocare te Supercælestem Deum Patrem et dicere: — Pater noster &c.

Quoniam tuum est Regnum, et potentia, et gloria, Patris et Filij et Spiritus Sancti nunc et semper, et in secula Seculorum. — Amen.

Conuersus benedicit: Pax + omnibus. — Et cum Spiritu tuo.

Diaconus Portam Sanctam ocludit.

Archidiaconus: Capita vestra Dño inclinate. — Tibi Domine

Pontifex capite inclinato secreto orat: Gratias agimus tibi Rex inuisibilis, qui immensa tua potentia cuncta creasti, et multitudine misericordiæ tuæ ex nihilo in esse produxisti cuncta, tu Dñe Cælitus respice ad inclinantes tibi ipsorum capita, non enim inclinarunt carni, et sanguini, sed tibi tremendo Deo, tu igitur Dñe proposita omnibus nobis in bonum dirigens pro cuiusque proprio usu, cum nauigantibus nauiga, cum peregrinantibus comes, ægrotos sana medice animarum et corporum.

Alta voce: Gratia et miserationibus, et pietate Unigeniti Filij tui cum quo benedictus es cum sanctissimo et optimo et Viuificante tuo Spiritu, nunc et semper, et in secula Seculorum.

Verum secreto, capite inclinato. Respice Dñe Jesu Christe Deus noster de sancto habitaculo tuo, et de throno gloriæ regni tui, et veni ad Sanctificandum nos, qui in excelsis simul cum Patre resides, et hic nobiscum inuisibiliter existis: et dignare potenti tua manu participes facere nos immaculati corporis tui et pretiosi Sanguinis, et per nos totum populum.

Служители. Здѣ діаконъ со свѣщоносцомъ дастъ о[illegible] на двухъ святителехъ отъ левое страны. Литъ

Архиерей [illegible] Боже очисти мя грѣшнаго и помилуй мя.

Сотворитъ.

Архидиаконъ. Святитель возноситъ святый агнецъ надъ дискосомъ.

Архиерей возглашение. Святая святымъ.

Почтвенно. Единъ святъ, единъ господь, Іисусъ Христосъ во славу Бога отца. Аминь.

Также. Причастникъ дневи или святомъ.

Архидиаконъ двери райския затворитъ: отходитъ во олтаре вратами сѣверскими и станетъ при святителю.

Архидиаконъ. Раздроби владыко святый хлѣбъ.

Архиерей раздробляя святый агнецъ. Раздробляется и разделяется агнецъ божий, сынъ отечь, раздробляемъ и неразделяемъ, и всегда ядомъ, и николиже снедаемъ, но причащающихся освящая.

Также. Познаста тебе господи ученика въ преломлении хлѣба: даждь и намъ познати тебе во свѣтъ вѣчномъ.

Архидиаконъ. Исполни владыко святую чашу.

Архиерей едину часть святаго агнеца оземъ, творитъ с нею крестъ верхъ святыя чаши, и вметаетъ вню.

Архиерей. Исполнение + вѣры святаго духа.

Архидиаконъ. Благослови владыко теплоту.

Приимъ теплоту отъ пономаря.

Архиерей [illegible]. Яко + божественнаго порождения словомъ сотворилъ [illegible] естество, точно испытахаши [illegible] отъ нетлен[illegible] и проводимыхъ ти рекъ, [illegible] слово на[illegible] теплотою духа.

Также. [illegible] благословенна теплота святыхъ твоихъ всегда нынѣ [illegible]

Архидиаконъ вливаетъ въ святую чашу + мало. Теплота вѣры исполнь духа святаго. Аминь.

47

Celebrantes. | Chorus.

S. Chrysostomus

Archidiaconus cum Acolythis ... aquam manibus Pontificis ... te sinistra.

Pontifex adorat ter: Deus munda me peccatorem et miserere mei

Archidiaconus alta voce: Attendamus.

Pontifex elevat Sanctum Agnum supra Patinam.

Pontifex alta voce: Sancta Sanctis

Cantus: Unus Sanctus, unus Dominus Jesus Christus in gloriam Dei Patris. Amen.

Postea canunt Versiculum Communionis de die, vel de ... Archidiaconus autem dicto [Attendamus] vadit ad Altare per portam Septentrionalem, et assistit Pontifici.

Archidiaconus secreto: Frange Domine Sanctum Agnum Panem.

Pontifex frangens: Frangitur et dividitur Agnus Dei Filius Patris partitus et non divisus: qui ubique editur, nec umquam absumitur, Sed communicantes sanctificat. Item. Cognoverunt te Domine Discipuli in fractione panis: dones quoque nobis ut cognoscamus te in vita aeterna.

Archidiaconus: Impleas Domine Sanctum Calicem.

Pontifex unam partem Sancti Agni sumens, exprimit cum illa Crucem supra S. Calicem, et immittit in illum.

Pontifex: Plenitudo Fidei ✠ Spiritus Sancti

Diaconus, accepta aqua calida: Benedic Domine calidam hanc

Pontifex benedicit aquam: Lavacrum ✠ Divinae generationis Verbo ... humanae generationis abundanter effundis mihi rivos, ex incorruptibili et transfixo tuo latere, o Dei Verbum consignans fervore Spiritus. Item: Benedictus sit fervor Sanctorum tuorum ubique nunc. &c.

Pontificale Armen.

S. Chrysost.

Diaconus infundit aquam in Calicem: Fervor fidei plenus Spiritu Sancto. Amen.

Pontificale Arm.

S. Chrysost.

Служители архиерей ота.

\+

Лит.

Верую Господи и исповедую, яко ты еси
Христос, Сын Бога живаго, пришедый в мир
грешных спасти, от них же первый есмь аз.
Вечери твоея тайныя днесь Сыне Божий, причасть:
ника мя приими, не повем бо врагом твоим
тайны, ни лобзания ти дам яко Иуда, но яко
разбойник исповедую ти; помяни мя Гос:
поди во царствии твоем. Да не в суд
или во осуждение будет мне причастие свя:
тых твоих тайн Господи, но во исце:
ления души и тела, и в жизнь вечную.

творит поклон.

Боже милостив буди мне грешному, Боже
очисти грехи моя и помилуй мя.
Честное и пречистое тело Господа Бога
и спаса нашего Іс Ха преподаеться мне рабу
Божию архиерею N. во оставление гре:
хов моих и в жизнь вечную.

Потребляеть Святый агнец. Поклоняеться и причащаеться кровии Хвой.

Честная и пресвятая кровь Господа Бога &
Се прикоснуся устнам моим, и отъи:
мет беззакония моя, и грехи моя по:
требит, всегда, ныне &.
Егдаже сия творит архиерей, вси со:
служители иереи и диакони целуют
руце свои: диакони же ораром своим пер:
вязуються крестаобразно. И тако вси
стоят около престола, ожидающе свя:
таго причастия.
Затем есть презвитер новоставляемь:
ый напред престола, и отъложивше свя:
тую часть, юже сам посвятивше есть, на свя:
той дискос, приемлет иную от свя:
тителя посвященную.
И престольнов з десныя страны архипрезвитер и вси
сослужители иереи и диакони, и десную простирают
на престоле близ святаго дискоса. Глаголют же:

S. Chrysost.

Celebrantes

Pontifex Secreto:

Chorus 48

S. Chrysost.

Credo Domine et Confiteor: quoniam tu es Christus Filius Dei vivi, qui venisti in mundum ut peccatores salvos faceres, ex quibus primus sum ego. Cœnæ tuæ mysticæ hodie Fili Dei participem me facias, non enim dicam inimicis tuis mysterium, neq osculum tibi dabo quemadmodum Judas Sed ut latro confiteor tibi; Memento mei Dne in Regno tuo. Non sit mihi in Judicium vel condemnationem comunio SS.rum tuorum Sacramentorum Dne, sed in medelam animæ et corporis, et in vita æterna. Deus propitius esto mihi peccatori, Deus munda peccata mea et miserere.

Plures hic dicuntur Orationes sed illæ apud Ruthenos ex devotione adduntur tantum, non de necessitate, sicut hæ quæ scripta sunt.

Adorat Sancta:

Consumit S. Agnum.

Pontificale Ruthenum

Pretiosum et castissimum corpus Dni Dei et Salvatoris nostri Jesu Christi datur mihi servo Dei N. Episcopo in remissionem peccatorum meorum, et in vitam æternam.

S. Ruthenum

Communicat Sanguinem Dni

Pretiosus et Sanctissimus Sanguis Dni Dei et Salv. &c.

S. Chrysost.

Hoc tetigit labia mea, et auferet iniquitates meas et peccata mea tollet, ubiq nunc &c.

S. Chrys.

Hæc autem absolvente Pontifice, omnes concelebrantes, Sacerdotes et Diaconi: lavant manus suas: Diaconi præterea stolis suis se præcingunt in modum Crucis: Atq ita omnes consistunt circa S. Mensam, expectantes S. Comunionem. At si est Sacerdos recens consecratus, primo accedit, et reponens suam particulam (quam ipse consecraverat) in Sanctam patinam, accipit illam a Pontifice consecratam. Tu accedunt Archipresbyter a parte dextra, et omnes concelebrantes Sacerdotes et Diaconi dextram porrigunt supra Altare iuxta Sanctam patinam. Dicunt ergo:

+

Сослужители

Архиерей. Иерею [или Диакону] проговорит. Лит

Сослужитель. Преподаждь ми Владыко честное и пресвятое тело Господа Бга и Спаса нашего Іиса Ха.

Архиерей. Преподается рабу Божию Иерею [или Диакону] честное и пресвятое тело Господа Бга и Спаса нашего Іи Ха во оставление грехов его и в жизнь вечную.

И тако дает часть Святую в руки Сослужителю: он же абие целует руку и ланит Святителев.

Архиерей. Христос посреде нас.

Сослужитель. Есть, и будет.

Ставшеже окрест престола Святаго потребляют глаголюще молитвы вышеписанныя. Верую Господи и исповедую &c.

Паки Архиерей. Иерею [или Диакону] проговорит.

Сослужитель. Се прихожду ко безсмертному царю.

Архиерей. Причащается раб Божий Иерей [или Диакон] честныя и пресвятыя Крови Господа Бга и Спаса нашего Іи Ха.

Даетже Святую чашу да пиет мало по единому от них. Причастившеся всех, поставляет Святая на трапезе, и поклон со умилением творит. Вступившеже на левую страну престола. И единому от священников пренесши сия перести свою руку вливает.

Архиерей. втай. Благодарим тя Владыко Человеколюбче, Благодателю душ наших, яко и в настоящий день сподобил еси нас небесных твоих и безсмертных таин. Исправи наш путь, утверди нас во страсе твоем всех, соблюди наш живот, утверди наша стопы, молитвами и молением славныя Богородицы и приснодевы Марии, и всех Святых твоих. Аминь.

…ntifex: Sacerdos [uel Diacone] accede.

…ncelebrans: Porrige mihi Dñe pretiosum et castissimum corpus Dni Dei et Saluatoris nostri Jesu Christi.

…ntifex: Datur seruo Dei Sacerdoti [uel Diacono] pretiosum et castissimum corpus Dni Dei et Saluatoris nostri Jesu Christi in remissionem peccatorum illius, et in vitam aeternam. Atq ita dat particulam sanctam in manum Concelebrantis: qui autem osculatur manum et genam Pontificis. — Pontif. Ant.

…ontificale Ant.

…d in sumptione … S. Chrysostomo … ad missam

…ontifex: Christus in medio nostrum.

Concelebrans: Est et erit. Ac circum Altare stantes sancta consumunt, dicentes orationes supra scriptas: Credo Dñe &c.

…um Pontifex: Sacerdos [uel Diacone] accede.

…ncelebrans: Ecce accedo ad immortalem Regem.

…ntifex: Communicat seruus Dei Sacerdos N. [uel Diaconus N.] pretioso et sacratissimo Sanguini Domini Dei et Saluatoris nostri Jesu Christi.

Dat ergo sanctum calicem, ut bibat parum quilibet eorum. Denique communicatis omnibus, collocat sancta in sacra mensa, et reuerentiam cum humilitate exhibet.

Postmodum recedit ad partem sinistram Altaris, allato sacro vino, per unum ex Acolythis digitos utriusque manus abluit.

…S. Chrysost. — S. Chrysost.

…Pontifex secreto: Gratias agimus tibi Domine benignissime, benefactor animarum nostrarum, quoniam et praesenti die dignos fecisti nos caelestium tuorum, et immortalium mysteriorum, dirige nostrum iter, confirma nos in timore tuo omnes, custodi nostram vitam, fac securos gressus nostros, precibus et intercessione gloriosae Dei parae et semper Virginis Mariae, et omnium Sanctorum tuorum. Amen.

…Pontificale

Священник | Тогда приемлет архидиакон покров свя-
тым сотворяет, и возвысъ святый дискос со-
мещает губою зело опасно во святый потир вся части сущая на дискос, яко едино
и тожде есть тело Христово да ни едино вдрузе остати на дискосе. Сотворше же покрывает святую
чашу малым покровцем. Также и на дис-
кос возлагает звезду и покровец. И по-
клонився встает, и рцет. [illegible]: такожде
и прочии иереи же и диакони. Отвлагают же
диакони орари своя на левое раме по
первому. Но и свещоносцы со свещами
исходят северными враты, и пред царскими [illegible] преклонше обращаются на
святое [illegible]. После диакон святые врата отверзает. Архиерей же взяв
святый потир дает архидиакону. Сей же
приемлет и, износит и станет посреди врат
святых, возвысъ и показуя людем святая.

Архидиакон возглашает. | Со страхом Божиим и с верою приступите.

Чтецы. Благословен грядый во имя Господне, Бог Господь, и явися нам.

Архиерей. | Спаси Боже люди своя, и благослови
достояние твое. | Ис полла эти

Певцы. | Видехом свет истинный, и при-
яхом духа небесного, обретохом веру ис-
тинную, нераздельной святей Троице покла-
няющеся, та бо нас спасла есть.

Святитель абие взяв от архидиакона
святую чашу, поставляет ю на престоле.
Приимше же [illegible] [illegible] дары
святая.

Архиерей втай. | Вознесися на небеса Боже и по всей земли слава твоя.
Отдав же архидиакон [illegible] со дис-
косом сиже относит и на жертвенник. Сам
взем святый потир благословляет им людей.

Возглашает. | Всегда, ныне и присно и во веки веком. | Аминь

Tunc accedens Archidiaconus Sancta [illegible] et eleuans Sanctam Patinam, detergit Spongia [illegible] in Sanctum Calicem omnes particulas quae sunt in patina, tanquam vnum idemque Corpus Christi, vt ne vna quidem [illegible] maneat in Patina. Postquam vero detexerit, operit Calicem [illegible] velo. Similiter super patinam ponit Stellam et vela. Et facta adoratione recedit [illegible] lauat, prout etiam alij Sacerdotes et Diaconi. [illegible] ponit etiam Diaconi stolas suas supra sinistrum brachium secundum prius. Sed et Ceroferarij cum candelis veniunt per Portam Septentrionalem, et [illegible] expectant Sanctam eleuationem. Postea Diaconus Sanctam Portam aperit.

Pontifex accepto S. Calice, dat Archidiacono. hic vero accepto illo effert, et conuersus in medio Sanctae Portae Eleuans et ostendens populo Sancta.

S. Chrys.

Archidiaconus alta voce: Cum timore Dei, ac fide accedite. — S. Chrys.

Canitur: Benedictus qui venit in nomine Domini, Deus Dominus, et illuxit nobis.

Hic si communicantes adsunt, communicant Corpori et Sanguini Domini.

Pontifex: Saluum fac Deus populum tuum, et benedic hæreditati tuæ. — In multos annos Domine.

Cantus: Canitur: Vidimus lucem veram, et suscepimus Spiritum Cælestem indiuisibilem Sanctam Trinitatem adoramus, hæc enim saluos fecit nos.

Tum Pontifex accepto ab Archidiacono [illegible] collocat in Sacra mensa. Susceptoque thuribulo cum thymiamate incensat Sancta.

Pontifex secreto: Eleuatus es super Cælos Deus, et per vniuersam terram gloria tua.

Denique reddens Archidiacono Thuribulum cum Patina (qui refert illa ad Altare Propositionis) ipse accepto Sancto Calice benedicit illo populum.

Alta voce: Vbique nunc, et semper, et in secula seculorum. — Amen.

Святители пения.	Поется. Да исполнятся уста наша ~~[illegible]~~ твоего Господи похвалы, яко сподобил еси нас причащатися святых, безсмертных пре:чистых и животворящих твоих таин. Ты нас вобще соблюди во твоей святыни по вся дни поучатися правде твоей. Аллилуия.	Лик.
	Архиерей обращься отдает святыю чашу Архипрезвитеру. Который приемъ ю отъ:носитъ и поставляетъ на жертовникъ, предъ нимже Архидиаконъ. Иже отдав наши: наше потребляетъ святая. Же сослужащии отходятъ в олтарь северными враты. Диаконже взявши митру на святителя исходитъ и ставъ пред царскими враты.	
Диаконъ.	Прости приимше божественных, святых, безсмертных, пречистых и животворящих таинъ достойно благодаримъ Господа.	Господи помил
	Заступи, спаси, помилуй и сохрани нас Боже твоею благодатию.	Господи помил
	День весь совершенъ свят, миренъ, и безгре:шенъ испросивше сами себе другъ друга, и весь животъ нашъ Христу Богу предадимъ.	Тебе Господи
Архиерей возглашаетъ.	Яко ты еси святыня наша, и тебе славу возсылаемъ, Отцу и Сыну и Святому Духу нынъ и присно, и во веки веков.	Аминь
Диаконъ.	Со миромъ изыдемъ.	О имени Господни
	Господу помолимся.	Господи помил
	~~[illegible]~~ Абие диаконъ входитъ в олтарь враты северными: Архипрез:витерже изшед царскими станетъ пред амвоном.	

Celebrantes
Cantus

Canitur: Impleatur os nostrum laude tua Dñe quoniam dignos fecisti nos Communione Sanctorum, immortalium, immaculatorum et vivificantium tuorum Sacramentorum. Tu nos Deus conserva in tuo Sanctuario omnibus diebus ad meditandum iustitiam tuam. Alleluia.

Pontifex conversus reddit Sanctum Calicem Archipresbytero. Hic vero suscipiens refert illum et collocat in Altari Propositionis, quem praecedens incensat Archidiaconus. Qui reddito Thuribulo consumit Sancta. Hic Ceroferarij redeunt ad Altare per Portam Septentrionalem. Diaconus vero imposita Mitra Pontifici egreditur et consistit ante Regiam Portam.

Chorus
S. Chrysost.

Chrysostomus
Diaconus: Erecti communicantes divinorum, Sanctorum, immortalium, Celestium, et vivificantium mysteriorum, digne gratias agamus Domino. — Domine Miserere.

Suscipe, salva, miserere et conserva nos Deus tua gratia. — Dñe miserere.

Diem totum, perfectum, Sanctum, pacificum, et absque reatu deprecantes, nosmetipsos et invicem, ac omnem vitam nostram Christo Deo committamus. — Tibi Dñe.

Pontifex altâ voce: Quoniam tu es Sanctificatio nostra, et tibi Gloriam damus Patri et Filio, et Sancto Spiritui, nunc, et semper, et in Secula Seculorum. — Amen.

Diaconus. In pace procedamus. — In nomine Dñi

Dominum deprecemur. — Dñe miserere

Et recedit ad Altare Porta Septentrionali. Archipresbyter autem egressus per Sanctam Portam consistit ante Ambonam.

Священнослужители. Благословляй благословящих тя Господи, и освящай Лик.

Архипресвитер уповающия на тя, спаси люди своя, и благослови

Молитву глаголет достояние твое, исполнение церкви твоея сохрани,

Высочайшим. освяти любящих благолепие храма твоего, ты тех

возпрослави божественною силою твоею, и не остави

нас уповающих на тя. Мир мирови твоему даруй, церк-

вам твоим, иереем, великому королю нашему N. воин-

ству, и всем людем твоим. Яко всяко даяние благо, и вся-

кий дар совершен свыше есть сходяй от тебе отца све-

тов, и тебе славу, и благодарение, и поклонение возсы-

лаем, отцу и сыну и святому духу, ныне и пр. Аминь.

Честнейшую трижды. Буди имя Господне благословенно

от ныне и до века. Псалом 33. Благословлю Господа на всякое время и пр.

Архиерей. Исполнение закона и пророк, сам сый Христе Боже наш, ис-

полнивый все отеческое смотрение, исполни радости

и веселия сердца наша. Всегда ныне и пр.

Зде архиерей раздает дары, сиречь частицы от прос-

фор благословенных.

Ста... Щедр и милостив Господь, даяй пищу боящимся его.

Благословит Благословение Господне на вас тем благодатию всегда ныне и пр. Аминь.

люди.

Архидиакон Премудрость. Честнейшую х...

Архиерей. Слава ти Христе Боже наш упование наше, слава тебе. Слава отцу

Архиерей. Воскресый из мертвых Христос истинный

В неделю Бог наш, молитвами пречистыя его матере,

силою честнаго и животворящаго креста

Господня, молением святых славных и

всехвальных апостол, иже во святых от-

ца нашего архиепископа Константина

града Иоанна Златоустаго, и всех святых

помилует и спасет вас, яко благ и

человеколюбец Бог.

Во прочия дни. — Христос истинный Бог наш молитвами

х настоящаго пречистыя его матере святаго N. иже

во святых отца нашего и пр.

V. [illegible] Chrysost.

celebrantes. Qui benedicis benedicentes te Domine, et san- Chorus.

...praesbyter orat ...ce altiore: ctificas in te confidentes, salva populum tuum et S. Chrysost.

benedic hæreditatem tuam, plenitudinem Ecclesiæ tuæ custodi, sanctifica diligentes decorem
domus tuæ, tu ipsos vicissim glorifica divina
tuâ potentia, et ne derelinquas nos sperantes in
te. Pacem mundo tuo tribue, ecclesiis tuis, sacerdotibus, regibus nostris, exercitui, et cuncto populo tuo, quoniam omne datum optimum, et omne
donum perfectum desursum est, descendens à Patre luminum, et tibi gloriam, et gratiarum actio-
nem, et adorationem damus, Patri, et Filio, et Sancto Spiritui nunc et semper, et in sæcula sæculorum. Amen.

...legitur ter: Sit nomen Dñi benedictum ex hoc nunc et usq. in seculum.

Psalmus 33. Benedicam Dominum in omni &c.

Pontifex: Plenitudo legis, et Prophetarum, tu ipse existens
Christe Deus noster, qui complevisti omne paternum
mandatum, expleas gaudio, et hilaritate corda nostra
usq. nunc &c. R. Amen.

...ntifex ... [illegible]: Hic Pontifex distribuit dona, hoc est particulas panium
Propositionis benedictorum: Misericors et misera-
tor Dominus escam dedit timentibus se.

...Secreto ...edicit Populum: Benedictio Domini sit super vos omnes, usq. nunc &c. Amen.

...chidiaconus: Sapientia. Venerabiliorem Cherubim. &c.

...ntifex: Gloria tibi Christe Deus noster, spes nra gloria tibi. Gloria Patri et Filio &c.

...e die Dominico: Qui resurrexit à mortuis Christus verus Deus noster,
precibus castissimæ Matris suæ, virtute pretio-
sæ, et vivificæ Crucis Dominicæ, supplicationibus
Sanctorum gloriosorum, et laudatissimorum Apostolorum, Sancti Patris nostri Archiepiscopi Constantino-
politani Joannis Chrysostomi, et omnium Sanctorum, misereatur et salvet vos ut bonus et clemens Deus.

Alijs diebus: ...ntis: Christus verus Deus noster precibus castissimæ suæ Matris
Sancti, N. et Sancti Patris nostri &c.

Отпусты за усопшихъ.

Иже животомъ и мертвыми обладаетъ Христосъ Литъ.
истинный Богъ нашъ молитвами пречистыя
его Матере и всѣхъ Святыхъ душу преставльша-
гося раба Божия N. в нѣдрахъ Авраама, Исаака,
и Иакова упокоитъ, и насъ помилуетъ и спасетъ
яко благъ и человѣколюбецъ Богъ.

Пѣния понеувное.

Почтѣся: Утверди Боже православную
християнскую вѣру. Соблюди Господи во
православной християнской вѣрѣ Святѣйшого
Короля нашего N. Спаси Господи Митро-
полита или Архиепископа или Епископа
нашего Кир N. и вся православныя христи-
аны Господи спаси.
Тогда диякони преходятъ под руцѣ Святителя, послѣдствующу ему иерею. Который
Ставъ на амвонѣ облачившися со всѣми со-
дѣйствуй Святительскими глаголя всю пѣснь
Исаиино. Ныне отпущаеши. Также
Святый Боже, Отче нашъ. и прочая по предписанному: Тропарь и кондакъ Святому или
Златоустому, или настоящему, или дневи.
Господи помилуй ві. Честнѣйшую. Слава и нынѣ:
Пѣсть отпустъ: За молитвъ Святыхъ
Отецъ нашихъ Господи Иисусе Христе Боже нашъ
помилуй насъ.
И совершивъ вся сия, во свое Святи-
тельство Мантию отходитъ со всѣми
народъ благословляя. Сослужителие же
вси со олтаря облачатся.

celebrantes. | Chorus.

defunctis: Pontificale ...

Qui vivorum et mortuorum dominatur Christus verus Deus noster, precibus Castissimæ Suæ matris, et omnium Sanctorum, animam defuncti servi Dei N. in sinu Abraam, Isaac et Iacob col„locet, et vestri misereatur ut bonus et clemens Deus.

Cantus finalis

Canitur: Confirma Deus orthodoxam Christiano„rum fidem. Conserva Domine in orthodoxa Chri„stiana fide Magnum Regem nostrum N. Salvum fac Domine Metropolitam, vel, Archiepiscopum, vel, Episcopum, nostrum Dominum N. et omnes orthodoxos Christianos Domine Salva.

Tunc Diaconi deducunt, manus fulcientes, Pontificem Subsequentibus Sacerdotibus. Ille vero consistens in Ambo„na, deponit totum amictum Pontificiis. Dicens totum Can„ticum Simeonis; Nunc dimittis &c. Item: San„cte Deus &c. Pater noster &c. vel suprascriptum. Antiphonas de SS.ti vel Chrysostomo, vel ocurrente, vel de die. Kyrie Eleyson duodecies Gloria Patri &c. Venerabiliorem Seraphim &c. Denique Conclusio Precibus SS. Patrum nostrorum Dne Iesu Christe Deus noster, miserere nostri.

Atque ita finitis his omnibus, amictus suo Episcopali pallio abit ex Ecclesia populum benedicens: Con„celebrantes vero in Altari sacras deponunt vestes.

SOURCES AND SELECT BIBLIOGRAPHY

Aničenka, U. V., *Biełaruska-ukrainskija piśmova-moŭnyja suviazi,* Minsk, 1969.

Archeografičeskij Sbornik Dokumentov otnosjaščychsja k istorii Severo-Zapadnoj Rusi, t. XII, Vilna, 1900.

Archivo Vaticano = Arch. Vat.:
Processus Datariae, Vol. 31.
Consist., Acta Misc., 40, t. 10.
Miscellanea XIII, Vol. 33.
Secretariatus Brevium Apost., 1095.

Arsen'jev, A. V., *Slovar' pisatelej drevnego perioda Russkoj literatury, IX-XVII veka* (862-1700). In Russia 1882; Letchworth, 1969.

Batjuškov, P. N., *Pamjatniki Russkoj Stariny,* Vyp. 6, SPb, 1874.

Beljajev, I. S., *Praktičeskij kurs izučenija russkoj skoropisi dla čtenija rukopisej XV-XVIII stoletij,* Moscow, 2nd ed., 1911.

Benedetti, E., 'Le vicende di un decreto della Propaganda sul passagio dei Ruteni al rito latino', *Stoudion,* t. I, Rome, 1923-24.

Bocian, I., 'De modificationibus' = 'De modificationibus in textu slavico liturgiae S. Ioannis Chrysostomi apud Ruthenos subintroductis', *ХРУСОСТОМIКА,* Rome, 1908, pp. 929-969.

Boniecki, A., *Poczet rodów,* Warsaw, 1887.

Braun, J., *Die liturgische Gewandung im Occident und Orient,* Freiburg im Br., 1907.

Brique, C. M., *Les Filigranes. Dictionaire historique des Marques du papier dès leur apparition vers 1282 jusqu' en 1600,* Vol. I, Amsterdam, 1968.

Brückner, A., 'Spory o Unię w dawnej literaturze', *Kwartalnik Historyczny,* rocznik X, Lvov, 1896, pp. 578-644.

Brumanis, A. A., *Aux origines de la hiérarchie latine en Rusie. Mgr. Stanislas Siestrzencewicz-Bohusz, premier Archevêque-Metropolitain de Mohilev (1731-1826),* Louvain, 1968.

Bułyka, A. M., *Razvićcio arfahrafičnaj sistemy, starabiełaruskaj movy,* Minsk, 1970.

Bylanych, J., *Synodus Zamostiana an. 1720,* Rome, 1960.

Ceremony of Consecration and the Pontifical Divine Liturgy of N. N. Savaryn, Toronto, 1943.

Chojnackij, *Zapadnorusskaja C. Unija* = Chojnackij, A. O., *Zapadnorusskaja Cerkovnaja Unija v jeja Bogosluženii i obrjadach,* Kiev, 1871.

Choma, I., 'Naris istorii chramu Žyrovickoj Bohomatery', *Bohoslovija,* t. 35, Rome, 1971, pp. 129-173.

Combaluzier, F., 'Sacres épiscopaux à Rome de 1565 à 1662' = 'Sacres épiscopaux à Rome de 1565 à 1662. Analyse intégrale du Ms. Miscellanea XIII, 33 des Archives Vaticanes', in: *Sacris Erudiri,* 18, 1967-68.

Čerepin, A. V., *Russkaja paleografija,* Moscow, 1956.

ČAD = *Čin Archierejskago Dejstva Božestvennych Liturgij,* Moscow, 1668.

ČAS = *Činovnik Archierejskago Svjaščennosluženija,* Moscow, 1890.

ČAS = *Činovnik Archierejskago Svjaščennosluženija,* Warsaw, 1944.

ČAS = *Činovnik Archierejskago Svjaščennosluženija,* Jordanville (USA), 1965.

De Backer, A. — Sommervogel, Ch., *Bibliothèque des Ecrivains de la Compagnie Jésus,* t. III, Louvain-Lyon, 1876.

De Meester, 'Les origines' = Dom Placide de Meester, OSB, 'Les origines et les développements du texte grec de la liturgie de S. Jean Chrysostome', *XPYCOCTOMIKA,* Rome, 1908, pp. 245-357.

De Meester, P., OSB, *La Divina Liturgia,* Rome, 1925.

Diomidov, S., *Ukazatel' porjadka archierejskich služenij,* Samara, 1916.

Dobrianskij, F., *Opisanije rukopisej Vilenskoj Publičnoj Biblioteki,* Vilna, 1882.

Dolnyckyj, I., *Pidručnyk* = *Pidručnyk dlja pitomciv seminara duchovnoho,* Lvov, 1907.

Dmitrievskij, A., *Bogosluženije* = *Bogosluženije v Russkoj Cerkvi v XVI v.,* Kazan, 1884.

Dmitrievskij, A., 'Bogosluženije v Russkoj Cerkvi za pervyje pjat' vekov', in: *Pravoslavnyj Sobesednik,* 1882, č. III.

Dmitrievskij, I. I., *Istoričeskoje, dogmatičeskoje i tainstvennoje izjasnenije na Liturgiju,* Moscow, 1812.

Elementa ad fontium editiones = Wyhowska De Andreis, Wanda, *Elementa ad fontium editiones,* t. VII, pars 2, Rome, 1962.

Estreicher, S., *Bibliografia Polska,* cz. III, t. 17, Cracow, 1930; cz. III, t. 31, Cracow, 1936, pp. 492-95.

Filaret Ieromonach, *Čin Liturgii Zlatousta po drevnim staropečatnym, novoispravlennym i drevlepis'mennym služebnikam,* Moscow, 3rd ed. 1899. Also in: *Bratskoje Slovo* 1876, I-II knigi.

Gauchant, P., *Hierarchia Cattolica Medii et Recontioris Aevi sive Summorum Pontificum, S. R. E. Cardinalium, Ecclesiarum Antistitum Series,* Vol. IV, Monasterii, 1935.

Goar, *Euchologion* = Goar Jacobus, *Euchologion sive Rituale Graecorum complectens Ritus et Ordines Divinae Liturgiae, Officiorum, Sacramentorum... juxta usum Orientalis Ecclesiae,* Venice, 1730.

Golenčenko, G. J., *Bibliografičeskij spisok belorusskich staropečatnych izdanij XVI-XVIII vv.,* Minsk, 1961.

Golubinskij, E., *Ist. R. C.,* = *Istorija Russkoj Cerkvi,* t. I, Moscow, 1904.

Habert, I., *APXIERATIKON, Liber Pontificalis Ecclesiae Graecae,* Paris, 1676.

Hanssens, J., *Institutiones* = *Institutiones liturgicae de ritibus orientalibus,* t. II, Rome, 1930; t. III, Rome, 1932.

Heawood, E., *Watermarks, mainly of the 17th and 18th centuries. Monumenta chartae papyraceae historiam illustrantia,* Hilversum, I, 1950.

Hofmann, G., 'Wiedervereinigung der Ruthenen mit Rom', *Orientalia Christiana,* Vol. III-2, 1925, pp. 125-172.

Hofmann, G., 'Briefweksel zwischen Gabriel Severos und Anton Possevino', *OChP,* Vol. XV, 1949.

Horbač, O., *Try cerkovnoslovjans'ki liturhični rukopysni teksty Vatykans'koi biblioteky,* Rome, 1966.

Il'inskij, G., 'K voprosu o proischoždenii nazvanija "Belaja Rus'" ', *Slavia,* VI, 1927-28, pp. 388-93.

Jankoŭski, F., *Histaryčnaja hramatyka biełaruskaj movy,* č. I, Minsk, 1974.

J(atulis), P., 'Skuminavičius Teodoras', *Lietuviu Enciklopedija,* t. 28, Boston, Mass., 1963.

Jocher, A., *Obraz bibliograficzno-historyczny literatury,* t. III, Vilna, 1857, p. 559, nr. 9494.

Jucho, J., 'Pra nazvu "Biełaruś" ', Połymia, Nr. 1, Minsk, 1968, pp. 175-182.

Jugie, M., *Theologia Dogmatica Christianorum Orientalium,* t. I, Paris, 1926.

Jugie, M., 'La Messe dans l'Eglise Byzantine après le IX-e s.', DTC, t. X, pp. 1332-1346.

Karatajev, I., *Chronologičeskaja rospis' slavjanskich knig,* SPb, 1861.

Karataev, I., *Opisanije Slavjano-Russkich knig napečatannych kirillovskimi bukvami, t. I, s 1491 po 1652 g.*, SPb, 1883.

Karskij, E. F., *Belorusy. Jazyk belorusskogo naroda,* t. II, vyp. 1, Moscow, 1955.

Karskij, E. F., *Trudy po belorusskomu i drugim slavjanskim jazykam,* Moscow, 1962.

Karskij, E. F., *Slavjanskaja kirillovskaja paleografija,* Leningrad, 1928.

King, J. G., *The Rites and Ceremonies of the Greek Church in Russia,* London, 1772.

Korolevskij, 'Le Pontifical' = Korolevskij, C., 'Le Pontifical dans le rite byzantin', *OChP,* Vol. X, Rome, 1944, pp. 202-215.

Kot, S., *Rzeczpospolita Polska w literaturze politycznej Zachodu,* Cracow, 1919.

Kovaliv, P., *Molitovnik-Služebnik = Molitovnik Služebnik pamjatka XIV st.*, New York, 1960.

Krajcar, J., 'The Paschalia printed at Rome in 1596', *Oxford Slavonic Papers,* Vol. III, 1970, pp. 107-118.

Krasnoselcev, N. T., *Materialy dla istorii činoposledovanija Liturgii Sv. Ioanna Zlatoustago,* Kazan', 1889.

Krasnoselcev, N. T., *Svedenija o nekotorych liturgičeskich rukopisjach Vatikanskoj Biblioteki,* Kazan', 1885.

Kucharek, C., *The Byzantine-Slav Liturgy = The Byzantine-Slav Liturgy of St. John Chrysostom. Its origin and evolution,* Alleluia Press (1971).

Kurczewski, J., 'Archidyakonat białoruski', *Podręczna Enc. Kościelna,* t. I-II, Warsaw, 1904, p. 311.

Kurczewski, J., 'Wileńskie bpstwo', *Podręczna Enc. Kościelna,* t. 31, Płock, 1911, pp. 203-330.

Kurczewski, J., *Biskupstwo Wileńskie = Biskupstwo Wileńskie od jego założenia aż do dni obecnych, zawierające dzieje i prace biskupów i duchowieństwa djecezji Wileńskiej, oraz wykaz kościołów, klasztorów, szkół i zakładów dobroczynnych i społecznych,* Vilna, 1912.

Lamanskij, V. I., 'Belaja Rus'', *Živaja Starina,* I, 1891, nr. 3, pp. 243-250.

Lappo, I. I., *Litovskij Statut 1588 goda,* t. I-II, Kaunas, 1934-1938.

Leibnitz, G. G., *Specimen demonstrationum politicarum pro eligendo Rege Polonorum; novo scribendi genere ad claram certitudinem exactum.* Auctore Georgio Ulicovio Lithuano. Juxta exemplar editum Vilnae 1659. In: Dutens, L., *G. G. Leibnitii Opera Omnia,* t. IV, Genevae, 1768, pp. 522-630.

Leonid, Archimandryt, *Bibliografičeskaja zametka o služebnikach vilenskoj pečati XVI veka,* SPb, 1882.

Likowski, E., *Unia Brzeska = Unia Brzeska r. 1596,* Warsaw, 1907.

Lozovei, P., *De Metropolitarum Kioviensium potestate (988-1596),* Rome, 1962.

Luk'janenko, V. I., *Katalog belorusskich izdanij kirillovskogo šrifta XVI-XVII vv.*, Vyp. I (1523-1600), Leningrad, 1973. Vyp. II (1601-1654), Leningrad, 1975.

Makarij, Mitr. Mosk., *Istorija Russkoj Cerkvi,* SPb, 1883, t. 12.

Mandala, P. M., *La Protesi della Liturgia nel Rito Bizantino-Greco,* Grottaferrata, 1935.

Mansvetov, I., *Mitropolit Kiprijan v jego liturgičeskoj dejatel'nosti,* Moscow, 1882.

Martinov, J., *Annus Ecclesiasticus — Annus Ecclesiasticus Graeco-Slavicus,* Brussel, 1863.

Marusyn, M., *Božestvenna Liturhija v Kiivskyj Mitropolii po spisku Isydorovoho Liturhikona z XV st.* Extractum from *Bohoslovia,* t. XXV-XXVIII (1964). Rome, 1965.

Marusyn, M., *Čyny Svjatytel's'kych Služb v Kiivs'komu Evcholohioni z počatku XVI st.,* Rome, 1966.

Mateos, J., *La célébration de la parole dans la Liturgie Byzantine. Étude historique,* Rome, 1971.

Muretov, S., *Istoričeskij obzor činosledovanija proskomidii do 'Ustava Liturgii' Konstantin. Patriarcha Filofeja,* Moscow, 1895.

Nevostrujev-Gorskij, *Opisanije* = Nevostrujev, K. — Gorskij, A., *Opisanije slavjanskich rukopisej Moskovskoj Sinodalnoj Biblioteki,* Otdel 3, knigi Bogoslužebnyja, č. I, Moscow, 1869.

Nikolskij, K., *Posobije* = *Posobije k izučeniju Ustava Bogusluženija Pravoslavnoj Cerkvi,* SPb, 1907.

Ohijenko, I., 'Rozmežuvannia pamiatok ukrainskich vid biloruskich', *Zapiski ČSVV,* č. 1-2, 1935, pp. 258-287.

Ostrowski, Wiktor, *About the origin of the name "White Russia",* London, 1975.

Petrov, S. O., Birjuk, J. D., Zolotar', T. P., *Slavjanskije knigi kirillovskoj pečati XV-XVIII vv.,* Kiev, 1958.

Petrovski, A., 'Histoire de la rédaction slave' = *'Histoire de la rédaction slave de la Liturgie de S. Jean Chrysostom', ΧΡΥCOCTOMIKA,* Rome, 1908, pp. 859-928.

Petrovskij, A., 'Učitel'noje izvestije pri slavjanskom služebnike', in: *Christijanskoje Čtenije,* t. 235, 1911, č. I, pp. 552-572.

Petruševič, A., *Archijeratikon Kijevskoj Mitropolii s poloviny XIV st. po spisku s konca XVI st.,* Lvov, 1901. (Offprint of *Bohosl. Vistnyk,* 1900-1901, I-II).

Praszko, I., *De Ecclesia Ruthena Catholica sede metropolitana vacante 1655-1665,* Rome, 1944.

R.A.P. (= Proctor, R.A.), 'Astronomy', *The Encyclopaedia Britt.,* 9th ed., Edinburgh, 1875, Vol. II, pp. 744-822.

Rabikauskas, *Relationes* = Rabikauskas, P., *Relationes Status Diocesium in Magno Ducatu Lituaniae.* 1. Dioeceses Vilnensis et Samogitiae, Rome, 1971.

Raes, A., 'La premiere édition romaine de la Liturgie de Saint Jean Chrysostome en staroslave', *OChP,* Vol. VII, N. 3-4, Rome, 1941, pp. 518-526.

Raes, A., 'La Liturgicon Ruthène depuis l'Union de Brest', *OChP,* Vol. VIII, N. 1-2, Rome, 1942, pp. 95-143.

Raes, A., 'Le dialogue après la grande entrée', *OChP,* Vol. 18, Rome, 1952, pp. 38-51.

Riccioli, John Baptist, *Chronologiae Reformatae et ad certas conclusiones redactae,* Bologna, 1669. Vol. I-III.

Rud, 'Liturhija' = Rud, Stepan, 'Liturhija sv. Ivana Zolotoustoho v peršyj polovyni XVII st.', in: *Opera Societatis Theologicae Ucrainorum Leopoli,* t. XI-XII, 1937, pp. 168-201.

Sauget, J. M., *Bibliographie des Liturgies Orientales (1900-1960),* Rome, 1962.

Savva, Jepiskop Možajskij, *Ukazatel' dlja obozrenija Moskovskoj Patrijaršej (nyne Sinodal'noj) Riznicy,* ed. 4th, Moscow, 1863.

Semenov, V. P., *Polnoje geografičeskoje opisanije,* t. IX, SPb, 1905.

Skuminovič, Theodorus, *Przyczyny=Przyczyny porzucenia disuniey, przezacnemu narodowi Ruskiemu podane* a Jaśnie Wielmożnemu Panu Jego Mości Panu Abrahamowi Woynie, z Bożej y Apostolskiey Stolice łaski Biskupowi Wileńskiemu, Patronowi y Dobrodzieiowi swemu ofiarowane od Theodora Skuminowicza w Wilnie, w Drukarniey Akademiey Societatis Jesu. Roku pańskiego 1643.

Skuminovič, Theodorus, *Epistola Paschalis = Epistola Paschalis Theodori Skvminowicz Episcopi Gratianopolitani SS. D.N.P.P. Praelati Assistentis, Suffraganei et Archidiaconi Albae Russiae, Cantoris Vilnensis.* In qua Graeco-Ruthenum antiquum Calendarium conformiter Gregoriano, aequatione Solis et Lunae praevia corrigitur, per aureum numerum suo loco restitutum, ad normam veteris Romanae et Alexandrinorum supputationis, cum *Responsione* ad eam A.R.P. Ioannis Baptistae Riccioli S. J. Astronomicis voluminibus celeberrimi. Dantisci Apud Georgium Försterum S.R.M. Bibliopolam, Anno 1659.

Skuminovič, Theodorus, *De Jure Personarum* = Theodori Scuminovii Episcopi Gratianopolitani, SS-mi D.N. Praelati Domestici, et in Capella Assistentis per Albam Russiam Suffraganei et Archidiaconi, cantorisque Vilnensis *De Jure Personarum, Seu In Primum Instit. Justinianearum Librum Catholica Explicatio,* Theologicis, Naturalibus, Politicisque rationibus, et Canonico, Civili Antiquiori ac Novissimo, et Consuetudinario Europae Jure, cum perpetua Triboniani in meris Civilibus defensione, Probata. Nunc primum in lucem prodit: Opus Theologis, Iuristis, et Politicis aeque necessarium ac jucundum. Bruxellae, Typis Joannis Mommarti. 1663. Superiorum permissu.

Slovnik Jazyka Staroslovenskego, Praha, 1973-1977, A-P.

Služebniki = Service Books:

Venice,	1519.	
Vilna,	1583.	
Vilna,	1598.	
Moscow,	1602.	
Stratyn,	1604.	
Vilna,	1617,	Mamonič edition.
Vilna,	1617,	Confraternity of Holy Trinity edition.
Kiev,	1639.	
Jevje,	1641.	
Kiev,	1646,	Euchologion of Mohila.
Kiev,	1653.	
Moscow,	1668,	Čin Archijerejskago Dejstva Liturgij.
Lvov,	1691.	
Vilna,	1692,	with the Suprasl Supplement in 1695.
Lvov,	1712.	
Suprasl,	1716,	Pontifikal si jest' Služebnik Svjatitel'skij.
Suprasl,	1727.	
Kiev,	1762.	
Suprasl,	1763.	
Počajev,	1765.	
Vilna,	1773.	
Moscow,	1794.	
Lvov,	1886,	Služebnik Svjatitel'skij.
Rome,	1942.	
Warsaw,	1944,	Činovnik Archijerejskago Svjaščennosluženija.
Rome,	1952.	
USA,	1965,	Činovnik Archijerejskago Svjaščennosluženija.
Rome,	1973-75,	Archijeratikon ili Služebnik Svjatitel'skij.

Solovey, M. M., *The Byzantine Divine Liturgy. History and commentary.* Translated by D. E. Wysochansky, OSBM, Washington, 1970.

Solovij, M., *De reformatione liturgica Heraclii Lisowskyj Archiepiscopi Polocensis (1784-1809),* Rome, 1950.

Solovjev, A., 'Belaja i Černaja Rus'', reprinted from *Sbornik Russkago Archeologičeskogo Obščestva,* t. III, Belgrad, 1940, pp. 29-66.

Statut Velikoho Kniastva Litovskoho, Drukovano v Domu Mamoničov, Vilna, 1594.

Svencickij, I., *Katalog knig cerkovno-slavjanskoj pečati,* Žovkva, 1908.

Szostkiewicz, Z., 'Katalog Biskupów obrz. łac. przedrozbiorowej Polski', in: *Sacrum Poloniae Millenium,* t. I, Rome, 1954, pp. 391-608.

Taft, R. F., *The Great Entrance = The Great Entrance. A history of the Transfer of Gifts and other Preanaphoral Rites of the Liturgy of St. John Chrysostom,* Rome, 1975.

Trebnik, part 2, Rome, 1946.

Tyszkiewicz, M., *Materyały historyczno-genealogiczne do monografii domu Tyszkiewiczów, wieki XV i XVI 1413-1599,* Warsaw, 1911.

Vakar, N. P., 'The name "White Russia" '. *American Slavic and East European Review,* Vol. VIII, New York, 1949, pp. 201-213.

Veselovs'ka, Z. M., *Naholos u schidno-slovjans'kich movach počatkovoi dobi formuvannja rosyjskoi, ukrains'koi ta bilorus'koi nacyj (kynec' XVI- počatok XVIII stolit').* Charkiv, 1970.

Vinogradov, A., *Pravoslavnaja Vilna,* Vilna, 1904.

Welykyj, A. G., *Documenta Unionis = Documenta Unionis Berestensis eiusque auctorum (1590-1600),* Rome, 1970.

Welykyj, A. G., 'Procuratores Negotiorum Ecclesiae Ruthenae in Urbe', *Analecta OSBM,* Ser. II, Vol. I(VII), fasc. 1, Rome, 1949, pp. 57-78.

Wijuk Kojałowicz, *Herbarz = Herbarz rycerstwa W. X. Litewskiego,* Cracow, 1897.

Zernova, A. S., 'Tipografija Mamoničej v Vilne (XVII v.)', in: *Kniga,* sb. I, 1959, pp. 167-222.

Zernova, A. S., Gorbunov, T. S., 'Knigopečatanije v Belorussii XVI-XVII vv.' In: *400 let russkogo knigopečatanija,* t. I, Moscow, 1964, pp. 99-110.

Žuraŭski, A. I., 'Ab biełaruskim varyjancie carkoŭnasłavianskaj movy', in: *Typałohija i historyja słavianskich moŭ i ŭzajemasuviazi słavianskich litaratur.* (Tezisy dakładaŭ i paviedamleńniaŭ). Minsk, 1967, pp. 18-21.

——oOo——

THEODORE SKUMINOVIČ

EPISCOPUS GRATIANOPOLITANUS,

ARCHIDIACONUS ET SUFRAGANUS VILNENSIS

PER ALBAM RUSSIAM (1610?-1668).

HIS LIFE AND WORK

On the first page of MS BL there appear the signature and handwriting of one Bishop Theodore Skuminovič, the suffragan of Vilna for Byelorussia. This raises the following questions: what was the suffraganate for Byelorussia? who was Bishop Theodore Skuminovič? and what is the content and significance of this unusual document?

Whilst all Byelorussians had been Christians of the Byzantine Rite since the end of the 10th cent., it was not until the end of the 14th cent. that the Lithuanians, under the Grand Duke Jahajla, who was simultaneously king of Poland, became Catholics of the Latin Rite.

At about this time a Latin bishopric was founded in Vilna under the Archbishop of Gniezno (1386). The Latin clergy soon started to convert not only pagan Lithuanians, but also their neighbours the Orthodox Byelorussians. On Byelorussian territory they built many Catholic parish churches. In the 14th c. some Latin churches had already been founded: in Abolcy (1386), Hajna, Miensk (1390), also in Pinsk (1396). By the 15th century another 10 new Latin churches had sprung up[1]. According to a report of George Tyškievič, bishop of Vilna, dated 13 Jan. 1652 — this report Theodore Skuminovič, who at that time was the Archdeacon for Byelorussia, brought to Rome — the diocese of Vilna had established 26 deaneries comprising 354 parish churches with a Catholic population of about 3,000,000. At the same time the diocese of Samogitia had 60 parishes only[2].

*

The better to provide for the spiritual needs of the faithful in the extensive diocese, Bishop Volovič (1616-1630) founded an archdeaconry for the eastern Byelorussian territory in the town of Abolcy[3]. Abolcy, formerly called Oblče, in the eastern part of Byelorussia to the west of

1) Kurczewski, *Biskupstwo Wileńskie,* Vilna, 1912, pp. 22, 102. — Sipovič, 'The Diocese of Minsk, its Origin, Extent and Hierarchy', *JBS,* II, 2 (1970), p. 177.

2) Rabikauskas, *Relationes Status Dioecesium in Magno Ducatu Lituaniae.* 1. Dioceses Vilnensis et Samogitiae, Romae, 1971, p. 91. When Bishop Tyškievič says: "cum *soli catholici* tres circiter conficiant si non superant milliones, haereticis, schismaticis, Iudeis et Tartaris exceptis, qui eundem adaequant numerum" — it seems he includes all Catholics of both Rites, Latin and Eastern.

3) Abolcy — today a village in the district of Tałačyn, Viciebskaja vobłaść, BSSR. Grand Duke Ladislaus Jahajła had founded in Oblče (Abolcy) the first Catholic church of the Latin Rite in 1386 (?1388). On the same site another church was built in 1707 in honour of the Holy Name of Our Lady (SS-mi Nominis BMV) by Viečarkoŭski, the Archdeacon of Byelorussia. Up to 1921 the parish priest of this church was the well-known Byelorussian poet Father Alexander Astramovič (Andrej Ziaziula). The same church, without a priest and in decay, was still recognizable in 1939. See: Semenov V. P., *Polnoje geografičeskoje opisanije,* t. IX, SPb, 1905, p. 397. — Vićbič J., 'Boh i Baćkaŭščyna, 1878-1968. U 90-ja ŭhodki ad naradžeńnia Andreja Ziaziuli', *Božym Šlacham,* Nr. 6 (111), pp. 12-15. — *Elenchus Cleri et Ecclesiarum Archidioceseos Mohiloviensis,* Warsaw, 1931, p. 15; Warsaw, 1932, p. 30.

Orša, was endowed with the first Latin church, founded by the Grand Duke Jahajla in 1386 (or 1388).

In documents such as the reports of the Bishops of Vilna to the Holy See, the *Processus Canonicus* of Bishop Skuminovič (1652), and MS BL, we find in the original Latin such expressions as "Russia Alba", Archidiaconatus "Russiae Albae", Suffraganeus "per Russiam Albam", or in Italian "Russia Bianca". Although etymologically "Biełaja Ruś", "Biełaruś", "Byelorussia" are the equivalent of "Russia Alba", "Russia Bianca", in the 16th-17th centuries it had a more restricted geographical and ethnic connotation. At that time the ethnic Byelorussians occupied a larger territory than that known as "Russia Alba". In fact the latter comprised only $^1/_4$ of the Grand Duchy of Lithuania, and included the palatinates of Mścislaŭ, Viciebsk, Połack and parts of Miensk. The Viciebsk palatinate included the towns of Orša and Abolcy.

Moreover, like other ethnic groups in the Grand Duchy of Lithuania, the Byelorussians were also described as "Lithuanian" in the political sense. For example, two Dominicans in Rome, Jacobus Kolarz Koroski and Jacobus Sgorecki, called as witnesses during the *Processus Canonicus* of Skuminovič, are described as "Lituanus". Either or both might have been ethnically Byelorussian, Lithuanian or Polish whilst at the same time being citizens of the Grand Duchy of Lithuania. They both came from Vilna.

Biełaruś — White Ruthenia, Byelorussia and other equivalents were the old names (15th c.) for a part of **Ruś**, but the ethnographic significance of this name is of fairly recent origin, and its present geographical definition is even more so.

These notes on the terminology concerning "Byelorussia"[4] will, it is hoped, help to prevent confusion, and will explain the significance of offices and titles in the very

4) Some works about the names of Byelo-Russia: Lamanskij, V. I., 'Belaja Rus', *Živaja Starina*, 1891, I, Nr. 3, pp. 245-250. — Iljinskij, G., 'K voprosu o proischoždenii nazvanija "Belaja Rus"', *Slavia*, VI (1927-28), pp. 388-93. — Vakar, N. P., 'The name "White Russia"', *American Slavic and East European Review*, Vol. VIII, New York, 1949, pp. 201-213. — Solovjev, A., 'Belaja i Čornaja Rus' reprinted from *Sbornik Russkago Archeologičeskogo Obščestva*, t. III, Belgrad, 1940, pp. 29-66. — Jucho, J., 'Pra nazvu "Biełaruś"', *Połymia*, Nr. 1, Minsk, 1968, pp. 175-182. — Nadson, A., 'The Memoirs of Theodore Jeŭlašeŭski, Assessor of Navahradak (1546-1604)'. Notes of introduction, *JBS*, Vol. I, Nr. 4, London, 1968, pp. 332-334. — The name of "Russia Alba" on the various historical maps see: Ostrowski, Wiktor, *About the origin of the name "White Russia"*, London, 1975. — Gregorovich, A., *Ukraine, Rus' and Muscovy.* A selected bibliography of the names, Toronto, 1971.

extensive diocese of Vilna having a mixed ethnic population, such as the Archidiaconate and the Suffraganate for Byelorussia. The author of MS BL Theodore Skuminovič was invested with both these functions.

*

Kurczewski, a reliable source, gives the year of foundation of the Archidiaconate for Byelorussia as 1619 together with the names of the first archdeacons[5]. Bishop George Tyškievč (1649-1656), in his report to the Holy See dated 1651, made this statement: "The Archidiaconate of Vilna was founded in 1623. The parish of Abolcy, from which it was founded, was formerly under royal patronage; this foundation Urban VIII, the predecessor of Your Holiness (Innocent X — C.S.), approved"[6]. An element of truth most probably lies in both these assertions: Bishop Vołovič initiated the formalities concerning the foundation of the Byelorussian Archidiaconate in 1619 and these were concluded in 1623.

After the Council of Trent[7] archdeacons were restricted in their jurisdictional prerogatives, which remained *potestas ab episcopo delegata* only, but still they were indispensable where the diocese was large, and the bishop needed any effective help. In the above-mentioned report of Bishop Tyškievič one finds the explanation for the foundation of the Archdiaconate for Byelorussia: "The Archidiaconate was founded because of the large extension of the diocese, including great distances from one parish to the other, particularly in that part of Russia[8], and because of a need for help in visiting half of the diocese; the Archdiaconate has the same jurisdictional rights as that of Vilna"[9].

Thus the territory of the Byelorussian Archdiaconate consisted of one half of the whole diocese of Vilna; this is nearly the same as the territory of 1/3 of the Byelorussian Soviet Republic today. This Archdiaconate enjoyed some of the privileges

5) *Biskupstwo Wileńskie*, pp. 102-103.
6) Rabikauskas, *Relationes*, p. 88.
7) Sessio 24, De reformatione, c. 3, 20. On the Archdeacons see: H. Leclercq, *DACL*, I, 2733-2736. A. Amanieu, *DDC*, I, 948-1004.
8) "Russia" here, no doubt, means the same as "Ruthenia", "Russia Alba" = Byelorussia.
9) Rabikauskas, *Relationes*, p. 88. See also o. c. notes 174, 184.

of the Suffragan of Vilna together with that property given by the bishop, namely the estate of Viadziec[10].

The first archdeacon for Byelorussia until 1634 was John Chrysostom Rožniatoŭski; he was then succeeded by Andrew Nadratovič, parish priest of Troki[11]. It seems that the third archdeacon was Theodore Skuminovič, mantioned for the first time as the archdeacon of Byelorussia in a document dated 20 Sept. 1651[12].

*

During the second half of the XVII cent. in the diocese of Vilna there were, apart from the bishop: 1) the Archdeacon of Vilna; 2) the Suffragan of Vilna; 3) the Archdeacon (of Vilna) for Byelorussia; 4) the Suffragan (of Vilna) for Byelorussia. Often these two offices were filled by the same person. Such was the case with Theodore Skuminovič.

The Byelorussian Suffraganate had been founded by Bishop Abraham Woyna (1631-1649), and Bishop Martianus Tryzna was the first Suffragan from 1639-1643. Being recommended by King Ladislaus IV and proposed by Bishop Woyna and his Chapter, Bishop Tryzna received from Pope Urban VIII a bull of preconization dated 28 Febr. 1638 appointing him to be the Coadjutor with the titular see of Mallo (Mallensis), and also to be the Suffragan cum futura successione[13]. Of him Kurczewski writes: "Martianus Tryzna was a Byelorussian nobleman by birth and had distinguished himself by an outstanding and gifted mastery of languages, especially of Greek. He also excelled in the art of oratory and was a fervent defender of the Byelorussians. In 1620 he became a member of the Chapter; in 1636 he took part in amending the Lithuanian Statutes; he accompanied King Ladislaus in his expedition to Moscow..."[14] Bishop Tryzna died in July 1643, waiting in vain for the succession to the episcopal see of Vilna.

10) Kurczewski, *Biskupstwo Wileńskie*, pp. 102-103.

11) L. c., p. 103. The same author: Archidyakonat białoruski' in *Podręczna Enc. Kość.*, t. I-II, 1904, p. 311.

12) The letter of Bishop George Tyškievič to Cardinal Orsini of 20 Sept. 1651. Archivio Capitolino, Arch. Orsini, 1651/0003. See *Elementa and fontium editiones*, VII, p. 2-da, Romae, 1962, nr. 149, p. 27. — The date of the death of the Archdeacon Rožniatoŭski is unknown. It is assumed that Skuminovič was nominated Archdeacon soon after his conversion, sometime about 1646.

13. Kurczewski, *Biskupstwo Wileńskie*, p. 83.

14) L. c., p. 83. See: Lappo, I. I., *Litovskij Statut 1588 goda*, t. I, part 2, p. 432.

From Bishop Tryzna down to the last Suffragan of Byelorussia, Bishop Stanislas Bohuš-Siestrencevič (1773-74), there were twelve Suffragans, and the last of them, by favour of Empress Catherine II, became in 1773 the Bishop of the Catholic Churches of Byelorussia, and later Archbishop and Metropolitan of Mahiloŭ[15].

Since their foundation the Archdiaconate and the Suffraganate for Byelorussia had always been mentioned in the reports of Vilna Bishops to the Holy See. By way of conclusion to this part of the chapter it is perhaps appropriate to quote from Bishop Michael Zienkovič's report dated 1749. He wrote: "Amplitudo diocesis extenditur ad milliaria 100 germanica et fere 20 in longitudinem, nec minus in latitudinem. Complectitur plane totam Lituaniam, praeter Brestensem palatinatum et Pinscensem districtum. Insuper includit in notabili parte Nigram et Albam Russiam. Pro Alba Russia est Suffraganeus et Archidiaconus: uterque iure patronatus ad me solum pertinet et successores meos. Posterior habet stallum in choro et utitur insignibus capitularibus ac habitu, videlicet cappa rubra, est extra stallum et vocem in Capitulo. Habet annexam curam animarum et ex parochia percipit fructus, de distributionibus ordinariis nihil participat. Eandem praerogativam habet Cancellarius et per omnia similem Archidiacono et est distinctae fundationis"[16].

*

Little is known about Theodore Skuminovič, apart from the fact that he was the Archdeacon and Suffragan of the Bishop of Vilna for Byelorussia. Up to the present time there have been only a few brief articles mentioning Theodore Skuminovič in various encyclopedias, and these are very far from providing a complete picture of his life and work; if anything they are rather misleading[17], — unlike Estreicher's bibliography which gives not only the

15) The names of the Byelorussian Suffragans are given by Rabikauskas, *Relationes,* pp. 15-16. One find them also dispersed in Kurczewski's *Biskupstwo Wileńskie,* and by the same author 'Wileńskie bpstwo' in *Podręczna Enc. Kościelna,* t. 31, Płock, 1911, pp. 203-330. — Szostkiewicz, Z., 'Katalog Biskupów obrz. łac. przedrozbiorowej Polski', in *Sacrum Poloniae Millenium,* t. I, Rome, 1954, p. 556: Skuminovič. All Byelorussian Suffragans except Stanislaus Bohuš-Siestrencevič p. 606. On him see: Brumanis, A. A., *Aux origines de la hierarchie latine en Russie. Mgr. Stanislas Siestrzencewicz-Bohusz, premier Archievêque-Metropolitain de Mohilev (1731-1826),* Louvain, 1968.

16) Rabikauskas, *Relationes,* pp. 170-171.

17) In chronological order they are: Stupnicki, H., *Herbarz Polski,* 1862, t. III, p. 65. *Enc. Orgelbranda,* Warszawa, 1884, t. X, p. 472. *Enc. Kościelna Nowodworskiego,* Warszawa, 1902, t. XXV, p. 515. *Podręczna Enc. Kościelna,* Warszawa, 1912, t. 35-36, p. 298. *Letuvių Enciclopedija,* Boston, Mass., 1963, Vol. 28, p. 109.

names of the books, but also an outline of their contents[18].

A valuable source for bibliographical details, without doubt, is the *Processus Canonicus* before the nomination of Skuminovič to Bishop[19], and his first published book *Przyczyny Porzucenia Disuniey* (Reasons why I forsook Disunity), Vilna, 1643[20].

It seems that Theodore Skuminovič's family goes back to Kalenik Myškovič (1437), from whom, through many ramifications, originated families from many corners of the Commonwealth (Byelorussia, Lithuania, Ukraine, Poland) such as Tyškievič (Tyszkiewicz), Skumin Tyškievič, Skumin and Skuminovič (Skuminowicz)[21]. Some of them played a significant part in the affairs of Church and State alike e.g. Theodore Skumin Tyškievič, voivode of Navahradak, who died in 1618[22].

From the *Processus* it is known that Bishop Theodore Skuminovič was born in Vilna about 1610. His father was also named Theodore and was a Catholic; when he died he left his teenage son under the guardianship of an Orthodox mother, who educated him according to her own faith. One may assume that his father was the abovementioned Theodore Skumin Tyškievič, who at first was hesitant in accepting the Union of Brest, but who finally became a Catholic. As yet there is no direct confirmation of this hypothesis, except the coincidence of the name, which was by no means a rarity in the family of Skumin Tyškievič, and some approximation in dates between the death of the voivode of Navahradak and the birth of the future Bishop.

Witnesses during the *Processus* assert that Theodore Skuminovič studied in Vilna, Cracow and Zamość for many years[23]. Moreover he himself asserts in his book *De iure personarum*[24] that at the time of his education in Louvain he came into contact with the works "deformatae religionis":

18) Estreicher, *Bibliografia Polska,* cz. III, t. XVII, Cracow, 1930, p. 210; t. XXXI, pp. 492-95. See also: Jocher, A., *Obraz bibliograficzno-historyczny literatury,* t. III, Vilna, 1857, nr. 9494, p. 559. — Likowski, E., *Unia Brzeska r. 1596,* Warsaw, 1907, pp. XVI, 43, 45.

19) Arch. Vat., Processus Datariae, Vol. 31.

20) The full name of the book is: *Przyczyny porzvcenia disvniey przezacnemu narodowi Rvskiemu podane i Jaśnie Wielmożnemu Przewielebnemu Panv Iego Mości Panv Abrahamovi WOYNIE z Bożey y Apostolskiey Stolice łaski Biskvpowi Wileńskiemu Patronowi y Dobrodźieiowi swemu ofiarowane od Theodora Skvminowicza.* W Wilnie, W Drukarni Akademiey Societatis IESV. Roku Pańskiego, 1643. (The Reasons to abandon Disunity, explained to the Most Honourable Ruthenian People and dedicated to the Most Reverend and Gracious Lord Abraham Woyna by the grace of God and the Apostolic See's Bishop of Vilna, my Protector and Benefactor from Theodore Skuminovič. Vilna, in the typography of the Society of Jesus. In the year of Our Lord 1643.) — Skuminovič's *Przyczyny* has a strange pagination: after the dedication and "Do czytelnika" (Ad lectorem), six pages in all, one side of the pages is marked with capital Gothic letters in the alphabetical order: A, A2, A3, and then no mark at all; then follow: B, B2, B3, and no mark and so on. For this reason I refrain from quoting the exact pages. — The book is rare today. The author is grateful to Cracow University Library for making the filmed copy available.

21) Tyszkiewicz, M., *Materyały historyczno-genealogiczne do monografii domu Tyszkiewiczów, wieki XV i XVI 1413-1599,* Warsaw, 1911. In the year 1507, nr. 102, p. 19 is mentioned Jeżyj Skuminowicz Tyszkiewicz. — In Vilna there were people of the middle class with the same family name, see: Batjuškov, P. N., *Pamjatniki Russkoj Stariny,* SPb, 1874, vypusk 6, p. 4. — Wijuk Kojałowicz, *Herbarz rycerstwa W. X. Litewskiego,* Cracow, 1897, p. 138. — Boniecki, A., *Poczet Rodów,* Warsaw, 1887, pp. 354-59.

22) Some authors give the year of his death as 1616: Estreicher, *Bibliografia Polska,* cz. III, t. 31, Cracow, 1936, p. 492. The Union of Brest was a matter of great concern to the palatine (=governor of province) of Novahradak. The exchange of letters between him, Metropolitan Rahoza and Constantin Prince of Ostrog etc. is clear evidence of this. See Welykyj, A. G., *Documenta Unionis,* Rome, 1970, pp. 78-79, 87-88, 91-92, 181-183.

23) Arch. Vat., Processus Datariae, Vol. 31. Zamość is mentioned by Father Sgorecki only.

24) For the full title see Bibliography under Skuminovič Theodore.

Borcholten, Minsynghen, Hunnius etc.[25]. His works bear witness to the fact that Bishop Skuminovič was a highly educated man. Small wonder that such a man attracted notice in the Orthodox Church, which under Metropolitan Mohila was passing from recession and stabilization to counter-attack. Skuminovič was nominated dean (błahačynny) of Ovruč, Mazyr and Rečyca in Paleśsie. Later he rose to the rank of ihumien (superior of a religious house), rector, and member of the Metropolitan Consistory. He also took part in the Kievian Synod under Mohila in 1640[26].

He was devoted to his ministry in the Orthodox Church, and his dedication helped him to see its needs, its weaknesses and its misery. Sharp polemical controversy between Catholics and Orthodox at that time sowed not only seeds of hatred, but also opened the eyes of many to the truth and shortcomings of both sides. Since 1642 Skuminovič had been seriously thinking of embracing Catholicism, and in May 1643 "he overtly shook off the dust of disunity", and became a Catholic of the Latin Rite. The reasons for this important decision, which affected his whole life, he explained thoroughly in his first work *Przyczyny* mentioned above, published in Vilna in 1643, which he dedicated to Abraham Woyna, Bishop of that diocese. Among the reasons he gave for changing his allegiance, some were personal grounds valid for Skuminovič alone; others were of more universal concern.

*

During his ministry in the Orthodox Church he had publicly spoken against the Catholic Church; in publishing his book he sought publicly to revoke his errors and his criticisms. In disunity he had achieved glory and wealth and "indubitata fide" (= by remaining Orthodox) he could have hoped for further promotion.

In spite of undoubted talent and ability

25) There were two Hunnius: Aegidius a Lutheran Theologian († 1603) and his son Helferich Ulrich († 1636), who became a Catholic. *Lexikon f. Theologie u. Kirche,* t. V, 1960, p. 540.

26. About the Synod of Kiev of 1640 Bishop Gembicki has published a book which was translated into Polish and published by the famous Cassian Calixt Sakovič in Warsaw, 1641. See Estreicher, *Bibliografia Polska,* t. XXVII, Cracow, 1929, p. 29.

among the Ruthenians there was — according to Skuminovič — a low standard of education, and the youth acquired such educational advantages as calves acquire as they grow into oxen.

Drawing on Greek and Ruthenian authors he gives his reasons why Union with the Roman Church prevailed in Ruś (Ruthenia) from the time of its baptism. The Kievian Metropolitans from Cemivlak (Tsamblak, 1415-1420) until Soltan (1507-1521) were in unity with Rome, but the other seven successors were in disunity. "After Michael Rahoza, the fourth Orthodox (= Catholic, C.S.) Metropolitan[27] now governs in happiness and with an increase of Holy Unity the sheep entrusted to him by God and the Holy Roman See".

Skuminovič criticises the disunited monasteries, on the grounds that there was not one religious house in which the Rule of St. Basil was read or known. He found himself in the dilemma of being vested in a monk's habit, but not sure of his salvation. Echoing a medieval scholastic, he says: "As **substantia non potest esse vel operari sine accidentibus**, in the same way the religious profession cannot exist without Rules and order". Skuminovič demanded that in Eastern monasteries there should, before the religious profession, be a time of trial and novitiate, as was the case in the Western orders. Those in disunity call such criticism "sycophantia" or slander, but — Skuminovič asks — to give a monk's habit to a simple peasant who has no idea about perfection or the religious order, is that "sycophantia"?[28]

Of the priesthood in the Orthodox Church he writes: "My priesthood in disunity was doubtful, although **in schismate suscepti ordines** might be true, but **quo ad executionem** they are always **irriti,** as was stated a long time ago in canon law and clearly repeated by Clement VIII in his Bull: "ordinati pravi, ab episcopis schismaticis

27) Metropolitan Anthony Sielava (1642-1655).
28) The Greek word *sykophantia* means false accusation, slander.

correcti vel emendati reconciliandi sunt, et absolvendi cum paenitentiis salutaribus". Subsequently Skuminovič draws a very severe conclusion, not followed by present-day theologians: since the priesthood in disunion is uncertain, "every one when he celebrates the Liturgy or serves some other priestly office, each time commits sin".

From this statement it appears also that Skuminovič had been a monk and was ordained priest of the Orthodox Church or, as he says, in Disunity. In spite of this, in the *Processus* it is clearly stated that he was ordained by Bishop Abraham Woyna: "So che é sacerdote da 10 anni e piú che so fu ordinato da Monsignore Abramo Woyna giá Vescovo di Vilna et per haverlo visto molte volte celebrare"[29].

Because Skuminovič was uncertain about the priestly orders he had received in Disunity, and because of the statements of two witnesses during the *Processus*, it seems likely that he was in fact ordained again by Bishop Woyna, possibly *sub conditione*, though there is no firm evidence of this.

*

In the same booklet *Przyczyny*, Skuminovič upbraids the Orthodox archimandrites and superiors (ihumieny) on account of their poor knowledge of theological questions such as the procession of the Holy Spirit, the glory of Saints, personal judgement, purgatory, the use of unleavened bread, the head of the Church, and the form of the Eucharist. Whatever they knew they had borrowed from protestant or "orthodox" authors such as Kleryk and Zizani, or from such books as *Antigraphe, Lament* and *Antidotum*[30].

In discussing various religious problems, he quotes from the Western and Eastern Fathers of the Church: Augustine, Ambrose, Chrysostom, Athanasius, Cyril of Alexandria, Epiphanius, and Simeon Metaphrastes. He uses historical and theological reasons to show that the Catholic Church

---

29) Arch. Vat., Processus Datariae, Vol. 31.

30) Kleryk published in 1588 a polemical work *O jedinoj pravoslavnoj vere i o svjatoj sobornoj apostolskoj Cerkvi*, sočinenije Ostrožskago svjaščennika Vasilija, Reprinted in *Pamjatniki polemičeskoj literatury v Zapadnoj Rusi, Russkaja Istor. Bibl.*, t. II, col. 633-938. See Jugie, M., *Theologia Dogmatica*, t. I, p. 560. S. Zizani, the author of writings against the Union of Brest: *Objasnenije Nikejskago Soboru, 1595; Sobranije slov Kiryla Ierusalimskago, 1599.* — Likowski, *Unia Brzeska*, pp. 194 note 1, 318. — Jugie, o. c., p. 560. *Antigraphe, Lament* — the abbreviated names given by Skuminovič of rather longer titles of the two books written by the same Meletius Smatrycki (Smotrzyski): *Antigraphe*, Vilna, 1608; *Lament or Threnos*, Vilna, 1610, — when he was still Orthodox and a vehemently anticatholic polemicist. The third one *Antidotum*, against him, of which the full name is: *Antidotum przezacnemu narodowi Ruskiemu, albo warunek przeciw Apologii* jadem napełnionej, kturą wydał Melecy Smotrzysky, niesłusznie Cerkiew ruską prawosławną w niej pomawiając Herezyą i Dyzunią dla niektórych scribentów, przez W-go Ojca Nadrzeja Mużyłowskiego ze Słucka roku 1629. — The true author was Gizel. See Likowski, o. c., p. 319 note 3.

is the only true Church. For instance, when he writes of the feast of the translation of the relics of St. Nicolas from Asia Minor to Bari, he quotes the fact that this feast was instituted by Pope Urban II in 1096 after the official separation (1054) and it was still accepted by the Metropolitan of Kiev Ephrem into Slavonic liturgical books. Not only this! In Vilna there was a church of St. Nicolas under this same title[31].

*

Przyczyny was written in the Polish language of the 17th cent., which is often far from correct, bring interspersed with whole sentences in Latin and with Church-Slavonic idioms. These flourishes render the style less lucid and show that the author was not of Polish origin, even though the use of the Polish language at that epoch was common among Catholic and Orthodox Byelorussians. At the same time Skuminovič does not turn his back on his own people. He calls them "the most honourable Ruthenian people", gifted with many talents; he desires to bring them into unity with Rome. The book concludes with a beautiful prayer to Jesus Christ for unity among Christians.

Why did Skuminovič become a Catholic of the Latin Rite, instead of the Eastern Rite, which was familiar to him?

The answer is not known. There was a trend among Byelorussian nobles to be received into the Latin Church[32]. The Uniate hierarchy and Rome protested against this usage but without much success[33]. It seems that Skuminovič was no exception to the prevailing fashion. It is certain that he was never opposed to the Catholic Uniate Church — judging from the evidence of *Przyczyny,* MS BL and of *Epistola Paschalis.* After all, his new task was to work among Byelorussian Orthodox and those of Latin Rite. Bishop Tyškievič wrote on 6 May 1652 to the Cardinals in Rome: "...et in Suffraganeum (Skuminovič)... deputari

31) About St. Nicolas church in Vilna see: Vinogradov, A., *Pravoslavnaja Vilna,* Vilna, 1904, pp. 51-54. The translation of the Relics was in 1092; the feast is celebrated by the Slavs only. See Martinov, J., *Annus Ecclesiasticus,* dies IX Maii, p. 125.

32) Likowski, *Unia Brzeska,* pp. 268-70, 328.

33) Benedetti, E., 'Le vicende di un decreto della Propaganda sul passagio dei Ruteni al rito latino', *Stoudion,* t. I, Rome 1923-24, pp. 12-16, 41-45, 65-68, 129-135, 167-72.

possit cuius motivum habeo, quod ad refutandos Schismaticos errores tum ad eos alliciendos ceteris aptiorem video"[34]. At that time the Latin-Rite Byelorussians already formed a significant proportion of the Vilna diocese.

After his reception into the Catholic faith, Skuminovič was not immediately put into harness. From the same letter of Bishop Tyškievič of 6 May 1652 we learn that after his admission to the Catholic Church, Skuminovič was subjected to a kind of strict apprenticeship, lasting two years: "per biennium tirocinium egit modisque omnibus probatus"[35].

Quite possibly, he also continued his philosophical and theological studies. Later, he became a parish priest in Abolcy, then Archdeacon of Byelorussia and the representative of the Bishop of Vilna in that region[36].

On 20 Sept. 1651, Bishop Tyškievič wrote to Cardinal Orsini (Ursus), protector of Poland, asking him to receive his messenger Skuminovič, "Albae Russiae in mea dioecesi existentis Archidiaconus", and graciously to listen to his petitions[37].

*

The real purpose of the mission of the Archdeacon Skuminovič to Rome was to bring to the Holy See a report on the Vilna diocese from Bishop Tyškievič, who was unable to make his journey **ad limina** in person[38], and receive his own nomination and approval to the Suffraganate of Vilna for Byelorussia[39]. It is not known how long Skuminovič stayed in Rome, but the purposes for which he came were accomplished.

On 27 May 1652 in the palace of Cardinal Orsini in Rome there took place the *Processus super qualitatibus* R. D. Theodori Skuminowicz[40]. The witnesses included the two "Lithuanian" Dominicans, members of the community at Santa Maria sopra Minerva, both by name Jacobus and both

34) Arch. Vat., Processus Datariae, Vol. 31, p. 133v.

35) L. cit., p. 133.

36) One of the witnesses during the *Processus* says: "So che ha essercitato la cura delle anime essendo Parrocho Obbolcense et é stato ancó Archidiacono di Bianca Russia et ancó officiale per Monsignore Vescovo di Vilna in Alba Russia et in tutte queste cariche si é passato benissimo", Arch. Vat., Processus Datariae, Vol. 31, p. 130. — One can see in this short text two names for the same region: Russia Bianca (Italian) and Alba Russia (Latin).

37) Archivio Capitolino, Arch. Orsini, 1651/0003. — See note 12.

38) This report of Bishop Tyškievič is published by Rabikauskas, *Relationes*, pp. 84-93.

39) A copy of the letter of Bishop *Tyškievič* of 6 May 1652. Arch. Vat., Processus Datariae, Vol. 31, pp. 133-133v.

40) Arch. Vat., 1. c., p. 128 etc.

sons of John: Jacobus Kolarz Koroski aged about 31 and Jacobus Sgorecki, Sacrae Theologiae Magister aged 31. Their rather scanty information has already been quoted above. Perhaps the most important parts of their testimony are the place of birth of Skuminovič (Vilna), the name of his father (Theodore), the fact that his mother was Orthodox and that he worked in Abolcy. There are no details about his exact date of birth, his date of ordination, his mother's maiden name, and so on.

On the same day Skuminovič made and signed his "iuramentum professionis fidei"[41]. One month later on 27 June 1652 there took place a session of the Holy Inquisition before Pope Innocent X in the Quirinal Palace, where the letter of Bishop Tyškievič dated 6 May 1652 was read, petitioning for the dispensation and nomination for Skuminovič to the Suffraganate of the whole diocese and particularly for the province of Byelorussia. This was duly granted[42].

On 12 August 1652, once again in the Quirinal Palace, there was a session of the Privy Council (Consilium Secretum) in the presence of Pope Innocent X. On the proposal of Cardinal Orsini, provision was made to give the Bishop, in the person of Theodore Skuminovič, the vacant See of Gratianopolis *in partibus infidelium*[43], and also to assign to the Bishop of Vilna a second Suffragan "ad exercendum Pontificalia in civitate, et dioe(cesi) Vilnensi et pr(a)esertim in Provincia Albae Russiae, et Terrarum tractu illi adiacente cum reservatione pro eius congrua pensionis annuae trecentos duc. auri de Ecclesia super fructibus et Mensae Episcopalis ecclesiae Vilnensis"[44].

On the nineteenth Sunday after Pentecost, 29 Sept. 1652, in the Basilica of Santa Maria Maggiore, Theodore Skuminovič was consecrated Bishop by Cardinal Mark Anthony Franciotti, assisted by the Archbishop of Benevento John Baptist Foppa

41) L. cit., pp. 131-137.

42) L. c., pp. 132-132v, 135. — "... ut a Sanctissimo peterem alium mihi Suffraganeum adiungi pro tota Diocesi mea ac praesertim pro provincia Albae Russiae praecipua Schismaticorum sede et eidem muneri praefici Admodum Rev. D. Theodorum Skuminouiz (sic) eiusdem Albae Russiae Archidiaconum virum etiam undequaque aptissimum. Ipse familia radicitus magnae nobilitatis ortus patrem Catholicum, matrem vero Schismaticam...", 1 c., p. 133.

43) Arch. Vat., Consist., Acta Miss., 40, t. 10, pp. 202-202v. Let us note the lapsum calami: "S-mus D-nus N-r referente eodem Rev-mo D-no Virginio Cardinali Ursino providit Ecclesiae Gratianopolitanae in partibus infidelium certo modo vacan. de Persona R. D. Theodori Skuminowicz Praesbyteri Viln. Dioc., et Archidiaconi *Abbatiae* (instead of: Albae) Russiae Theologi fidem Catholicam professi..."

44) Arch. Vat., Consist., Acta Misc., 40, t. 10 p. 202v.

and Bishop Ranutius Scotti. Two other Bishops were consecrated at the same time: Philip De Jacob of Policastro and Martin Dentatus of Strongoli. Also recorded as being present at the solemn ceremony were Andrew Jacob Cinamo and Nicola de Michaelibus, archpriest[45].

*

On 21 April 1653 Bishop Skuminovič was honoured with the dignity of Assistant to the Apostolic Throne (Solio Pontificio Assistens)[46]. Was he still in Rome at this time? If so, where had he been staying?

From Roman documents it is known that the *Processus Canonicus* took place on 27 May 1652. Therefore it can be assumed that his arrival in the Eternal City was at least one or two weeks earlier (say about 14 May). He certainly stayed until 29 September 1652, when he was consecrated Bishop. It seems reasonable to suppose that he was still in Rome when he was nominated Solio Pontificio Assistens, and he may have stayed on for a time, in order to exercise this privilege.

Since 1639 the Basilian Fathers, "Rutheni", had been in possession of the church of the holy martyrs Sergius and Bacchus. Attached to this church was the office of the procurator of the Catholic Metropolitan of Kiev. The first holder of this office was Father Novak, originally from Miensk[47]. Skuminovič presented his precious MS of the Liturgy of St. John Chrysostom to this church, the first "Ruthenian" Catholic church in Rome. Certainly this was done after 29 Sept. 1652 since he signed it as Episcopus Gratianopolitanus. This appears to indicate that he had a close connection with the church, and its guardians the Basilian Fathers. It seems reasonable therefore to suppose that Skuminovič stayed in Rome with them; possibly in his free time during his long stay he prepared the Pontifical Liturgy, and when

45) Arch. Vat., Miscellanea XIII, vol. 33, fol. 220. — Combaluzier, F., 'Sacres épiscopaux à Rome de 1565 à 1662. Analyse intégrale du Ms. Miscellanea XIII, 33 des Archives Vaticanes', in: *Sacris Erudiri*, 18, 1967-68, p. 234. See also pp. 252, 284, 295. — In the Vatican Ms we read: "... Theodoro Skominouicz (sic!) Polono electo Gratianopolitano ..." For anybody in the Roman Curia it was enough to arrive from Poland to be Polish.

46) Arch. Vat., Secretariatus Brevium Apost., 1095, f. 765.

47) Welykyj, A. G., "Procuratores Negotiorum Ecclesiae Ruthenae in Urbe', *Analecta Ordinis S. Basilii Magni*, Ser. II, Vol. I (VII), fasc. 1, Rome, 1949, pp. 57-78. About Father Nicolas Novak pp. 62-78.

it was completed he presented it to them as his *aeternum monumentum.*

*

Let us now look closely at MS BL.

It is on paper, has 58 leaves of size 27,8 cm. × 20,3 cm., of which 5 are left blank. There is a total of 106 pages, leaves alone are numbered, and not each page. There are three blank leaves in front, one between leaves at the 10 and 11 and one at the end. Waterstains are apparent on the upper and lower margins, but not to the extent that they destroy it. However a copious use of ink has caused significant damage to the text on page 14. The paper used for the MS is of good quality.

The MS contains two watermarks. The first, in the front flyleaf, is a six-pointed star in a circle surmounted by a Latin cross of double outline, similar to Heawood Nr. 3879 (Rome, 1646) but with a figure resembling an inverted 4 below the circle. Briquet says of this mark: "On trouve des étoiles surmontées de la croix du même style que le Nr. 6089, souvent accompagnées d'initiales, dans l'Italie méridionale durant tout le XVII s."[48].

The second mark is found in the paper of the main body of the MS. It consists of a roughly oval shield bearing three unidentified objects with a bishop's (or cardinal's) hat above. The mark resembles Heawood's Nos. 791 and 792 (Rome, 1639 and 1635)[49].

It has a binding of old vellum, characteristic of the XVII c., particularly used for books and archives of the Congregation De Propaganda Fide and other papal offices. On the very first page we read the solemn inscription:

БОЖЕСТЪВЕНЪНАЯ ЛІТУРГИЯ
Иже во Святыхъ Отца Нашего
ІОАНЪНА ЗЛАТАУСЪТАГО
Егъда служытъ святитель
По усътаву
Церъкви Восъточъное Кафолическое
Митрополии Киовъское
И всея Росъсийския Земъля.

48) Briquet, C. M., *Les Filigranes. Dictionnaire historique des Marques du papier dès leur apparition vers 1282 jusqu'en 1600*, Amsterdam, 1968, Vol. I, nr. 6089, p. 353.

49) Heawood, E., *Watermarks, mainly of the 17th and 18th centuries. Monumenta Chartae Papyraceae historiam illustrantia*, Hilversum (Holland), I, 1950, p. 82.

Then follows the Latin translation with a very interesting correction: instead of "Divinum Sacrificium", as was originally written, there is:

DIVINA LITURGIA
Sancti Patris nostri
JOANNIS CHRYSOSTOMI
Quando celebrat Pontifex
Secundum Ordinem
Ecclesiae Orientalis Catholicae
Metropoliae Chioviensis
Et omnium Terrarum Russiae.

The correction was an improvement because "Liturgia" sounds more accurate and more Eastern than "Divinum Sacrificium".

In this inscription is expressed the old name of that very extensive Church province of Kiev and of all the Russian (Ruthenian) Lands. One should notice the archaic wording: »всея Росъсийския Земъля«, — all the Russian Land.

Although originally (X cent.) the Metropolitan Province of Kiev extended throughout the territories of Ukraine, Byelorussia and Muscovy, after it was divided in 1448 it comprised the Ukraine and Byelorussia only. Again, after the Union of Brest (1596), the Catholic Metropolitans continued to use the same title with the addition of Halič, the full title being: "Metropolitan of Kiev, Halič and of All Russia"[50]. Later, when the Orthodox Hierarchy was restored, the Orthodox Metropolitans of Kiev considered themselves to be the legitimate holders of the same title of Kiev and All Russia.

It would then appear that Bishop Skuminovič used the title: "Metropolitanate of Kiev and of All the Russian Land" to refer to the local Church and to the "Ustaŭ" (the liturgical Order) used in that Church. As far as we know there is no other Pontifical Service Book with such a solemn inscription, expressing the idea of the local Church which is ruled by its own "Ustaŭ" (Order).

50) Pelesz, J., *Geschichte der Union,* t. I, p. 156. Lozovei, P., *De Metropolitarum Kioviensium potestate (988-1596),* Rome, 1962, pp. 117-118.

There is no reason to doubt that the use of this grandiloquent title to describe the content of the MS is due to Skuminovič's genius.

What of this name "The Eastern Catholic Church of the Metropolitanate of Kiev and of All the Russian Land"? Does it imply that for the entire territory, defined by that name, there was one single "Ustaŭ"? Depending on the political situation this territory frequently changed not only its borders but also its population. For example when Skuminovič prepared his MS "the Eastern Catholic Church of the Metropolitanate of Kiev and of All the Russian Land" comprised only part of the old Kievan Metropolitanate and did not include several large dioceses such as Lvov and Pieremyšl; the whole of Byelorussia had a mixed population of Orthodox and Catholics.

It is too early to answer this question. A more careful analysis of our MS will reveal that in spite of local liturgical differences and customs, the Pontifical Liturgy handed down by Skuminovič was accepted generally by Catholics and Orthodox territorially and liturgically throughout the Metropolitanate of Kiev (Byelorussia, Ukraine) and, before the reforms of Patriarch Nikon, in Muscovy also. Therefore Skuminovič could quite properly write: "The Divine Liturgy of Our Father Among the Saints John Chrysostom celebrated by the Bishop according to the Ustaŭ (Order) of the Eastern Catholic Kievan Metropolitane and All the Russian (Ruthenian) Land."

Po Ustavu — iuxta Ordinem, according to Statutes or Rules, is a juridical and liturgical insertion. It can be at once supposed that the same Liturgy of St. John Chrysostom has different Statutes or a different Order (in Greek — diataxis) for the Kievan Church. As we shall see later MS BL gives some very old liturgical prayers which were in use in 12th-17th centuries in the Metropolitanate of Kiev.

Just under the title there is written, it seems in the same hand, one sentence in dedication: "Ecclesiae SSm Sergij et Bacchi in Urbe offero aeternum mei obsequij monumentum. Theodorus Skuminowicz, Episcopus Gratianopolitanus, Suffraganus Vilnensis per Albam Russiam m(anu) p(ropria)". This sentence is indeed the most important key to the date, region and authorship of MS BL. What a pity that Bishop Skuminovič overlooked one fact so important for us now — the date!

*

We should now draw attention to the letter of Bishop Tyškievič to Cardinal Orsini from 20 Sept. 1651, not because of its content, which is simply a matter of administrative routine, but because it was written by Theodore Skuminovič himself, the signature alone being that of the Bishop of Vilna. It is in the same handwriting as appears on the title page of MS BL in its dedication to the church of Saints Sergius and Bacchus in Rome. Again, the dedication and this letter offer further evidence that the whole MS was written by the same hand of the same person — Theodore Skuminovič, Suffragan of Byelorussia.

It is worth while illustrating a few of the more striking graphological similarities in the two MSS.

MS BL — Dedication (1652)		Letter of Bishop Tyškievič 20 Sept. 1651
E — Ecclesiae, Eps	=	E — Eminentissimo
Theodorus[51] Skuminowicz	=	Theodorus Skuminowicz
ff — offero, Suffraganus	=	affectu, faciles, officiorum
p — Eps, Gratianopolitanus	=	Princeps, comparebit, pro etc.
Viln. — i without dot	=	Vilnae — i without dot
aeternum[52]	=	praebere

It seems that the same similarities are characteristic of the Latin part of MS BL[53] and there is other evidence that the same hand was responsible for the Slavonic text also[54].

There are two texts: the Church Slavonic and the Latin translation of it on facing pages. Each page has in the upper part a little cross. Both texts have marginal notes, which usually show by whom parts of the Holy Liturgy are sung or read, e.g. by Archbishop (usually called Archierej or Svjatitel), by Priests, by Archdeacon, Deacon or Choir.

In the margins of the Latin text, apart from those corresponding to the Slavonic, there are such notes as: "Pontificale Rutenum" or "S. Chrysostomus". They are proofs that somebody studied this MS carefully and compared it with the Greek Liturgy of St. John Chrysostom. Note "Pontificale Rutenum" means that a part so marked is peculiar to the Byelorussian and Ukrainian Rite, at that time called Ruthenian, and could not be found in the Greek liturgical books in current use.

On pages 30v and 31 there are two handmade, rather careless, sketches to explain the way the bishop or priest should put on the discos the particles of leavened bread, which later will be consecrated. How these sketches were done, carefully or not, is of little importance because they explain clearly enough this particular rite, at that time, in our Church; but if you look at them attentively there seems no doubt that they were made by the same hand at the same

51) Skuminovič writes "d" in two ways: here it is written "∂". In the Letter in such words as *protegendum, ornandum, illustrandum* "d" is written identically with the form in the *Dedication*. In such words as *Theodorus, diocesi, Reverendis* the normal Latin "d" is used. In the Latin text of MS BL both forms of "d" occur.

52) The similar graphological signs: *ae*ternum, pr*ae*bere.

53) The graphological similarities between MS BL's *Dedication*, the *Letter* of Bishop Tyškievič and the *Latin text* of MS BL are in the following letters: E, T, S, V, p,q.

54) See MS BL pp. 30v-31: the sketch explaining the order of the particles on the paten (diskos). There can be no doubt that it was outlined on both sides by the same hand.

time. Therefore one may justifiably conclude that the copyist of both texts is the same person. The fact that the corrections of both texts are made in the same manner supports the same conclusion. This copyist, as we said above, is Bishop Skuminovič.

On page 14 of the Latin text, we can read in the margin the note: "Cantus. Habetur etiam in Missa S. Jacobi 2° Thomo Bibliothecae Graeco-Latinae editae Parisiis 2°. 1624"[55]. No doubt this note was added by the man who studied our MS and compared it with the known Paris edition. At the same time it is proof that the MS is not earlier than 1624. As we said before, its origin could be rather later, perhaps the year 1652, when Skuminovič stayed in Rome.

In spite of some corrections and deletions MS BL can be read without difficulty. It has small but clear lettering. The hand which wrote it was steady and sure and the writer not lacking in attention to a moderately aesthetic appearance in calligraphy. The distances between lines are the same. There are some pages of 32, 34, 36 and others of 28 lines.

MS BL is written in a Byelorussian cursive, with the characteristics proper to the late XVI and XVII centuries[56]. The most characteristic orthographical features of our MS show its link with the orthography of contemporary Byelorussian secular writings.

Finally, it is worth while noticing that in our MS there are practically no abbreviations, if one excepts IS (Iisus), BE (Bože), and sometimes HDI (Hospodi). There are also very few instances of writing letters above the lines, even in such words as "ot", usually written as "$\overset{\text{т}}{\text{o}}$". It is probable that the author consciously refrained from using all "shorthand" devices, knowing that the MS was to be in Rome and to be used by those not sufficiently familiar with the Church Slavonic tradition in writing.

55) La Bigne (Margarini de la Bigne) published in 1575 in Paris *Bibliotheca SS. Patrum supra Codices*... 8 volumes plus one volume in 1579 *Bibliothecae Appendix*. A new edition appeared in 1589, 9 volumes under the name: *Bibliotheca Veterum Patrum et antiquorum scriptorum ecclesiasticorum;* then again the same work was published in 1609 with the *Auctarium* (Supplement) in 1610. Fronton Ducaeus (Duc, S.J.) in 1624 in Paris produced a new edition in 9 volumes plus a *Supplement* of two volumes. In the second volume of this *Supplement* is the Mass of St. Jacob, about which there is a marginal note in MS BL.

56) On the Byelorussian cursive the following works provide information:
Sbornik paleografičeskich snimok s drevnich gramot i aktov, Vilna, 1884. — Beljaev, I. S., *Praktičeskij kurs izučenija drevnej russkoj skoropisi,* Moscow, 1911. — Karskij, E. F., *Belorusy. Jazyk belorusskago naroda,* t. 2, č I, Moscow, 1955. — The same author, *Slavjanskaja kirillovskaja paleografija,* Leningrad, 1928. — Možejko, N. S., *Drevnerusskij jazyk,* Minsk, 1970. — Bułyka, A. M., *Razvićcio arfahrafičnaj sistemy, starabiełaruskaj movy,* Minsk, 1970. — Jankoŭski, F., *Histaryčnaja hramatyka biełaruskaj movy,* č. I, Minsk, 1974. — Čerepin, A. V., *Russkaja paleografija,* Moscow, 1956.

Thanks to this we have today precious examples of the complete spelling of certain words, which in other MSS and printed Service Books at that time are found in abbreviated form only.

It would be interesting to make a grammatical study of MS BL. This, we hope, will be done by specialists who will use the original or this edition of it.

*

On 18th May 1661 was held the official inspection of the church of SS. Sergius and Bacchus and of the religious house attached to it. At this time a Catalogue was made of various items, including the books. Among these were found: triodion, octoich, the Gospel and the *Church Slavonic MS Missal (Służebnik)*[57]. Was this the one presented by Bishop Theodore Skuminovič? Not enough is known about this Missal to identify it with the present MS, which certainly later in some mysterious way came from the same church of SS. Sergius and Bacchus in Rome to Great Britain and was for the first time sold by Sotheby of London from the Guilford Collection in 1830; for the second time from the Phillips Collection in 1966 and for the third by the same Company on 27 June 1972 to the Francis Skaryna Byelorussian Library and Museum in London at a price of £140.00 (one hundred and forty pounds)[58].

When Bishop Skuminovič returned to his country, he was engaged in various activities. But the times were not at all propitious for any work either pastoral or scientific. Moscow, under Tsar Alexy, occupied the whole of Byelorussia. At the end of July 1655 the Cossack Zolotorenko entered Vilna with his grisly army. During this war the Byelorussian people endured terrible destruction of their cities and of their cultural achievements. It was the beginning of Byelorussia's national decline[59].

In the year 1657 Bishop Skuminovič was living in Brest (Bieraście), where he wrote

57) Choma, 'Naris istorii chramu Žyrovickoj Bohomatery', *Bohoslovija,* t. 35, Rome, 1971, p. 155.

58) *Catalogue of Auction* by Sotheby and Co., Tuesday, 27 June, 1972, Nr. 299, p. 51.

59) According to A. M. Karpačev and P. G. Kozlovskij, 'Dinamika čislennosti naselenija Belorussii vo vtoroj polovine XVII-XVIII v.', in *Ježegodnik po agrarnoj istorii Vostočnoj Jevropy, 1968 g.*, p. 92: during the period of war 1650-1667 Byelorussia lost more than half of its population (53%). — See: P. N. Batjuškov, *Belorussija i Litva,* SPb, 1890, pp. 254-264. — M. Hruševs'kyj, *Istorija Ukrainy-Rusi,* t. IX, New York, 1957, chapter VIII. — S. M. Solov'jev, *Istorija Rossii,* kn. V, t. 10, Moscow, 1961, chapter IV. — *Historyja Biełaruskaj SSR,* t. I, Minsk, 1972, pp. 328-330.

FRONTISPIECE: EPISTOLA PASCHALIS, GDAŃSK 1659.

his book **Epistola Paschalis**[60], and was at the same time responsible for the Archives of the Chapter of Vilna, which were transferred to Brest, then to Warsaw in order to save them from destruction[61]. He appears also to have lived in Braševičy, a village 12 km. distant from Drahičyn. Braševičy was a property of the Chapter of Vilna. In 1658 he there restored the parish church. To assist that church he assigned a part of the income from the Stemploviane tenement in Vilna which he had restored at his own expense[62].

Bishop Skuminovič was an official spokesman of the Vilna Chapter on two solemn occasions: the installation of Bishop Biełazor on 15 June 1664 and that of Bishop Sapieha on 16 Aug. 1668[63].

*

Apart from *Pryczyny* (Vilna, 1643) and the Pontifical Liturgy of St. John Chrysostom (= MS BL), which he left in Rome, Skuminovič published two other books in Latin. *Epistola Paschalis* (Gdańsk, 1659), and *De Jure Personarum* (Brussels, 1663)[64].

Epistola Paschalis is further proof that Bishop Skuminovič, in spite of his transfer to the Latin Church, was still concerned with problems of the Eastern Rite Church in Byelorussia.

The question of the Julian and Gregorian calendars — the latter came into force in Catholic countries in October 1582 — had been thoroughly discussed in the preliminary negotiations before the Union of Brest and afterwards, by both Catholics and Orthodox[65]. The Articles pertaining to the Union with the Roman Church signed by the Metropolitan Rahoza and his Bishops in 1595 include the following relevant passage: "We will accept the new calendar if the old one cannot be retained, without infringement however of Easter and our feastdays"[66]. When Meletius Smatrycki (alias Smotrzyski) became a Catholic he did not oppose the introduction of the new

60) At the end of *Epistola Paschalis:* "Datum ad Brescian Lituaniae. Anno 1657 Apr. 8". *Lietuvių Enciclopedija,* Boston, Mass., 1963, Vol. 28, p. 109.

61) *Lietuvių Enciclopedija,* 1. c., p. 109.

62) *Wizerunki i roztrząsania naukowe.* Poczet Nowy Drugi. Tomik 14, Vilna, 1840, pp. 12-14, note 1. About this Stemploviane house has been said: "Domus acialis murata, dicta lapidea Sztęfloviana, in platea a S. Joanne ad PP. Dominicanos tendente", 1. c., p. 12. note 1. — Kurczewski *Biskupstwo Wileńskie,* p. 84.

63) Kurczewski, 1. c., p. 84.

64) *Epistola Paschalis* is to be found in the British Library, 531.k.3(4). In the catalogue Skuminovič's bishopric is given but instead of "Gratianopolitanus" there is "Bishop of Grenoble". It is true that Grenoble in the south-east of France was known in Roman times as Gratianopolis, in honour of the Emperor Gratian, but it was never a titular city for bishops *in partibus infidelium.* Again Gratianopolis in the Mauretania Caesariensis, the titular see of Bishop Skuminovič, was never called Grenoble. — Under Riccioli's name in the same catalogue Skuminovič's book is indicated also. — *De Jure Personarum* is to be found in the Louvain University Library, L 5A 55845.

65) Articuli ad Unionem Ecclesiae Ruthenae cum Ecclesia Romana pertinentes, 6, in: Hofmann, G., 'Die Wiedervereinigung der Ruthenen', *Orientalia Christiana,* Vol. III-2, p. 143 Polish text; p. 151 Latin text. — Welykyj, A. G., *Documenta Unionis,* p. 62 Polish text; pp. 68-69 Latin text. See also 1. c. pp. 77, 108, 128, 194. — Pope Gregory XIII sought to convince Jeremiah, Patriarch of Constantinople, that he should accept the new calendar. On their part Jeremiah and the Patriarch of Alexandria had written to the Prince of Ostrog (1582) suggesting that he should not accept this innovation. Šeptyckyj, A., *Monumenta Ucrainae Historica,* Vol. I, pp. 29-33. See also Vol. IX-X, p. 95. — Hofmann, G., 'Briefweksel zwischen Gabriel Severos and Anton Possevino', *Orient. Chr. Periodica,* Vol. XV, 1949, p. 432. — Krajcar, J., 'The Paschalia Printed at Rome in 1596', *Oxford Slavonic Papers,* Vol. III, 1970, pp. 107-118.

66) Welykyj, A. G., *Documenta Unionis,* pp. 62, 68-69.

calendar, since it was not an article of faith[67].

During the Anti-Synod in Brest (1596) it was insisted by its adherents that the new calendar could not be accepted because it would be against the canons of the Church[68]. Later, Hierodeacon Leontius in 1608 wrote: "It is heresy to celebrate any feast according to the new calendar"[69].

In Bishop Skuminovič's time the subject of the calendar attracted numerous scholars of different denominations from different countries; this is amply proved by the books published at that time. Mention need only be made here of those who were nearest to him as regards rite, country and, perhaps, polemic stubbornness. These include: Cassian Calixtus Sakovič and the Archimandrite John Dubovič, both contemporaries of Skuminovič, who both wrote books on the old and new calendars[70].

Epistola Paschalis was written in April 1657 in Brest, and then was sent to Father Riccioli, who wrote a reply dated 3 August of the same year. the *Epistola Paschalis* came into the hands of the printer George Foerster only much later, and was published by him in Gdańsk at the end of March 1659. Foerster included a dedication from himself as publisher to Bishop Daŭhiała Zaviša (1656-1661), Bishop of Vilna, whom he calls "the supreme Hierarch of Lithuania having under his jurisdiction a large number of people of the Greek Rite". This is not exactly true: in the Vilna diocese there were, indeed, many persons of the Greek (Ruthenian) Rite but they did not came under the jurisdiction of the Latin Bishop of Vilna.

The *Epistola Paschalis* opens with magniloquent compliments to Riccioli: "te tanquam luminarium coelestium veneremur". It was, in fact, Father Albert Kojałovič, Rector of the College and of the Academy in Vilna, author of the *Annales Lituaniae* who had suggested that Bishop Skuminovič

67) Likowski, *Unia Brzeska*, pp. 323-24.
68) Likowski, l. c., p. 152.
69) 'Sočinenije ierodiakona Pečerskogo monastyrja Leontija', in: *Akty otnosjaščijesja k ist. Južnoj i Zapadnoj Rossii*, SPb, 1865, t. 2, pp. 271, 277.
70) Jocher, A., *Obraz bibliograficzno-historyczny literatury*, t. III, Vilna, 1857, pp. 345-349. Among various calendars the author mentions Skuminovič's *Epistola Paschalis.* — Cassian Callixt Sakovič, *Okvlary Kalendarzowi Staremu ...*, Cracow, 1644. — Estreicher, *Bibliografia Polska*, cz. III, t. XVI, Cracow, 1929, p. 28.

should contact Riccioli, the famous Italian astronomer[71].

Before Skuminovič starts to expound his new Ruthenian Calendar he — as Suffragan of Byelorussia — tries to explain to Riccioli what is meant by "Russia". It is interesting to see what a Bishop, Byelorussian by descent and now Latin by culture and rite, thought about "Russia" or rather "the Russians" in the middle of the seventeenth century. He speaks very little about the geographical significance of the term, but says a great deal within a short compass about the approach of the two "Russias" (Muscovy and Byelorussia) toward the Catholic Church and towards freedom and a new way of life.

Skuminovič writes: "As you probably know, dear and Very Reverend Father, there are two Russias: one is the Lesser, which embraces the freedom of the Kings of Poland and the Grand Dukes of Lithuania. The other is the Greater, which is at will subservient to the Grand Dukes of Muscovy, formerly excluded by immemorial laws, as is the case of China, from the society of neighbouring peoples. Both (Russias), by reason of the Eastern Rites, are involved in schism.

"One of these, Russia Minor, is everywhere entirely open to the preaching of the Catholic truth. The other, Great Russia, has always been difficult of approach. But thanks to recent contact with our people, the inhabitants of Great Russia seem to be now to some extent becoming more civilised and beginning to recognise the harshness of their own outlook. It seems that they are beginning to look with admiration and approval at the freedom and more civilised way of life which we enjoy. Thus, they now reject and even condemn some of their own rites and practices such as the rebaptism of the baptized[72], which has been condemned for centuries but yet found favour with them right up to the present year.

71) "Riccioli, a Jesuit, born at Ferrara in 1598, contributed to the progress of astronomy... His *Novum Almagestum* is a collection of observations, opinions, and physical explanations of the phenomena, together with all the methods of computations then known... He gave to the principal spots of the moon the names which are now used by astronomers" — writes R.A.P., 'Astronomy', *The Encyclopaedia Britt.*, 9th ed., Vol. II, Edinburgh, 1875, p. 754. — See also: De Backer, A., Sommervogel, Ch., *Bibliotheque des Ecrivains...*, t. III, Louvain-Lyon, 1876, col. 182-186. Here are given 17 titles of the various books published by Riccioli "l'un des plus savants astronomes du 17e siecle"", l. c., col. 183.

72) See Makarij, *Istorija Russkoj Cerkvi*, t. 12, p. 195.

"It is evident from many indications, so far as human reason can judge, that many inhabitants of both Russias are in error not so much through sour obstinacy as through ignorance (an ancient ignorance, as has been said). It happens sometimes with them that they protest, yet at the same time they believe the same truth which the Catholic Church believed and believes. Hence those very articles of faith of the Church which through ignorant error they think are false, from another point of view they do in fact believe and hold in a general and implicit way".

What precisely did Skuminovič understand by "Russia Minor"?

Is it the same as "Małaja Ruś", "Little Russia"? It would appear not. Estreicher[73] states categorically that the distinction is simply that between schismatic Muscovy (Great Russia) on the one hand, and Byelorussia on the other. Certainly Skuminovič's "Minor Russia" includes Byelorussia (in the sense explained above), but it would seem that he extends the term to the whole of "Ruś" within the Commonwealth; hence according to modern terminology it would cover both Byelorussia and the Ukraine. Estreicher, and not he alone, occasionally applied the term "Byelorussian" to the Ukrainian territory and language. It should be noticed also that the Ukraine, when Skuminovič wrote his book, was outside the Grand Duchy of Lithuania.

There is no doubt, however, about another aspect of Skuminovič's two "Russias". The "Minor" is more open to the Catholic truth and more civilized. Here one might fully agree with Skuminovič.

*

Skuminovič proposes a new version of the Gregorian Calendar specially adapted to the Eastern Rite, which he calls *Calendarium Ruthenicum,* with a detailed scientific discussion on ecclesiastical astronomy ("ecclesiasticae meae astronomiae") in order to help the devout Ruthenian people:

73) *Bibl. Polska K. Estreichera,* cz. III, t. 31, Cracow, 1936, p. 495.

"obsequio et utilitati gentis Russiacae devotae". He understands why the people are so attached to the old calendar: "non per inacia magis, sed ignorantia, eaque (ut vocant) antecedente errare..."

The existing Ruthenian Calendar which had been drawn up, not without Greek subtlety, had become useless only because during the course of time it had not received the necessary revision, and now therefore should be restored once again to its pristine vigour. The Orthodox think that the Council of Nicaea drew up the Church Calendar. This is especially true, he says, of the Muscovites who are "a philosophicis theologisque studiis, occlusa exotis disciplinis regione, alieni". To prove this opinion false it is sufficient to recall that the Ruthenian alphabet with its 35 letters was formulated by SS. Cyril and Methodius, who lived more than 400 years after the Council of Nicaea; and this alphabet lies at the basis of the calendar. Nevertheless Skuminovič fully understands the tenacity of the traditionalists and therefore proposes to proceed with the new calendar very prudently.

He goes on to discuss the differences between the Julian and Gregorian calendars, and explains the cycles of the sun and moon with diagrams and tables. He asks Riccioli to read and consider his proposals for his new-style Ruthenian Calendar, to express his approval or disapproval and to make any necessary additions; all this should serve "to the greater elegance of the Church militant, which dressed in brocade without any wrinkle stands before the face of the Lord" (quae sine ulla ruga circumamicta varietate stat in conspectu Domini).

Epistola Paschalis ends with a trope reminiscent of the dedication of the MS BL: "Quo beneficio certe mihi suavissima *perennis* tibi deferendae gratitudinis *obsequium*".

*

Riccioli answered Skuminovič's letter, albeit somewhat briefly[174]. First of all he

74) The answer of Fr. Riccioli in the form of a letter may be found published at the end of the same book *Epistola Paschalis.*

gently waives the Bishop's compliments as regards his own person, attributing them to his esteem for the Jesuit Order. Then he extols the Bishop's virtue of humility since he sought the judgement of Riccioli, a master turning to a pupil. Riccioli declined to express a definitive opinion concerning those matters which referred to the Ruthenian Calendar only, but in general terms he expresses his interest in Skuminovič's proposal. "I have read and re-read", he says, "your most learned treatise about the revision of the Graeco-Russian Calendar and I could not fail to admire such a profundity which is apparent simultaneously with clarity of style in discussing most abstruse matters, and reveals such ability".

Riccioli also praises the diagrams and tables, and notes that he himself had elaborated certain similar questions in the third and fourth books of his *Almagesti*. He also promises to mention the Ruthenian Calendar in his new book *Chronographia reformata*.

Even if Riccioli's remarks about Bishop Skuminovič's proposed calendar may be attributed simply to the elegant but conventional baroque compliments customary at that time in such a letter, nevertheless it is clear that he, Riccioli, had a genuine appreciation and professional interest in the Skuminovič proposals. This is corroborated also by the fact that he kept his promise and inserted in his important work *Chronologiae Reformatae* (Bologna, 1669, t. I, ch. XXIII, p. 51)[75], the following recapitulation about Skuminovič's newly proposed Calendar: "Ruthenians and Muscovites generally use the Julian Calendar, which has 365 days in the year, 366 in a leap year. They use also the names of the months and their number according to the Romans. So says Joseph Scaligero, Origanus, p. 1, Ephem. c. 2. But as the Most Illustrious and Most Reverend Lord Theodore Skuminoroicz (sic!), Bishop of Gratia-

75) *Chronologiae Reformatae et ad certas conclusiones redactae.* Tomus primus continens doctrinam temporum auctore R. P. Io. Baptista Ricciolio Ferrariensi Societalis Iesu Illustrissimi Collegii Parmensis Nobilium Convictoribus dedicatus. Bononiae, 1669. There are three volumes: t. I, pp. XV+404; t. II, pp. 236; t. III, pp. 324 — in folio.

nopolis and Suffragan of Byelorussia (Albae Russiae Suffraganus) has said to me in writing, the Ruthenians, to find the date of Easter, use the Alexandrian cycle; but (Skuminovič) devised an ingenious method, through which, while preserving the appearance of the Old Calendar, one could in essence produce the effect of the Gregorian Calendar. He has written to me at length about this method. I still do not know whether he prevailed with the Ruthenians or not".

No doubt, Riccioli's appreciation of Skuminovič's work and his proposal for a New Ruthenian (Byelorussian) Calendar, which would eventually satisfy both Orthodox and Catholics, gave it great support and publicity. But the real judgement on the value and utility of Bishop Skuminovič's work is still awaiting serious examination.

*

There is a further book *De Jure Personarum* written by Skuminovič which bears as the date of its dedication 2 February 1663, Louvain, but was published in Brussels during the same year[76]. It concerns law, and is intended as a text-book for theologians, lawyers and politicians: "Opus theologis, iuristis et politicis aeque necessarium ac jucundum".

The work is dedicated to John Paul Sapieha, the palatine of Vilna. The author mentions his victories over Muscovites, particularly the liberation of Słonim; and over Rakoczy and the Swedes. He refers also to Leo Sapieha and his merits in the edition of the *Lithuanian Statutes:* "Magnus ille Leo, Illustrissimae tuae familiae decus immortale". The entire book comprises 26 chapters, of which each is divided into paragraphs in the following form:

Titulus primus: De justitia et jure;

Titulus secundus: De jure naturali, gentium et civili;

Titulus tertius: De jure personarum;

76) For the full title see Bibliography under Skuminovič, Theodore.

Titulus quartus: De ingenuis;

Titulus quintus: De libertinis,

Etc.

Skuminovič is familiar with the usual literature of the XVI and XVII centuries. Sometimes he compares the law in Poland with that of the Grand Duchy of Lithuania, e.g. in Poland noblemen could not engage in trade, and in Lithuania they could. It seems he had in mind the *Lithuanian Statutes*[77].

Skuminowič's *De Jure Personarum* is the third book published after *Przyczyny* and *Epistola Paschalis* and is of a totally different character. No doubt it is of the greatest importance, and illustrates both the wide scope of his interests and a degree of scholarship of a Western European level. This work was quoted as an authority by the German philosopher Leibnitz[78].

In the end of the book *De jure Personarum* there are two ecclesiastical approvals of the work: one by Jacobus Pontanus, Doctor of Divinity, Professor and Censor of books (Louvain, 4th Febr. 1663); another by J. Ceron, Parish Priest of St. Mary's de Capella, Archpresbyter of Brussels and Censor of books. Because the latter contains an evaluation of the work, we should like to quote it in full:

"Feliciter in publicum usum prodeat haec *Catholica Explicatio Lib. I. Instit. Iustiniani,* in qua Illustmus Gratianopolitarum Praesul non tantum Juris Civilis sincerum ac solertem agit interpretem; sed etiam ea quae ex Jure Naturali, Divino, et Ecclesiastico ad rem faciunt, opportune interserit; quaeque a Triboniano Ethnico, vel a Lutheri et Calvini discipulis, Christianae Religioni vel sacris Ecclesiae sanctionibus adversa prodierunt, quantum ad ea, de quibus in primo Institutionum Libro agitur, pertinet, valide et succincte refellit. Elegans est, amoenum, acutum, nervosum, et varia solidaque eruditione, praesertim Jurisprudentiae studiosis, expetendum, utiliter-

---

77) See: 'Handel', *Encyklopedia Staropolska,* Warsaw, 1939, t. I, p. 414: Sejm z r. 1633 uchwalił, że "każdy szlachcic szlachectwo traci, jeśli będąc w mieście osiadły handlami i szynkami się bawi". According to the Statutes of the Grand Duchy of Lithuania, 1588, chapter 3, art. 25, if for some reason a nobleman went to a town and engaged in trade or commerce, he would forfeit the privileges of his estate so long as he was engaged in the said occupation.

78) After the abdication of King John Casimir (1668) there were various parties promoting their candidates in order to gain the throne of the Republic. Young Leibnitz (when only 22 years old) tried to promote the Prince of Neuburgh as the best candidate. For this occasion he wrote a political-juridical treatise in the Latin language: *Specimen demonstrationum politicarum pro eligendo Rege Polonorum; novo scribendi genere ad clarum certitudinem exactum.* Auctore Georgio Ulicovio Lithuano. Juxta exemplar editum Vilnae 1659. See Dutens, L., *G. G. Leibnitii Opera Omnia,* t. IV, Genevae, 1768, pp. 522-630. As is explained by the editor of the *Opera Omnia* of Leibnitz both the name of the author of the pamphlet and the place of edition were invented. In fact it was published in Danzig (Gdańsk) in 1669. When Leibnitz asserts that the cities of Cracow, Vilna and Danzig have the same privileges as the nobles *(Specimen demonstrationum,* l. c., p. 525), he refers to the text from Skuminovič's book *De Jure Personarum* (Brussel, 1663, p. 69). Leibnitz himself has not mentioned Skuminovič's book; Dr. S. Kot has reached this conclusion *(Rzeczpospolita Polska w literaturze politycznej Zachodu,* Cracow, 1919, p. 146), and it was supported by Estreicher *Bibliografia Polska,* cz. III, t. 31, Cracow, 1936, p. 494). Here are the texts:

1) of Skuminovič: "Magistratus tamen in pluribus locis est nobilis, ut in Germania passim; in Polonia Cracoviensis, Vilnensis (in Polonia? — C. S.), Dantiscanus";

2) of Leibnitz: "Magistratus urbani: Cracoviensis, Vilnensis et Dantiscanus, Nobilibus comparatur".

que ac jucunde lectum iri existimo". (Brussels, 10th July 1663).

*

Bishop Theodore Skuminovič died on 24 Sept. 1668 in the presbytery of Łyntupy during his journey to Haduciški[79].

In the documents of the Vilna Chapter one can read about him: "Vir integritate vitae, probitate morum et annorum gravitate decorus, ac conspicuus, sacrae et profanae doctrinae eruditione insignis, variarum peritus linguarum"[80].

After all that is said about the life and work of Bishop Skuminovič we can support, no doubt, this brief, but significant epitaph. Its author was a contemporary and knew Bishop Skuminovič better than we can from the distance of over 300 years.

To summarize on reflection we may conclude:

1) All that we know from the various sources about Bishop Skuminovič bears witness that he was a highly educated man in such widely differing fields as liturgy, history, theology, astronomy and law. He knew several languages, and he was also a good Priest and Bishop.

2) Bishop Skuminovič holds a particular place in the history of the Byelorussian Catholic Church. He was educated in the Orthodox Church, but, because of his sincere desire to find the truth, he changed his denomination and rite, although it seems he never severed all ties with the Eastern Rite (his connection with the Basilian Fathers in Rome, his MS of the Lithurgy of St. John Chrysostom, his Ruthenian Calendar intended as a link between Catholics and Orthodox) or with Byelorussians. He worked among them as an Orthodox Priest, then as the Archdeacon and the Suffragan of Byelorussia.

3) The MS BL of the Liturgy of St. John Chrysostom merits special attention. Despite many difficulties we have decided to render it accessible to the larger number of people who may be interested in it, publishing it in fascimile copies made possible by modern methods. Our observations and commentaries, on some of its parts only, although far from perfect, may, we hope, be of some small addition to its permanent value.

*

79) Kurczewski, *Biskupstwo Wileńskie*, p. 84.
80) Kurczewski, loc. cit., p. 84.

EXPLANATORY LITURGICAL NOTES

Entrance Prayers

In the process of the evolution of the Liturgy of St. John Chrysostom the Entrance Prayers are of a later date[1] and among the Eastern Slavs their number and content were subjected to change under the influence of various circumstances. Two factors were here undoubtedly decisive: the reforms by Patriarch Nikon of liturgical books in Russia, and the Union of Brest in Byelorussia and the Ukraine. In each of these countries there existed also local traditions which found their expression in the manuscript and printed Service Books (Służebniki).

Although MS BL was composed at the middle of the XVII century, it would not, however, be a mistake to assert that in its traditions it embraces roughly two centuries, i.e., from the second half of the XV century to the second half of the XVII century, which gave it time to take root in the Metropolitan See of Kiev. Thus it is of equal interest to Catholics of Eastern Rite (Uniates) and Orthodox. Each fragment of it — if one can use such an expression here — is both interesting and important for the student.

In the preparatory part of the Liturgy, which is called the Entrance Prayers, three parts can be distinguished:

1) The meeting of the bishop and his proceeding to the doors of the church.
2) Prayers, reverences and the kissing of icons before the Royal Doors.
3) Entrance into the sanctuary, and prayers before vesting in the sanctuary.

In our MS one can easily distinguish all three parts, as shown on the scheme below: 1) A, 1-10; 2) B, 11-31; 3) C, 32-34, but it should be noticed that in the first part according to the MS the bishop proceeds straight to the iconostasis. The pause before the doors of the church with the prayer "The impassable door", which was brought later into prominence in the Suprasl (1716) and Lvov (1886) Archieratica, does not exist in MS BL.

For a Pontifical Liturgy, the first and last parts appear to be the most characteristic, because the second or middle parts, which came down almost unchanged to our present times and became customary, are identical for the Liturgy of a bishop and a priest.

A. Dmitrijevskij[2], in order the better to analyze the sequence and content of the Entrance Prayers in many manuscripts and printed Service Books of the XVI century, divided them into seven groups. Besides this he gave also the Entrance Prayer for a Pontifical Liturgy, taking them from three manuscript Service Books.

Among the Service Books, there are those that have only one Entrance Prayer: "Lord stretch forth your hand"[3], but there are also those that have two, three... twenty, and even more Entrance Prayers[4]. Depending upon their number Dmitrievskij divided them into groups. As has already been mentioned in the introductory remarks, he placed the Entrance Prayers of the Vilna Service Book of 1583 into a fifth and separate group[5].

Because the Entrance Prayers of MS BL are similar to the prayers not only of one Vilna Service Book but of two dated 1583 and 1598, it is worth while here to devote a little further consideration to them.

A more precise examination reveals that A. Dmitrijevskij apparently confused the Vilna Service Books, because the Entrance Prayers placed by him in the fifth group correspond more to those which are found in the Service Book of 1598 than to those of 1583[6]. Thanks to his parallel method, however, he has brought us along a path which again leads to a very important conclusion, namely, that the Entrance Prayers of MS BL belong to the same group as the prayers of the first two Service Books printed in Byelorussia at the end of the XVI century, despite the fact that they present only the ordinary Liturgy for the priest and not the pontifical.

Thus, the Entrance Prayers of the Pontifical Service Books given by the same author[7], even though they offer numerous similarities to MS BL, are somewhat closer in their composition, number and content to the Muscovite pre-Nikon Service Book of 1602. Wholy different is *The Order of Pontifical Ceremonies of the Divine Liturgies (= Čin Archijerejskago Dejstva Božestvennych Liturgij = ČAD)* of the Moscow Patriarchate of 1668, which all subsequent Pontifical Service Books of the Russian style (Archijerejskija Činovniki) follow, including the most recent[8]. They do not contain even one prayer from the first and third parts of the above mentioned Entrance Prayers.

Because the liturgical heritage, and the evidence of the further evolution of the Liturgy enshrined in MS BL, appear also in the so-called Uniate Pontificals or Archieratica it is worth while examining the similarities and differences between them. Reference will be made to the Archieratica edited in Suprasl in 1716, in Lvov in 1886, and the Archieraticon in Rome in 1975[9].

*

Let us look at the ceremonies and prayers according to MS BL. A hierarch (svjatitel) about to celebrate the Liturgy, when the time has come, puts on the mantiya (bishop's mantle) and klobuk[10]. Leaving his place of residence[11], he meets "the deacons who are vested in liturgical robes with a thurible and incense, and the candlebearers carrying lighted candles who await him" (MS BL, p. 1v). By deacons is meant an archdeacon and a deacon who, during the entire time, take part in the Liturgy.

The archdeacon "holding the incense and the thurible turns to the bishop and asks: Bless, master, the incense"[12]. The bishop, blessing the incense, recites the prayer: "We offer you incense", ending with "Amen", after which he immediately adds: "Praise, children of the Lord, praise the name of the Lord". The archdeacon (inclining his head again" (caput rursum inclinans), goes before the bishop, incenses and sings alternately with the people: "Blessed be the name of the Lord from now and unto eternity". During this time, the bishop advances reciting the folloving prayers:

My feet lead me in the path of your truth... (Effusi sunt gressus mei in justitiam, memor fui Domini...)[13].

But I, so great is your love, may come to your house...[14]

The impassable door...[15]

Ps. 22 (23): The Lord is my shepherd...[16]

Arriving at the Royal Doors, he bows down saying: "O God, be merciful to me a sinner". The archdeacon removes the bishop's klobuk and hands it "to those standing around", and the bishop begins to recite the usual Entrance Prayers beginning with: "Blessed be our God" and "Heavenly King"[17]. There follows: "For yours is the kingdom", "Lord have mercy" repeated 12 times etc.

Entering into the sanctuary, the bishop "with the deacons supporting him under the arms and candlebearers standing before the Royal Doors" recites the prayer: "Lord remove from me all my transgressions... O Lord our God send down your hand from your dwelling on high..."[18] In the sanctuary the priests in their vestments await the bishop, "the prothesis being already completed on the side altar by the archpriest or one of the priests"[19]. This signifies that, in the Greek custom, the priest in the higher dignity prepares the gifts, and not the youngest as is done in the Russian rite down to the present time.

The bishop kisses the holy Gospel; then "the archdeacon or deacon, taking the Pontifical Service Book[20], holds it up before the bishop from his left side", and the bishop reads a lengthy prayer: "Lord God Almighty, you do not desire the death of sinners..." This is one of the most ancient prayers. It is to be found in the Service Book of Anthony the Roman († 1147)[21], and in the Prayerbook of the XIV century published by Kovaliv[22]. The Vilna Service Books (1583, 1598) also have it, although according to these the priest recites it after he is already vested, but before the washing of hands. It also appears in XVIth century MSS Service Books for Bishops[23], as well in the Muscovite printed edition of 1602, and in the Suprasl (1716), Univ (1740) and Lvov (1886) Archieratica, but not in the Roman edition of 1975. It would be interesting to make a study of the content and language of this old prayer, which the Uniate Pontificals have handed down to us and which Chojnacki — who criticised "all and everything" — failed to notice in his book *Zapadnorusskaja Cerkovnaja Unija.*

*

When one compares this part of the Liturgy of MS BL with the rites and prayers of the Uniate Archieratica, which have been published later in Byelorussia and the Ukraine, one finds much that is common, but also quite a few things that are different.

First, what is common are certain episcopal prayers of which today in some Pontifical Service Books there is not even a trace, although they have behind them a long tradition. All Catholic Archieratica have: "Praise, children of the Lord", "Blessed be the name of the Lord...", "My feet lead me in the path of your truth...", "The impassable door...", Psalm 22 (23).

Common to all Greek and Slavonic Service Books is also that part of the Entrance Prayers which is recited before the iconostasis, although it should be noted that in no single known Service Book is there such detail and accuracy in the indication and sequence of these prayers as in MS BL.

The differences of MS BL from the other Uniate Archieratica are in the ceremony of meeting the bishop, and in the number and sequence of prayers recited. MS BL does not include among the entrance prayers one which is known from other sources: *"The voice of joy..."* (Гласъ радости и веселія горѣ взыйде къ Отцу небесному...). Since this prayer seems to be inseparable from the other Entrance Prayers, and is found as far back as MSS of the XV century and in the later MSS and printed Service Books of the XVI cent. (Vilna edition 1583, 1598), and also in all the Uniate Archieratica, — it seems certain that this prayer has been omitted from MS BL either as the result of a scribal error or owing to a lacuna in the source.

The other Pontificals except the Roman (1975), under the influence of the Latin "Asperges me hyssopo", also provide, at the meeting with the bishop, for sprinkling with holy water and lying prostrate in the sanctuary, together with the recitation of Psalm 50 (51). Such features are entirely absent from MS BL.

ORDER OF THE ENTRANCE PRAYE

А — Аръхиерей Д — Аръхидиаконъ Л — Ликъ

	Text	Rubrics
A.	1. Д: **Благосълави Владыко кадило.**	А времени уже пришедшу облачитъся в манътию Святительскую, и тако исъходитъ ко церкъви. И изъшедъ обрѣтаетъ диаконы оболъчены во одежъду церъковъную со кадильницею и кадиломъ, свѣщоносъцы же со свѣщами возъженъными ожыдающыхъ его.
	2. А: **Кадило † ти приносимъ...**	
	3. А: **Хвалите † отроцы Господа...**	
	4. Д: **Буди имя Госъподъне благосълавенъно...**	Д главу паки прѣклонь идѣ прѣдъ Святителемъ кадя.
	5. Л: **Буди имя Госъподъне...**	и прочая пѣния
	6. А: **(Гласъ радости...)**	А идяй благосълавъляетъ люди, и втай глаголетъ
	7. А: **Пролиашася стопы моя...**	
	8. А: **Азъ множествомъ милости вниду...**	И паки
	9. А: **Непроходимая дверъ...**	
	10. А: **Господь пасетъ мя...**	Таже Псаломъ 22.
B.	11. А: **Боже милосътивъ буди мне грѣшному.**	А прышедъ предъ Святые Врата, творитъ поклонъ глаголя стихъ.
	12. А: **Благосълавенъ Богъ нашъ...**	Д веземъ с него клобукъ. Архиерейже отъкровенъну главу имущы, и во святыхъ Вратѣхъ стоящы.
	13. А: **Царю небесны...**	
	14. А: **Святый Боже...**	А творытъже поклонъ 3.
	15. А: **Слава и нинѣ.**	
	16. А: **Пресвятая Тройце...**	
	17. А: **Госъподи помилуй 3.**	
	18. А: **Слава и нинѣ.**	
	19. А: **Отъче наш.**	
	20. А: **Яко твое есть царсътво...**	
	21. А: **Госъподи помилуй 12.**	
	22. А: **Слава и нинѣ.**	
	23. А: **Прыйдѣта поклонимъся цареви нашему Богу...**	И паки творитъ поклонъ трижди глаголя
	24. А: **Помилуй насъ Госъподи...**	Таже глаголетъ тропары сыя.
	25. А: **Слава Отъцу и Сыну и Святому Духу.**	
	26. А: **Госъподи помилуй насъ, на тя бо уповахомъ...**	
	27. А: **И нинѣ и присно и во вѣки вѣкомъ. Аминь.**	
	28. А: **Милосердия дверы, отъверъзи намъ Благосълавенъная...**	
	29. А: **Пречестъному ти образу...**	Покланяется иконѣ Спасовѣ
	30. А: **Милосеръдия сущи исъточъникъ...**	Покланяетъжеся иконѣ Богородичънѣ
	31. А: **Боже очисъти грѣхи моя и помилуй мя.**	Покланяется ко прѣстолу
C.	32. А: **Госъподи отыйми отъ мене вся безъзакония моя, и прѣгрѣшения моя, да досътойно вниду...**	И тако входитъ в олътаръ диакономъ его подъ руцѣ держащымъ свѣщоносъцѣмъже предъ царъскими дверъми стоящымъ, и глаголетъ молитву входяй.
	33. А: **Госъподи Боже наш посъли руку твою отъ вышъняго жы-**	

руку твою [illegible] лица твоего, и укрѣпи мя...

Егъдаже присътупитъ ко святому прѣсътолу, диакони вземъше и поднесъше Святое Еванъгелие напрѣсътольное, даютъ е целовати Аръхиереови ничътоже отъверзъше.

34. А: **Владыко Госъподи Вседеръжытелю не хотяй смеръти грѣшъникомъ, но ожыдаяй обращения ихъ...**

По целовании же Святаго Еванъгелия аръхидиаконъ или диаконъ вземъ **Служебъникъ Святительский,** деръжытъ и прямо Аръхиерея з страны левое. Онъже чтетъ втай молитву сию. Скончавъже молитву и поклонъшеся исъходитъ царъскими враты и восъходитъ на амъбонъ.

candlebea[illegible]
Doors, recites the p[illegible]
A having reached the holy Altar the deacons lift the Gospel-Book and give it to the bishop to kiss, but they do not open it.

33. A: **O Lord, our God, send down Your hand from Your dwelling on high...**

After the kissing of the Gospel-Book the archdeacon, or deacon, taking *the Pontifical Service Book,* holds it up before the bishop on his left side. The bishop reads silently this prayer. Having finished the prayer, and bowed, he proceeds through the Royal Doors and goes up into the ambo.

34. A: **Lord God Almighty, You do not desire the death of sinners...**

CCORDING TO THE MS OF THE BL

A — Bishop   D — Archdeacon   L — Choir

	Text	Rubrics
A. 1. D:	**Bless, Master, the incense.**	When the time has come A puts on bishop's mantiya and so proceeds to the church. Leaving his place he meets the deacons who are vested in liturgical robes with a thurible and incense and the candlebearers carrying lighted candles who await him.
2. A:	**We offer you † incense...**	
3. A:	**Praise, children of the Lord...**	
4. D:	**Blessed be the name of the Lord...**	D again inclining his head goes before the bishop, incenses.
5. L:	**Blessed be the name of the Lord...**	and other antiphons
6. A:	**(The voice of joy...)**	A advancing blesses the people and silently recites.
7) A:	**My feet lead me in the path of your truth...**	
8. A:	**I in the multitude of your mercy will enter into your house...**	And this
9. A:	**The impassable door...**	
10. A:	**The Lord is my shepherd...**	Also Ps. 22(23).
B. 11. A:	**O, God, be merciful to me a sinner**	A arriving at the Royal Doors, bows down saying the verse.
12. A:	**Blessed be our God...**	D removes his klobuk. A bare-headed stands between the Royal Doors.
13. A:	**Heavenly King...**	
14. A:	**Holy God...**	A bows down thrice.
15. A:	**Glory be to the Father... now and always...**	
16. A:	**Most Holy Trinity...**	
17. A:	**Lord, have mercy.**	Thrice.
18. A:	**Glory be to the Father... now and always...**	
19. A:	**Our Father...**	
20. A:	**For yours is the kingdom...**	
21. A:	**Lord, have mercy.**	12 times.
22. A:	**Glory be to the Father... now and always...**	
23. A:	**Let us come and bow down to the King...**	And again bows down thrice and recites.
24. A:	**Have mercy on us, O Lord, have mercy...**	
25. A:	**Glory be to the Father...**	
26. A:	**Have mercy on us, O Lord, because we have trusted in You...**	Says also these troparia.
27. A:	**Now and always and for ever and ever. Amen.**	
28. A:	**Open the door of mercy for us, O blessed Mother of God...**	
29. A:	**We bow down to your most pure image...**	A bows down to the icon of the Saviour.
30. A:	**The fountain of mercy, O Mother of God...**	A bows down to the icon of the Mother of God.
31. A:	**O God, cleanse my sins and have mercy on me.**	A bows down to the Altar.
C. 32. A:	**Lord remove from me all my transgressions and all my sins...**	A entering into the Sanctuary with the deacons supportin[illegible] candlebearers

The bishop accompanied by the priests and deacons, who are already in their liturgical vestments, proceeds through the Royal Doors towards the ambo[24]. In our MS there is no mention that "Ton despotin" should be sung during the procession[25].

The archdeacon assists the bishop to robe. The vesting, like any other liturgical act, begins with: "Blessed be our God"[26]. The bishop silently recites the prescribed prayers[27].

Vesting himself with the *sticharion,* the bishop first blesses it, then kisses it. According to MS BL this is done with the sticharion only and not with each individual vestment. At least nothing is said about any action.

After the sticharion the bishop puts on the *paraman* (in Greek paramandy, in Russian paramand). Taking the paraman, he says: "The Lord said, My yoke is sweet and my burden light" (Mat. 11, 30). The parallel Latin text reads: "Sumens *humerale* dicens: Dixit Dominus † jugum meum suave, et onus meum leve".

The Latin translation is misleading, since "humerale" or "amictus" until recently was a part of the liturgical vestments of the bishop or priest of the Latin rite. The Catholic Archieratica and Service Books call it "naplečnik" and give a rubric for vesting in the manner of Latin priests: before the sticharion (alb). MS BL gives a different rubric: the paraman should be put *over the sticharion* and quite a different prayer should be recited from that used in putting on the "naplečnik"[28].

What is the paraman?

Bishop Savva explaines: "Paramand (paramandy) or analav is the quadrangular cloth with a cross, which was put on during the tonsure ceremony and worn by monks on the chest or on the arms under their clothes"[29]. As early as the Pachomian rule translated by St. Jerome a linen covering for the arms is mentioned[30]. It is possible that ancient monastic custom was adopted for the bishop's vestments too, and the fact that in the East bishops were usually monks seems to support this opinion. It is known that Patriach Nikon of Moscow (in 1657) used the paraman[31]. According to Braun, certain Western rites, i.e. the Ambrosian of Milan and the rite of Lyon, and also the Eastern Armenian rite, include the paraman among their liturgical vestments[32].

It may confidently be asserted that to Byelorussia as to Moscow the use of the liturgical paraman came from the East through Kiev. In the Church united to Rome it became "naplečnik" = "humerale" and as such — a clear Latin influence — has been omitted from the 1975 Roman Archieraticon.

After the paraman, the celebrant-bishop puts on the *epitrachelion, girdle, cuffs* and *epigonation,* and says the usual prayers common to all Service Books. Before the vesting with the sakkos our MS makes the following remarks: "If Archbishop take the sakkos, if Bishop — the phelonion". In the Latin: "Sumens saccum (si est Archiepiscopus) vel pluviale (si Episcopus)... (MS, p. 7).

The *sakkos* (a short tunic with half-sleeves) came into use not earlier than the XI century. It was first used by patriarchs and by them only on the feasts of Easter, Christmas and Pentecost. The earliest icons showing Saints wearing the sakkos date from the XIV cent. The vestment of distinction for higher hierarchs was the phelonion with crosses (polystaurion)[33]. The Metropolitans of Kiev originally — as Golubinskij says — "so far as liturgical vestments are concerned did not differ from the vestments of other bishops"[34]. Later, from the time of Metropolitan Photius

(1408-1431) they began to use the sakkos[35].

In the Catholic Church of the Eastern Rite the same question arises from time to time: who is entitled to wear the sakkos?

The Metropolitan Kiška (1714-1729), invoking the old euchologia, was of the opinion that only the Archbishop Metropolitan had the right to use the sakkos[36]. Pope Clement VIII granted the use of the sakkos to H. Paciej, Bishop of Vladimir, and most probably to C. Terlecki, Bishop of Łuck[37], but it is not clear whether the privilege was restricted to wearing the sakkos in their own dioceses only. For instance, during the consecration of the Metrophanes Drucki-Sakalinski, Bishop of Smalensk, when the Bishop of Vladimir appeared wearing a sakkos, the Metropolitan Cyprian Žochoŭski (1674-1693) ordered him to take it off.

The Bishops of Połack and Smalensk began at an early date to use the sakkos. Because the use of this vestment was considered a sign of distinction and of precedence, among other matters the Synod of Zamość had this question on its agenda[38].

MS BL is evidence of the old tradition of the Kievan Metropolis, where Archbishops Metropolitans used the sakkos, while all other bishops wore the phelonion. In Russia after the ukase of Peter I, 1705, all bishops at their ordination received the sakkos[39]. Today all bishops of Byzantine Rite use the sakkos.

Vesting in the *omophorion* the bishop says the same prayer as it is found in all Uniate Archieratica and in the Pontifical Liturgy of the Metropolitan Jonas of the XVII cent.[40].

MS BL is silent about both the *pectoral cross* and the *encolpion*[41].

One important feature of our MS is the omission of the *evangelical texts* during the vesting ceremony: these texts usually occur in the Ukrainian Service Books and in the Uniate Archieratica[42]. The Roman Archieraticon (1975) leaves these prayers to the discretion of the celebrant.

There is also no mention in our MS of the bishop's *ring*. Neither is there in the Roman Archieraticon.

The washing of the hands, the prayers of the prothesis.

After vesting, "if there are candidates the consecrating bishop will ordain them up to but excluding the deacon" (MS, p. 7v). The hierarch washes his hands and recites Ps. 25 (26), 6-12: "I will wash my hands among the innocent", priests and deacons serving at the ceremony: the archdeacon holds the prepared water, the senior priests the towel and the deacon the bowl.

Then, according to the Slavonic Archieratica, follows a blessing by the bishop: with the dikirion and trikirion (Russian) or with the dikirion and cross (Ukrainian). MS BL does not include this blessing but instead quite unexpectedly gives a short prayer which today is used at the beginning of the rite of preparation (prothesis): "You have redeemed us from the curse of the law" (Gal. 3, 13). Both the Slavonic and the Latin texts of this prayer are written in the same hand as the MS (pp. 7v, 8). Since both are written in the margin it may be postulated that they constitute a later addition or perhaps it shows some hesitation on the part of the compiler of this MS as to whether this is an appropriate place for this prayer.

However, this seems unlikely since the prothesis element is stressed still more explicitly by the next prayer. The archdeacon, having asked the bishop's blessing on the incense, then repeats: "For the oblation of precious gifts, let us pray to the Lord" (MS, p. 7v). The celebrant-bishop blesses the oblation and says these two prayers: "O God, our God, who sent Jesus

Christ..." This is the prayer of offering, the prayer of prothesis which is the oldest in the whole rite of preparation[43], but which occurs today at the end of the rite of preparation. Why then does it occur earlier in our MS in this place? The next prayer is also very ancient. It begins: "O Lord our Master and God, now I with a mind to ascend to this tremendous and wonderful mystery" (MS, p. 8v).

Surely the prothesis prayers at this place are a reminder of the fact that the preparation of the Holy Gifts was originally performed at the beginning of the Liturgy. This is also the conclusion of Taft in his research on the Great Entrance. According to him: "The presence of the prothesis prayer at the beginning of the Mass in the modern Archieraticon is a relic of the earlier rite as seen in *Codex Pyromalus* and the version of Johannibsberg, when the patriarch vested, offered his prosphora, and said the prothesis prayer in the outside skeuophylakion before entering the church at the introit"[44]. In the Russian recension of the Archieratica the same prothesis prayer is recited in silence by the celebrant-bishop at the same time as the deacon (protodeacon, archdeacon) chants the synapte. In the Archieratica of Suprasl, Univ, Lvov and Rome this prayer does not occur at all[45].

The other prayer mentioned above: "O Lord our Master and God, now I with a mind..." (MS, p. 8v) is found in the XII century Service Book of Anthony Roman[46], in the Service Books of the XIV cent.[47] and in the MSS of Archieratica from the XVI century[48].

According to the Pontifical Service Book of Metropolitan Jonas[49] after the bishop's vesting, lavabo and after two prayers there begins the prothesis, which is performed by the priest in the usual order. When the rite of preparation has been concluded the priest recites some troparia and prayers including: "O Lord our Master and God, now I..."

Thus one can rightly infer that in MS BL in this part of the Liturgy there remains only a trace of the prothesis and the greater part of it has been transferred to the place after the Cherubic Hymn.

Just before the beginning of the Liturgy proper, the bishop asks his concelebrants' forgiveness: "Forgive me, venerable Fathers..." After this short rite of forgiveness, he makes the Sign of the Cross and says: "Blessed be our God", "O heavenly King..." etc. "After this all the concelebrants approach the bishop... and the bishop puts his right hand on the head of each of them; thus they receive absolution, and having kissed his hand and bowed, they proceed to their places" (MS, p. 9v).

The dialogue: "It is time to sacrifice unto the Lord..." follows, after which the archpresbyter goes into the sanctuary, the archdeacon takes the place before the Royal Doors. Here he proclaims: "Bless, O Master!" The archpresbyter in the sanctuary: "Blessed is the kingdom of the Father and of the Son..." Whether at the same time he makes the Sign of the Cross with the Gospel-Book, as is specified in the rubrics of the Roman Archieraticon (1975), our MS does not say.

As we see, in this part of MS BL the prothesis element is stressed very explicitly. The sequence of prayers and ceremonies as given in this part of the Liturgy does not occur in precisely the same form in any Slavonic Service Book so far published.

Synapte, two short Litanies.

All prayers and ceremonies up to "Blessed is the kingdom" belong to the preparatory part of the Liturgy. In the MS of the BL it is distinguished by being preceded by three blank pages, and on the separate page in calligraphic capital is written:

СЛУЖБА БОЖАЯ (The Divine Service), and underneath also in capitals in Latin: SACRIFICIUM DIVINUM. The different parts of the Liturgy were shown even in the outward form of the MSS in the XVI-XVII centuries. The same practice still survives in Service Books for priests.

After the archdeacon's invocation: "Bless, O Master!", the archpriest sings: Благосълавенъно царсътво, Отъца и Сына и Святаго Духа, нинѣ и присъно и во вѣки вѣкомъ. In Latin: Benedictum Regnum Patris et Filii, et Spiritus Sancti, nunc et semper et in secula seculorum (MS, p. 12). The choir answers: Amen. Аминь.

During the synapte "the bishop will sit in the ambo" (MS, p. 11v). The choir answers each of the deacon's invocation with: Госъподи помилуй, which is translated in our manuscript's Latin text by the familiar Greek: "Kyrie eleison". The prayer is recited by all the concelebrants silently, the ecphonesis aloud by the archpriest.

The text of the MS is not pointed, hence it is impossible to say how it was pronounced, e.g. памо́лимся (Byelorussian way) or помоли́мся (Ukrainian way). Some conclusions may be drawn from other evidence. Since nearly all Service Books printed in Byelorussia, including the famous Liturgicon of Metropolitan Žochowski (Vilna 1692, Suprasl 1695), have the distinct Byelorussian accentuation: памо́лимся and since Byelorussians have an innate tendency to pronounce unstressed "o" as "a" (akańnie), it seems that MS BL should, considering its origin, also exhibit Byelorussian phonological features[50].

According to our MS, it is the archpriest who pronounces all the ecphoneseis (vozhłasy), i.e. after the synapte and after two short litanies[51]. All ecphoneseis in the Slavonic end *вѣкомъ* — dative case plur. When there was introduced into Byelorussia *вѣковъ* — genitive case plur., which was not used in the liturgical prayers among the Eastern Slavs till the XVII cent., it is difficult to establish. Maybe the Suprasl Pontifical of 1716 can represent the transitional period, as it has both: вѣкомъ вѣковъ. In Russia, from the time of Patriarch Nikon, вѣковъ began to be used, although the Old Believers even today use вѣкомъ in their liturgical books[52].

In the synapte (a collect prayer, usually called the great litany = vialikaja ekcienija, or litany of peace = mirnaja ekcienija) the archdeacon names among other petitions the metropolitan, archbishop and bishop according to who is celebrating, but not the Holy Father. He is, however, mentioned later in the Liturgy. Before the metropolitan and archbishop there are epithets: "Most Eminent", "Most Reverend", but in both Slavonic and Latin texts these epithets are crossed out (MS, pp. 11v-12). It seems that the compiler had serious doubts about the necessity for exaggerated titles for the hierarchs, which, however, still persist at this point.

Another petition characteristic of the period when our MS was written (or copied) is: "Let us pray for our Orthodox King, protected by God, for the whole palace *палата,* and for his forces"[53]. Instead of "King" originally "Tsar" was written, then corrected. One of the possible conjectures is that our MS was copied from an exemplar which read "Tsar".

The ecphoneseis of the archpriest after prayers recited in silence form conclusions to these prayers. The synapte is sung by the archdeacon, and the next two litanies by the deacons.

After the synapte the choir sings the first antiphon, which is Ps. 103 (104): "Bless the Lord, O my soul", and after the first short litany Ps. 145 (146). At the words: "Glory be to the Father" the bishop rises and stands without his mitre until the end of the hymn "Only-begotten Son"[54].

After the second short litany our MS

gives this rubric: “Here you should read the Beatitudes” (Ms, p. 14v). Instead of чтутъ originally was written ликъ, and in the Latin text “chorus” is corrected to “leguntur”.

Little Entrance, Epistle, Gospel.

The prayers, ceremonies and the liturgical chants of the concelebrants and of the choir during the *Little Entrance* and the *Holy God,* which forms an integral part of it, and then the *Epistle* and the *Gospel,* are extremely complicated and are performed in different ways according to the different traditions and thus to the different Service Books and Archieratica. Therefore to be clear and orderly in describing this part of the Holy Liturgy one has to adopt a tedious procedure using a precise comparison table. In the table below the rites and prayers are presented not only according to MS BL, but also according to the Suprasl Pontifical (1716) and Moscow Order (1668). The Ukrainian Archieratica (Univ 1740, Lvov 1886) follow the Suprasl Pontifical and the Russian recension follows that of Moscow.

MS BL is nearer to that of Suprasl, but in some matters either coincides with Moscow or goes its own way. No doubt all of them basically depend upon Greek tradition. We received the Roman Archieraticon (1975) only at a late stage in our research; it will seldom therefore be mentioned.

Again we must apologize for giving the whole table in the Slavonic only. This way of presentation seems to be not only easier for us but more practical for students specialising in liturgical matters.

The following abbreviations are used:

I = MS BL
II = The Suprasl Pontifical, 1716
III = The Moscow Order, 1668 = ČAD
A = Archbishop, Bishop
I = Archpriest, Protopresbyter
і = Priest
Д = Archdeacon, Protodeacon
д = Deacon
е = Subdeacon
с = Candlebearer
T = Trikirion
t = Dikirion
K = Cross
F = Censer, Incense
X = Choir

The ordinal numbers in the first line of each column indicate the order of prayers and ceremonies, those of the second row (in columns II and III only) correspond to the same prayer or rite in MS BL, e.g.:

II,6 = 5 — means that the same “Прійдѣте поклон.” sung by the choir is indicated in the MS BL under 5 (= I,5). “0” (zero) indicates that the relevant prayer, acclamation or rite is not present in our MS. The text (usually its beginning only) is given as far as possible in the original old orthography[55].

Let us be clear when we compare the texts and rites of the Suprasl Pontifical and ČAD with those of MS BL. With very few exceptions (e.g. “Peace be with you”; “Lord have mercy”), one cannot find an identity between them.

The numbers in the second and third columns of the second row show the localization and existence of similar rites. E.g., the taking of the omophorion from the bishop’s shoulders during the Epistle is found in all three columns (I,35 = II,36 = III,33), but the details of the ceremony itself are different in each text. The differences as to style, grammar and orthography appear substantial, even if one is familiar with the Old Slavonic of different recensions.

The LITTLE ENTRANCE properly begins with the exit from the sanctuary. According to our MS, when the lector starts to read the Beatitudes, the archpriest takes the book of the Holy Gospel from the altar and gives it to the archdeacon. Preceded by two candlebearers the deacon comes out carrying the thurible, followed by the archdeacon with the Gospel. The arch-priest comes last.

I
D
d
c c

Exit from the sanctuary

As soon as the archdeacon reaches the bishop, he asks him to bless the Holy Entrance (I,1). The Moscow ČAD and the Roman Archieraticon (1975) prescribe that the archdeacon should say: "Let us pray to the Lord" (III,1), which is followed by the prayer: "Lord, our God" (III,2).

When the archdeacon sings: "Wisdom! Stand up!" (I,4) there is no indication what he does with the Holy Gospel Book: whether he makes the sign of the cross or simply elevates it and holds it high for a short time. In the Moscow Service Books the rubrics contradict each other[56]; the Roman reads: the deacon "raises his hands a little and shows the Holy Gospel and says (why not sings? — C.S.) in a loud voice: Wisdom! Stand up!"[57]. In the Suprasl Pontifical the exclamations: "Wisdom! Stand up!" are not even mentioned. There is no doubt, however, of their use in practice. The Lvov Archieraticon (1886) gives evidence.

All Archieratica have, after the deacon's "Wisdom! Stand up'": 1) procession of all the concelebrants towards the sanctuary, 2) the singing of "O come, let us worship and bow down to Christ...", 3) reading or singing troparia and kontakia, 4) singing of "Holy God, Holy mighty One" (Trisagion).

MS BL says that after "O come, let us worship and bow down to Christ" the troparia (I,6) are *to be read,* while all the concelebrants enter into the sanctuary, the celebrant-bishop being assisted by two senior priests who take his arms. There is no mention of censing; the bishop at once says the prayer: "God the Holy One who abides in the saints" (I,8)[58]. Then he blesses the Gospel Book "with two lighted candles" reciting at the same time the troparion (I,9), which according to the Suprasl Pontifical is said during the blessing of the people: "O Christ, the true Light" (II,4). This is the first blessing (in our MS) of the Gospel Book and is similar to the rite for the blessing of a monastic refectory by the bishop[59].

But in MS BL there is another blessing which is identical with that of the Suprasl (II,15) and Roman (p. 41) Pontificals. This is found after the archdeacon's: "Bless, Sir, the time of Trisagion" (I,10). The prayer of this blessing is remarkable for its theological trinitarian content: "Father and Son and Holy Ghost in three distinct hypostases together blessed in one divinity and one essence" (I,11). This rite of blessing the Gospel Book is also found, in the same place, in certain Service Books of the XVI[60] and XVII cent.[61]. Traces of the same rite occur in the Moscow ČAD but without the prayer (III,22).

The Suprals Archieraticon prescribes the blessing by the celebrant-bishop of the faithful, which he gives with the pastoral staff in his left hand and the trikirion in his right saying: "O Christ, the true Light" (II,4). Then the bishop and all concelebrants go around the altar, singing: "Save us, O Son of God" (II,8).

The most solemn blessing of the Book of the Gospel is given in the Suprasl Pontifical. According to this, the bishop gives the blessing with the trikirion (three candles) and recites the prayer: "Lord, O Lord, look down from heaven"; meanwhile all concelebrants sing in Greek: "Hagios o Theos" (II, 19-21).

The Roman Archieraticon (pp. 38-39) preserves the blessing (without mentioning the staff and trikirion) and the prayer: "O Christ, the true Light", but omits the procession around the altar, prescribing instead the censing by the celebrant-bishop as is done in the ČAD (III, 9-10).

Neither MS BL nor any other Catholic Archieraticon has this deacon's acclamation alternating with the choir: "O Lord, save the devout people and have mercy upon us!" (III,12). Dmitrievskij observes here that nothing of this kind occurred in the old Service Books, since it was not used by the Greeks and Yugoslavs[62].

A feature of the Moscow ČAD, and of all others derived from it, is the rite of eulogy (encomium) (III,13). It is known also from the Suprasl Pontifical (II,12). MS BL does include this ritual accretion but in a different place i.e. after the exclamation: "І да будутъ милости..." (p. 42v), and the rubric seems to stress its somewhat rare use: "if there is a particularly solemn feast" — "аще есть нарочытый праздъникъ (p. 43v). K. Nikolskij writes about it, not without reason, as follows: "In manuscript Prayer Books of XIII-XVI cent. nothing is said about the performance of the eulogy"[63]. How and why did it occur that this rite became included in the Pontificals?

In all the Service Books before "Holy God" there is the ecphonesis: "For You are Holy, our God..." (I,13; II,15; III,17), but in our MS can be found the following rubric: "The bishop, having turned his face towards the people, will stand between the Holy Doors" (p. 17v). A similar direction is given by the Moscow Service Book of 1602 and that of Lvov of 1691, while the 1639 Service Book of Mohila very clearly states that the celebrant should recite this prayer "looking towards the east" i.e. facing the altar[64].

"Holy God, holy mighty one" in MS BL is intertwined with various exclamations and prayers which make this part of the Liturgy rather difficult and complicated. The bishop has to recite **twice** the troparion-prayer: "Lord, O Lord, look down from heaven". The first time is just after the ecphonesis: "For You are holy, O our God" (I,17), when he is holding the pastoral staff and the trikirion with which he blesses the people from the Royal Doors. The same rite is found in the Moscow ČAD (III,23) but here the bishop gives the blessings with the cross in his right hand and with the dikirion in his left. Moreover only one part of the prayer prescribed in our MS is given in the Moscow Činovnik.

The second time the bishop recites the same prayer (according to MS BL), standing before his throne and blessing the altar with the trikirion (I,27). It seems that the same rite also occurs in the Moscow ČAD (III,29), when the bishop blesses the altar with the trikirion. The proto-deacon, giving the trikirion to the bishop, repeats: "The apparition of the Trinity took place in the Jordan". MS BL does not have this text; neither the Suprasl nor Roman Archieratica.

One of the more interesting peculiarities of our MS is the **rite of blessing of the prothesis** (I,21), again part of the rite of the preparation. Unfortunately, the MS has not given us the prayer of blessing itself. This prayer, already known in MSS of the XV cent.[65], is found in the Byelorussian Service Books of Vilna (1583, 1598) and Jeŭje (1641); also in those of Moscow (1602), Lvov (1637)[66] and in the manuscript episcopal Archieratica of the XVI cent.[67].

At the very end of "Holy God, holy mighty one" our MS instructs the arch-deacon to say: "Is polla eti despota. Let us attend!" (I,30). Other Archieratica give at this point "Let us attend!" only (II, 32; III,30).

All Catholic Archieratica have the rite of blessing of the priests by the celebrant-bishop, and they have almost the same prayer: I,35; II,36. MS BL reads: "...во прѣподобии и правдѣ *славити* тебѣ" — "in holiness and in truth *to glorify* You". Other Archieratica have: in holiness and truth *to serve* You" — въ преподобіи и правдѣ *служити* тебѣ".

The ceremony of the removal of the omophorion is in all Archieratica: I,35; II,36; III,33, except the Roman (1975). The Moscow does not include the prayer of the blessing of the priests. The omophorion should be removed from the bishop's shoulders "by two priests of senior rank" (начальнѣйшыя), according to our MS (p. 18v); by priests Suprasl, by deacons — Moscow ČAD.

All Catholic Archieratica, except the recent one (Rome 1975), give the bishop's blessing, accompanied by the words: "Peace to all!", **only** before the Epistle, but not before the Gospel (I,31; II,33). Our MS, like the other Byelorussian Service Books (Vilna of the XVI cent.), follows the same practice.

It seems contrary to the usage of nearly all Eastern Churches that our MS prescribes *the reading of the Epistle by the deacon* instead of by the lector (I,35)[68].

According to our MS (I,42), Suprasl (II, 38, 42), Univ and Lvov, it is the archdeacon (deacon) who takes the Book of the Holy Gospel from the altar and carries it to the bishop, asking his blessing. The Moscow ČAD has the Gospel Book given to the protodeacon by the bishop celebrant, (III,48), while the Roman, following the more recent Russian Archieratica, ordains that the protopresbyter should give it to the protodeacon (p. 46).

MS BL is in this matter in the same tradition as the Greek, Serbian and Byelorussian Service Books[69].

During the reading of the Gospel the celebrant bishop stands holding the pastoral staff but without the mitre: I,46; II,48. The Moscow ČAD (III,59) gives the following rubric: "The bishop does not take off (the mitre), only the archimandrites do so". This is repeated, almost word for word by the Roman Archieraticon, although it is given in brackets! (p. 47), which do not change the rubric but simply make it more dubious.

In concluding this chapter let us note that on page 21 of our MS there is a text in the Latin: "Et si fuerit festum aliquod, legit duo Evangelia", which is missing in the Slavonic. Usually the Latin translation faithfully follows the Slavonic, but here apparently the compiler of this MS repeated just the same rubric as he has done previously for the reading of the Epistle (MS, pp. 18v, 19).

The Insistent Ektene — The Ektene for the dead — The Litanies over the catechumens — The Ektene before the hymn of the Cherubim.

In MS BL, as in the other Service Books, the Gospel is followed by the Insistent Ektene which begins with words different from those used today: "Рцѣмъ вси ко Госъподу. Отъ всея душа и от всего помышъления нашего рцемъ вси". (Let us all say to the Lord. Let us all say with our whole soul, and with our whole mind), MS, pp. 21v, 22[70].

After the archdeacon's *Again let us pray for our Orthodox and God-protected king N.*, the bishop having accepted from the deacon the candlestick with two lighted candles turns toward the people, standing between the Royal Doors; in the left hand he holds the staff and with the right hand he blesses the people with the candlestick three times, at the same time praying: "O Lord † save the Tsar and hear him in the day he calls upon You" (MS, p. 21v).

When the archdeacon in his petition prays for the metropolitan, archbishop or bishop who are actually celebrating, then all concelebrants respond with a three times repeated "Lord have mercy".

If the metropolitan celebrates he himself commemorates the Pope and at the same time he blesses with the candlestick and prays: "Lord, save † the universal Pontiff and hear him in the day he calls upon You"[71].

The ecphonesis which concludes the Insistent Ektene is said by the bishop celebrant (MS, p. 22v).

If there is a Liturgy for the dead, the proper ektene is given. MS BL orders the prayer "God of spirits and of all flesh" to be said by the bishop silently. After the litany the archdeacon adds: "The blessed dormition and the eternal peace" and the choir sings "Eternal memory" (MS, p. 24v)[72]. It seems that these additional prayers by deacon and choir were sung even when the litany for the dead was not, as we read in the MS, p. 24v: "This should be said *at every service* after the first bishop's ecphonesis". This rubric is not very clear, but it seems to refer to the one which follows immediately after the Insistent Ektene.

Then follow two litanies over the catechumens. After the first one during the ecphonesis by the archpresbyter: "That with us they too may glorify", *the priests* spread out on the altar the eiliton (corporal), MS, p. 24v[73]. "This is where it occurs in all euchology MSS and in the Slavic rubrics too" i.e. the spreading out of the eiliton[74]. According to our MS the eiliton is spread out by the priests. The Warsaw (1944) and American (1965) Archieratica have similar rubrics: "The concelebrants spread out the antimension, the bishop, however, touches it with his right hand". The Roman Archieraticon (1975, p. 54) orders the bishop only to spread out the eiliton.

Let us note that in MS BL the antimension has been not mentioned at all but only the eiliton.

The ektene before the Cherubicon ends with the bishop's ecphonesis: "So that, ever protected by your might" and the rubric directs *that he be turned towards the Holy Doors* (MS, p. 26v).

МАЛІТВЫ І ЦЫРЫМОНІІ У ЧАС МАЛОГА УВАХОДУ, АПОСТАЛА І ЕВАНГЕЛЬ

I. Рукапіс ББ[1])

1. Д Благослави Владыко св. вход.
2. А Благославен вход святых твоих.
3. AIi Владыко Господи Боже наш . . .
4. Д Премудрость, прости.
5. Зде поется. Прыйдѣте поклонимся и припадем ко Христу...
(аще неделя) Воскрес из мертвых.
(аще прочыя дни) во святых дивен сый.
(аще за усопшых) жывыми и мертвыми обладаяй.
6. Чтут же ся и тропары поряду.
7. А со всѣми сослужытельми входит волтар вѣдом под руцѣ от Иерей начальнѣйшых. Д св. Еванг. полагает на прѣстолѣ и станет одесную Святителя: Иереи окрест прѣстола.
8. А Боже Святый иже на Святых опочываяй...
9. Д дасть в руку десную т(осиальник) Святителеви.
А Благославляет Еванг. трыщы: Хрсте † Боже наш Свѣтѣ истинный... Да знамѣнуется † на нас свѣт... Направи † стопы наша на дѣло заповѣдей твоих...
10. Д Благослави Владыко время трысвятаго.
11. А Знамѣнует С. Еванг. десною. Отца † и Сына и Святаго Духа вкупѣ Богаславиму, во трѣх свойствѣх и Составѣх, едино Божество и едино Существо.
И абие А целует С. Еванг. д полагает е на св. трапезѣ.
12. Д Господу помолимся. Х Господи помилуй.
13. А Обращся лицѣм ко людем, станет во святых вратѣх.
Возглас: Яко Свят еси Господи Боже наш... и присно.
14. Д И во вѣком. Х Амин.
15. Зде поют трыжды Святый Боже. А обращся ко олтарю тры поклоны творит со сослужытельми, глаголя втай тожде: Святый Боже.
16. Д Даст Святителю Т. Вси же сослужытелѣ поют: Святый Боже.
17. А во ц. вратѣх, трыщи благославляет свѣщами людѣ держа левою посох. Господи † господи призри со небесѣ... Буду рука десная твоя на мужа... Господи † Боже сил обрати ны... Тройце † Трысвятая, Отче, Сыне, и Святый Душе.
18. А обращается и отходит со Т ко жертовнику вѣдом под руцѣ диаконома.
19. Д Повели Владыко.
20. А Повелением Господним небеса утвердышас.
21. Д Благослави Владыко прѣдложение сие.
22. А Благославен градый во имя Господне.
23. Д Благослави Владыко горнѣе сѣдалище.
24. А Благославен еси на прѣстоле Славы царствия твоего...
25. Святителеви последствуют вси Иереи крестаобразно... межы царскими дверми и прѣстолом идут.
Поется: Слава Отцу и Сыну... Амин. Святый безсмертный...
26. Паки Сослужытеле поют: Святый Боже.
27. А Благославляет трыщы престол став пред сѣдалищем трисвѣщником глаголя Господи, Господи призри...
28. Паки поется: Святый Боже...
29. д держа в руках Апостол, исходит от олтара сиверскими враты, и став пред царскими поклон сотворяет.
30. Д Ис полла ети деспота. Вонмем.
31. А Мир всѣм.
32. д И со духом твоим. Прокимен. Поется тожде трыжды.
33. Д Премудрость.
34. д Надписание Апостолу.
35. Д Вонмем. д чтет Апостол, и аще случытся празник який, два

II. Пан

1-1 д Благослови В
2-2 А Блгвенъ Въхо
3-0 д Аминь.
4-0 А вземлетъ въ
Осиялникъ, и
и Западъ, гля
Хе свѣте ист
Да знаменает
Направи стоп
Млтвами Прч
5-0 Х Осіявающу С
пота.
6-7 А въходит къ С
7-0 Д Архідіакон п
8-0 А а Стель лобз
3. около прес
коном и поющ
Семуже скон
9-5 Х на Хорѣ пою
10-0 II Крилошаном
11-0 А сѣдаетъ, на с
Трапезы,
12-0 Д взем Блгосло
т в руце, гл
Црскихъ стоя
Д 1) О коемжд
срцѣ своем
Х Пѣвцы поют
Д 2) Млстію Б
шему имк
Х Пвъцы поют
Д 3) Велѣкому
пребывані
съ всею П
Х Пѣвцы 3. пою
Д 4) Преосщен
рополѣти
приносящ
ншему. М
Здѣ аще С
лѣтствія
дритовъ. Г
Д 5) О мирѣ в
Црквей, о
Хрстолюб
Х Пѣвцы поют
Д 6) О спсені
семъ, пом
съгрѣшен
Х Пѣвцы поют
13-8 А востаетъ и ч
14-10 Д Блгослови В
15-11 А благословля
и Стаго Дха
сѣхъ, в куп
существо. Та
А Яко Сть еси

Апостолы чтет.

a) II два священницы начальнейшые приступуют ко А поклоньшежеся, и омофор над коленома целовавшы снимают и со Святителя.

b) А Господи Боже наш, благослови † свѣщенныя сия Иерея...

c) А Целует омофор.

d) II Иереиже возлажат и на левое рамо Д. И так совершается Апостол.

36. А Мир † ти.

37. д И со духом твоим. Псалом Давидов Аллилуя трыжды. Лик.

д возвращается волтар сиверскими враты.

38. Д взем у панамара кадильницу и фимиям приходит ко А.

Д Благослави Владыко кадило.

39. А Кадило ти † приносим...

40. Д Кадит по первому яко начыная Службу Божую.

41. А молитву: Восиа во сердцах нашых человѣколюбче Владико...

42. Д кадильницу отдав диакону станет у престола и взем обѣма рукама св. Еванг., держыт е прямо себе.

43. Д Благослави Владыко благовѣстити Святаго славнаго и всехвальнаго Апостола и Евангелиста Христова Н.

44. А Бог за молитов святаго славнаго и всехвальнаго...

45. Д идѣ Святыми враты со Евангелию предидущома ему свѣщоносцама, и д со кадильницею, и станет на амбоне, и полагает Св. Ев. на налойцу, от панамара... поставленном. Станут же окрест налойца свѣщоносцы. Но и д кадыт прямо Д и Евангелия.

46. I миру со А взем держыт ю аж до скончания Еванг.

47. д Премудрость, прости, услышим Св. Еванг.

48. Д От Н. Святаго Ев. чтение.

49. Х Слава тебѣ Господи.

50. д Вонмѣм.

51. Д Чтет Св. Еванг.

52. А стоящу и посох левою держащу.

53. А по Евангелии: Мир † ти и митру прыймает от Архипрезвитера.

54. Д втай: И со духом твоим.

Д и идет з амвона ко святым вратѣм.

55. Х Слава тебѣ Господи.

56. А исходит прямо Д и прыим Св. Еванг. и целовав поставляет на престоле.

57. Ii Иереи идут ко А по первому крестаобразно мимоходяще себе, межы прѣстолом и сѣдалищем святительским, и тако станут окрест престола.

58. Д поклон сотворше обращается от царских врат и станет на амвонѣ.

59. Д Рцѣм вси ко Господу.

60. Х Господи помилуй.

61. Д От всея душа и от всего помышления нашего рцем вси.

Д Господи вседержытелю Боже отец нашых...

Д Помилуй нас Боже по велицей милости твоей.

62. Х Г. П. 3.

63. Д Посем Д взем омофор з шуйцы своея, прыймает и обѣма рукама и разшырен держыт прамо себе.

Д Еще молимся о Благовѣрном и Богохранимом великом Короли нашем Н.

И абие сослужытели поют в олтары тры крат: Господи помилуй.

64. А Прыим от диакона осиальник со двѣма свѣщама возженнома обращается ко людем, и став во святых вратѣх, лѣвою убо держыт посох, а десною знаменует осиальником люди трыжды по выш писанному.

А Господи † спаси царя и услышы его в онже день аще прызовет тя.

1) "ъ" = Here the hard sign is omitted.

Оцу, и Сну,

А возглашае

16- 0 Д втай глетъ:

велегласно:

17-14 Д и въ вѣки в

18- 0 Х Поется 2. Ст

19- 0 АIiДд Ститель съ

Гречески Аг

20- 0 А Поему Трст

осіяеть Сто

творя знаме

21- 0 А Гди, Гди при

град свой, и

Гди Бже си

спасени буде

Трце Стая, С

Стаго твоего,

Сія рекъ А, .

22- 0 Д Воздадѣте сл

23- 0 Х Слава и Ннѣ.

24- 0 Х Таже на Хор

25-19 Д Повели Влко

26-20 А Повеленіемъ

27- 0 Д Блгослови В

28-22 А Блгословенъ

29-23 Д Блгви Влко г

30-24 А Блгословенъ

Херувѣмѣхъ.

31-26 АIiДд Пришедъ на

32-30 Д Вонмѣмъ.

33-31 А Миръ всѣм, †

34- 0 Д Премудрость.

35-35 Таже Проким

Въсіяй въ ср

35-35b) А блгословляя

ныя сія Іерея

37-36 А По прочтеніи

38- 0 Д Премрость во

39-38-42 Д Посем приход

40-40 Д кадитъ окрес

носцем, и вес

41-37 Х Ликъ же пое

42-43 Д стоящи у

блговѣстити

и Евлиста Хв

43-44 А стоя при Сѣ

славнаго...

44-47 I Старей Іерей

Стаго Ев.

45-48 Д стоя на Амбо

46-49 Х Ликъ: Слава

47-50 Іерей или діа

48- 0 Здѣ низлагаю

49- 0 А чтетъ тихо Е

женной на гл

идет А от гор

50-56 А тамо цѣловав

51-53 А Миръ ти блго

52-59 (Д) Ститель[2]) же

53- 0 Д Егдаже прійд

шомъ, Вселен

54- 0 IiДд Единым Сще

помлуй. 3.

55- 0 А Трема свѣща

таже на прав

Гди, Гди приз

56-63 Д Еще молимся,

57-64 А Ставъ въ Ца

свѣщами гля:

Гди спси Цр

призовемъ тя.

1) Here the title of abbreviation is omitte

2) Mistake in the original text. Should be

- PRAYERS AND CEREMONIES OF THE LITTLE ENTRANCE, EPISTLE AND GOSPEL

ър. 1716[1])

ый Въход.
х твоихъ.

) руку Патерицу, а въ правую
яетъ на Востокъ, Югъ, Сиверъ,

.. грядущагo въ миръ. †
іас свѣтъ... ти славы † .
, на дѣло заповѣдей твоихъ † .
и Мтре, Хе Бе ншъ, спси насъ † .
Пѣвцы поютъ: Исполла ети дес-

ратом
іет их мало,
поклонся пред престолом, кадит
редходящим Сщенником: и Діа-
легласно: Спаси насъ Сне Бжій.
я,
дѣте поклон.
цимъ Тропары, и Кондаки,
Сѣдалищи, по лѣвом углѣ Стыя

А, многолѣтствуетъ, и вземши
елегласно, внутръ при Вратехъ

цим помышленіе, о своихъ, въ
ѣшеніихъ, и о всѣх, и за вся.
сѣхъ, и за вся.
Вселенскому Архиерееви Стѣй-
Римскому, многая лѣта.
ая лѣта.
о нщему имкъ, держава, побѣда,
здравѣе, и оставленіе грѣховъ,
его. Многая лѣта.
огня лѣта.
рхіеппу нщему, Кіръ имкъ Мет-
ому, Галицкому, и всея Россіи,
етныя и стыя дары, Гдеви Бгу
ѣта.
изволитъ, мощно и более много-
ити, за Еппов, и за Архиман-
іетъ Д.
ра, и Блгостояніи Стых Бжіих
еніи, о утвержденіи, и утѣшеніи
оинства; и о всѣхъ и за вся.
сѣх, и за вся.
предстоящихъ въ Стомъ Храмѣ
щихъ, и млящихся, о своихъ
о всѣхъ и за вся.
ьх, и за вся.
тву: Бже Стый.
мя Трстаго.
сглае отвѣщаетъ: 9тца †, и Сына †
тріехъ свойственныхъ Ыпоста-
ровенно, едино Бжество, и едино
елегласно:
нашъ, и тебе славу возсылаем,

III. Чинъ Архіер. Дѣйства 1668[1])

1-0	Д	Гду помолимся.
2-3	А	Владыко Гди Боже наш...
3-1	Д	Благослави Владыко Всестѣйший, стый вход.
4-2	А	Благославенъ входъ стыхъ твоихъ, Гди...
5-4	Д	Премудрость прости. И воздвигет стое Евліе мало кртвуя.
6-0	А	з Тт
7-5		Пріидите поклонимся.
8-0	А	Вниду въ домъ Твой поклонюся...
9-0		Въ олтари: Исъ полла ети деспота.
10-0	А	кадитъ.
11-6		И сослужители стоятъ окртъ и поютъ отпустительныя тропари дне.
12-0	ДХ	Гди спаси благочестивыя.
13-0		Тогда полагается престолъ уготовленъ пред стою трапезою
	А	сядетъ къ народомъ.
	Д	глаголет похвалу.
14-0		Сослужители поют последний контакий.
15-10	Д	Благослави Владыко время тристаго:
16-12	Д	Гду помолимся.
17-13	А	Яко святъ еси Бже наш... и присно
18-14	Д	И во вѣки вѣковъ. Х. Аминь.
19-15	Х	Святый Боже.
20-8	А	Боже стый, иже во стыхъ почиваяй...
21-16	А	Сослужители: Святый Боже.
22-9	А	держа т въ левой творитъ крестъ надъ стымъ Евліемъ. Даже и метаніе творитъ.
23-17	А	з крестомъ и т: Призри съ небесе Бже...
24-19	Д	Повели Преосвящ. Владыко.
25-23	Д	Блгослови преосвщ. Влко горнее мѣсто.
26-24	А	Блгвенъ еси на пртолѣ славы цртвія...
27-0	Д	подаетъ А Т глаголя тропарь: Тройцы явленіе во Іорданѣ бысть...
28-26		И паки поютъ въ олтари: Св. Бже.
29-27	А	блгословляетъ съ Т трижды по чину.
30-30	Д	Вонмемъ.
31-31	А	Миръ всѣмъ.
32-32	Чтецъ:	И духови твоему.
33-35а	А	Отдаетъ омофорий, и изоблачаютъ его дд.
34-0	Д	Премудрость.
35-32	Чтецъ	Прокименъ: Псаломъ Двдовъ.
36-33	Д	Премудрость.
37-34	Чтецъ	надписаніе Апла.
38-35	Д	Вонмемъ.
39-36	А	Миръ ти.
40-37	Чтецъ:	И дхови твоему.
41-0	Д	Премудрость.
42-37	Чтецъ:	Аллилуя. Второй ликъ: Аллилуя.
43-38	Д	приемъ кадильницу, иный д ф.
44-39	А	Кадило тебѣ приносимъ...
45-40	Д	Кадитъ.
46-0	д	Гду помолимся.
47-41	Д	отдавъ кадильницу, приходит ко престолу, и пріемъ стое
48- 0	Д	Евліе (от А)[2]) приходит къ А и глаголет:
49-43	Д	Блгослови, преосвященнѣйшій Влко...
50-44	А	Бгъ, млтвами стаго, славнаго...
51-0	Д	Аминь.

духу, нпъ, и всегда. Егдаже сiе

и Благовѣрныхъ Хртiанъ. Посем

Х Аминь.

.

ики, и дiаконы поетъ, а. Тртое
Феосъ...
ически, Ститель трема свѣщами
Сщенникомъ поддержащимъ е,
кое 3. и гля:
Нбсе, и вѣждъ, и посѣти вино-
и и, егоже насади десница твоя †.
ати ны, и просвѣти лице твое, и

не, и Стый Дше, призри съ Нбсе
ослови всѣхъ насъ † .
етъ Стое Ев.
исту Бгу ншему.
Безсмртный помлуй насъ.
й Бже.

ь Нбса утвердишася.

й въ Имя Гдне.
Сѣдалище.
Престолѣ славы твоея, сѣдяй на

Сѣдалище глаголюще Стый Бже.

овляя люди.
емъ.
постолъ, и Млтва пред Евалаемъ:
ших чл вколюбче Влко...
ь †, Гди Бже ншъ, блгви сщен-

ла глетъ А: Миръ ти.
.
А с кадиломъ, и вземъ Блгвенiе
ола, предходящим двомъ свѣще-
й Олтаръ.
лилуя.
а возглашаетъ: Блгви Влко
славнаго, и всехвалнаго Аптола
.
и глетъ: Бгъ млитвами Стаго

: Премрость прости, услышимъ

т Iмк Стаго Евангелисты чтенiе.
и.
онмѣмъ.
итру съ главы Стителя,
о прочтенiиже Евлiя от д, возло-
Митры,
Сѣдалища, въ Великия Врата, и
глетъ къ Д:
ующему.
ктенiю велѣкую: Рцемъ вси.
до сего: Еще молимся о Стѣй-
Архiереи:
мъ, и дiакономъ поющим: Гди

вѣняетъ 3. на востокъ, на лѣвую,
рану, посемъ и людей гля:
Нбсе, и виждъ...
ѣкомъ Короле:
ь дверехъ, осiяетъ люди двѣма

услышши ны, вонже день аще

о.
ъ.

52-45 Д творитъ метанiе и целовавъ руку А отходитъ: предходящу предъ Евлiемъ д, нисущю омофорiй на обѣихъ рукахъ и два ыподiакона с Т т. Д нося Евлiе.

53-0 д держай омофорiй внутрь олтаря, стоитъ предъ стыми дверьми, зря къ народомъ:

54-47 д Премудрость, прости услышимъ стаго Евлiя.

55-0 А Миръ всѣм. Х И духови твоему.

56-48 Д От имкъ стаго Евлiя чтенiе.

57-49 Х Слава тебѣ Гди.

58-50 д Вонмемъ.

59-0 А шапки не отлагаетъ, токмо архимандриты.

60-55 Х Слава тебѣ Гди.

61-0 Х Исъ полла ети деспота.

62-53 А Миръ ти блговѣствующему.

63-56 А Цѣлуетъ св. Евглiе.

64-59 д Рцемъ вси от всея души...

1) Here the title of abbreviation is omitted: титло.
2) According to more recent Russian Archieratica: от перваго архимандрита или от протопресвитера.

The following subdivisions can be made of this part of the Liturgy:

1. The Cherubicon (The Cherubic hymn).
2. The Lavabo.
3. The prothesis.
4. The procession.
5. The dialogue.

To understand the Great Entrance and its historical evolution there is a new scholarly book by Fr. Taft: *The Great Entrance,* Rome, 1975, which has been indispensable for our research too, although our goal is rather restricted and limited to studying MS BL only.

1. The Cherubic hymn

When the choir sings the Cherubicon, the bishop silently recites *the Prayer of the Cherubic hymn:* "Nemo dignus", "No one is worthy"[75].

It is worth while to draw attention to the double text of the hymn, — the Slavonic and Latin, which are preserved in MS BL.

The same Slavonic text has been in use in the Liturgy through the centuries although we do not know who introduced it in this form or when and where. No doubt the Latin text is a translation by Bishop Theodore Skuminovič, as we suppose that he is the author of MS BL.

In the MS is the Old-Slavonic text which was accepted in the Kiev Metropolitan See and later on in that of Moscow also, until Patriarch Nikon changed it[76]. His text is now in use in the Russian Church and among Slavs who follow the Russian practice.

We give here the Slavonic text of the Cherubic hymn of which the first part is found in the MS, p. 26v and the second p. 33v. Here, for convenience, we put them together, as is usual in to-day's Service Books.

Иже херувимъ та"нѣ образующе, и жывотъворяще" тро"цы трысвятую пѣснъ прыносяще, всякую нинѣ жыте"скую отъверъзимъ печаль.

Яка царя всѣх подъемълюще, анъгельскими невидымо дароносима чынъми. Алълилуя, Алълилуя, Алълилуя.

Иже — There was an author who considered this word of many meanings to be superfluous for the translation of the Greek article "oi", which was accepted wrongly by some translators as the pronoun "oī"[77].

Херувимъ (not Херувимы) — The Hebrew kerubim pl., used in the Bible (Gen. 3. 24; Ez. 28. 14, 16) to indicate one of the Angelic Orders, has passed into Greek, Latin, English and Slavonic without changing the plural ending "-im". In the Slavonic it had a different spelling: херовимъ, хер8вимъ, хѣровимъ, хир8вимъ[78]. MS BL has the same Old-Slavonic noun but the spelling is nearer to the Hebrew.

Comparing the text of MS BL with that of the Roman Liturgicon (Rome, 1942, p. 230) one will find there quite a few differences, as can be seen from the following comparative outline.

	MS BL	LITURGICON 1942
1.	Тайнѣ (та"нѣ)	— тайно
2.	прыносяще	— припевающе
3.	нинѣ	— нынѣ
4.	отъверъзимъ	— отложимъ
5.	печаль	— попеченіе
6.	яка	— яко
7.	- - -	— да
8.	подъемълюще	— подимемъ
9.	дароносима	— дорыносима

Та" нѣ, яка — Perhaps under the influence of the local dialect. In this form they are unknown, at least in the Eastern Slavonic languages[79].

Прыносяще — grammatically similar to подъемълюще: maybe it comes from misreading Greek "prosagontes" (offering) in place of the correct "prosadontes" (singing)[80].

Нинѣ — always used in MS BL.

Отъверзимъ — to cast away, to throw away is stronger than отложимъ. This is a question of style.

Печаль, попеченіе — very near in meaning. Long ago the difference was negligible. Печаль Bishop Skuminovič translated as did Goar (text of Erasmus), sollicitudo. The adjectives житейски have the different translation: "temporalis" Skuminovič, "saecularis" Goar.

Дароносима — today дорыносима. Taft tries to explain it as a misunderstanding of the Greek language; that is, by wrongly translating "doryforoumenon" (escorted) as "doroforoumen" (we bear gifts)[81].

If this explanation be admitted the use by Bishop Skuminovič of "дароносима" could be understood only as his respect for the old tradition. The Service Books such as Vilna (1583, 1598, 1617), Jeŭje (1641), Moscow (1602) have all "дароносима"; Moscow has: "даро носима" and only one Alliluja[82]. That Bishop Skuminovič most probably knew the original Greek text one can see from his Latin translation: "Angelicis invisibiliter *stipatum agminibus*", which is again identical with Goar's translation (See below).

The Latin text of MS BL strictly follows the Old-Slavonic text. Here we give two Latin texts: of Goar[83] and of Bishop Skuminovič; both of them were made about the same time but independently of one another. A literal translation of the Greek textus receptus is given by Taft[84].

Goar

page 87.
... Omnem nunc mundi vitae sollicitudinem deponamus, ut omnium regem ordinibus Angelicis invisibiliter stipatum suscepturi.

page 92.
Qui Cherubim mystice repraesentamus, et vivificanti Trinitati, ter sanctum Hymnum canimus, omnem saecularem deponamus sollicitudinem;

tanquam regem omnium suscepturi,
Angelicis invisibiliter stipatum agminibus.
Alleluia.

Skuminovič

page 27.
Nos qui Cherubim mystice exprimimus et vivificae Trinitati ter Sanctum Hymnum afferimus omnimodam hodie temporalem abjiciamus sollicitudinem.

page 34.
Ut Regem omnium suscipientes Angelicis invisibiliter stipatum agminibus.
Alleluia, Alleluia, Alleluia.

2. The Lavabo

Our MS orders the first washing of the hands just after the vesting of the bishop (p. 7v), where the blessing of the water is mentioned and the prayer Ps. 25(26). After the prayer "Nemo dignus" (No one is worthy to come to You) "the archdeacon takes the wash-basin, then gives it to the nobles who will take their place before the Holy Door" (p. 28v). The bishop celebrant blesses the water saying the prayer "Lord our God, who has sanctified Jordan's waters".

Who were "the nobles" we do not know exactly. Probably some of the lords, or some of the founders of the church, or some of the bishop's family. In the Greek Church it is the duty of the subdeacons to serve at the washing of the bishop's hands, and in the Patriarchate of Constantinople this was reserved for the protonotary[85].

One can find the same prayer for the blessing of water "Lord our God" in the MSS Service Books for a bishop of the XVI cent.[86], in the Pontificals published in Suprasl (1716), Lvov (1886), Rome (1975); and in the Činovnik of Moscow (1798)[87], of Warsaw (1944), USA (1965) and Cholmogory (XVIII cent.)[88]. No doubt this prayer is very old (Codex Barberini 336 from VIII c.) and was used at the blessing of a church[89]. The text of MS BL and that in the other Pontifical Service Books mentioned above is adapted to the Liturgy. A similar prayer was used in the blessing of the swimming pool in Blacherne which is given in Goar's Euchologion from Bessarion's Codex in Grottaferrata near Rome[90].

Having blessed the water the bishop washes his hands and recites Ps. 25(26) "I will wash my hands in innocence". Then the archdeacon receives the basin from the lay nobles and the bishop puts on his arms the towel and offers the cross to the archdeacon and to the laymen to kiss. The same ceremony is in the Suprasl Pontifical, but that of Lvov (1886) omits the kissing of the cross and the Roman Archieraticon (1975), which follows the Russian Činovniks, is silent about both the kissing of the cross and the bishop's blessing.

Here one should pay attention to the differences existing between MS BL and the Russian Činovniks followed by the Roman Archieraticon. According to MS BL there are two different liturgical acts: the blessing of the water and the washing of the hands. According to the Russian Činovniks "and the bishop, washing his hands, says the prayer: Lord, our God" means that the prayer for the blessing of water is used simply for the washing of hands. Liturgically this is nonsense and without good reason this is repeated by the Roman Archieraticon which omits Ps. 25(26), although that is found in old MSS and in the Catholic Pontificals of the Eastern Church.

3. The Prothesis

Some prayers which are today said at the prothesis jointly with others, according to MS BL, are recited just after the vesting of the bishop and after the first "Lavabo". These prayers are:

You have redeemed us from the curse of the law... (MS, p. 7v in the margin).

O God, our God, who sent Jesus Christ... (MS, p. 7v).

O Lord, our Lord... (MS, p. 8v)[91].

As we said before, these prayers may be remnants of the rite which was performed before the Liturgy began. But now after the second "Lavabo" and after the kissing of the cross the bishop goes to the prothesis-altar, takes the lance (knife) and the prosphora and makes the commemorations, cutting it and putting the particles on the paten (diskos) (MS, p. 28v). The bishop himself, who began the rite of prothesis after his vesting, continues it now.

Our MS does not give the number of prosphoras to be used, but from the sketch made on both sides of the MS and from the prayers one can see which Saints were commemorated and how many particles were used. Here is given exactly the same sketch, except for the numbers, which show the succession of commemorations and the order of single particles. On the sketch there is a Lamb with a cross fixed with a beam and with the letters: IC XC NI KA = Jesus Christ conquers.

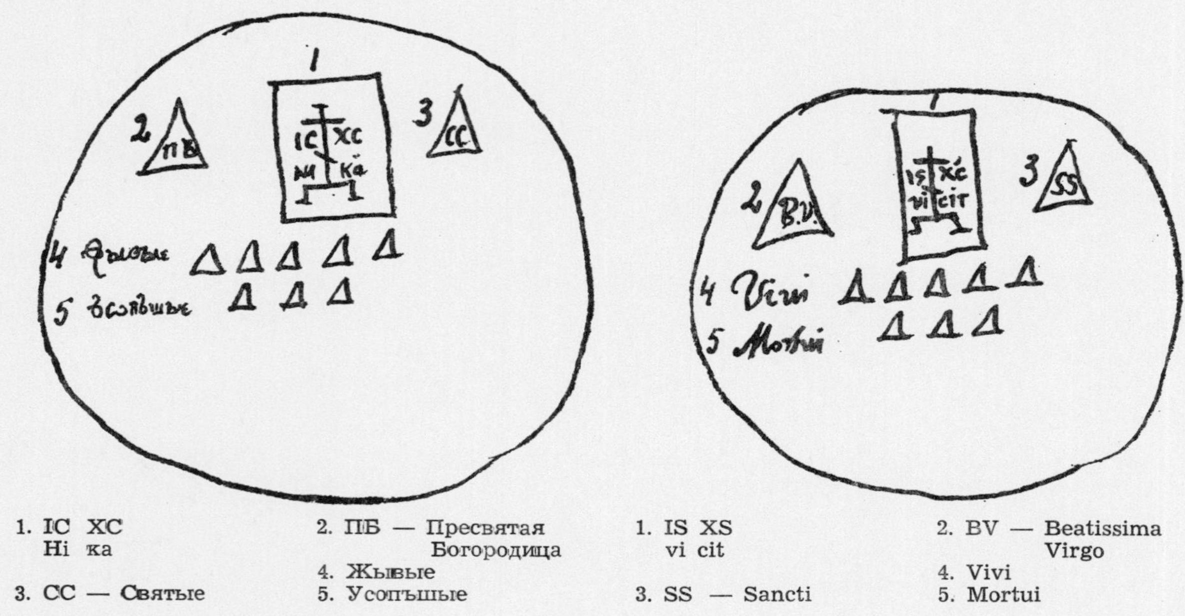

Facsimile of diagram, MS BL, pp. 30v, 31.

It is to be noted that verses from the prophets which refer to our Lord's passion: "He was led as a sheep..." are omitted in this MS. The prothesis starts with the placing by the bishop celebrant of a small part of the bread in honour of our Lady, which he lays on the right side of the Lamb and says: "To the honour and in memory of our most blessed Lady... The Queen stood at your right..." In the original sketch this particle is marked with ПБ Пресвятая Богородица = Most Holy Theotokos, Mother of God.

On the right side of the Lamb the bishop puts *only one particle* commemorating the Church triumphant. In the sketch it has the letters CC (Slavonic text) = SS (Latin t.) = Святые = Sancti = Holy. This is, so far as we know, a unique case, because in the sketches contemporary to MS BL, as today, one find nine small particles arranged in three vertical rows of three[92].

Below the particles representing the Lamb, our Lady and Saints the bishop lays in a horizontal line a few pieces of the same bread in order to commemorate the living and the dead.

The following is the order of the particles on the diskos according to MS BL:

Our Lady.

Saints:

The lifegiving Cross,
The Angelic Powers,
The Prophet and Forerunner John and all Prophets,
The Holy Apostles,
The Holy Hierarchs Basil, Gregory, John Chrysostom, Athanasius, Cyril and Nicolas,
The Holy Martyrs: Archdeacon Stephen, George, Demetrius, Theodore,

The Venerable and God-bearing Fathers: Anthony, Euthymius, Saba, Onuphrius, Arsenius,

The Holy Physicians and Moneyless ones: Cosmas and Damian, Cyrus and John, Panteleimon and Hermolaus, Samson and Diomedes, Phaleleus and Tryphon,

The Holy and just Joachim and Anne,

The Saint of the day and All Saints.

For the living:

Every Bishop of the orthodox faith,

The universal Pontiff,

The Metropolitan,

The honourable Priests, the Deacons in Christ, the Clerics of all ranks and monks,

The Orthodox Sovereign the great King, his Council and all his armed Forces,

The concelebrant Priests and Deacons and all our Brethren whom You have called into communion by Your mercy, All Gracious Lord,

The pious founders of the monastery, our benefactors, those who have asked our prayers, all orthodox christians,

Any living person whom the Priest wishes to remember.

For the dead:

The universal Pontiffs, Patriarchs, Archbishops, Bishops, Kings, Priests, Monks and all who have died in the hope of eternal life,

Any dead person whom the Priest wishes to remember.

For himself. — In the very last place the bishop puts a particle for himself.

From this we can see that after the commemoration of Our Lady follows the commemoration of the holy lifegiving Cross and the Angelic Powers just as during Vespers with aditional litanies (in Slavonic: licija). This is rare in Service Books of the XVI-XVII cent., and is non-existent in present-day Slavonic books but it is found in Greek liturgical texts[93].

The list of Saints includes in the group of venerable monks the little-known Arsenius[94] and among the physicians and poor (biezsiarebraniki) Samson and Diomedes, Phaleleus and Tryphon. Of these only Phaleleus is known to Martinov, but it is not certain that he is to be identified with the Phaleleus in the prothesis[95].

The list includes no Saints from the Kievan and Moscow hagiologies, which do, however, appear in the Vilna Service Book (1598)[96] and then later in the Service Books of Mohila and others[97].

While the bishop cuts the particles and places them on the discos there is no dialogue given between him and the deacon[98].

The contemporary Service Books including our MS try to prescribe with great precision how the particles should be placed on the diskos. The Stratyn Service Book (1604) even gives two diagrams: one showing an incorrect procedure (p. 24) and the other the correct (p. 26). In spite of these explanations certain Service Books still fail to elucidate the point[99].

No other Service Book, so far as we knew, gives the procedure laid down in MS BL. An unusual and original feature of it is that the nine Orders of Saints instead of nine have only one particle; one triangular piece of bread which is placed on the left side of the Lamb. On the sketch of MS BL this piece is marked with the two letters: CC in Slavonic text, SS in the Latin. This is also confirmed by the text which reads: "having taken the third (particle the bishop) puts it below the Lamb" (MS, p. 29v). There is no doubt that the third particle is "for every bishop". In all there are ten particles mentioned, the second of them being placed in honour of the Orders of Saints.

It seems a pity that this simpler manner of preparing the gifts has not survived to the present day.

Our MS, however, shows no similar restraint in dealing with individual Saints, the number of which was ever increasing. The Serbians introduced their own Saints, later the Moscow Service Books included Saints of their own. The most balanced in this respect were the Service Books published by Balaban (Stratyn 1604) and by Mamonič (Vilna 1617).

When the bishop has finished placing the particles on the diskos, he takes the thurible from the archdeacon, recites Ps. 50 (51)[100] and preceded by deacons carrying candles incenses the altar, the prothesis-altar etc. (MS, p. 31v). After incensing, the bishop, together with his concelebrants, recites three times the Cherubic Hymn. Then all the concelebrants kiss first the Cross held by the bishop over the altar, then the bishop's hand and then the altar. During this ceremony the bishop recites "Benefactor of all and Maker of all creatures" (MS, p. 31v). According to Goar's Euchologion this prayer occurs at the Little Entrance and was known there in the XII cent. and its present position in the Service Books dates from the XIV cent.[101].

A different order is given by Dmitrievskij. The bishop first recites the Cherubic Hymn, then goes to the prothesis, blesses the concelebrants with the Cross, says the concluding prayer (adpust), recites "Benefactor of all...", then the priests and deacons come out of the sanctuary to make the Great Entrance[102].

According to the Suprasl and Lvov Archieratica the bishop recites the prayer "Benefactor of all..." while remaining in the sanctuary during "the usual Entrance". The Russian Archieratica and the Roman (1975) omit this prayer.

4. The Procession

The archpriest incenses the prothesis. The archdeacon places the omophorion on the stretched hands of the deacon and the latter turning towards the archpriest says: "Take it Lord". The archpriest puts the veil over the shoulders of the second priest in rank, he also gives the diskos to the archdeacon and he himself takes the chalice and chants: "In peace lift up your hands (see Ps. 133 (134), 2) and bless the Lord. May the Lord bless you now and for ever..." (MS, p. 32v).

We observe here the very important part played by the archpriest; his invocation is longer than in any modern bishop's Service Book, and nowadays the equivalent part is said by the bishop himself, not by the archpriest.

The procession, according to MS BL, goes from the sanctuary to the centre of the church before the iconostasis in this order:

A l t a r

Bishop Celebrant

Iconostasis

7. i the fourth priest with the mitre
6. ı the third priest with the hand Cross
5. i second priest in rank with the veil
4. I archpriest with the chalice
3. D archdeacon with the diskos
2. d deacon with omophorion
1. cc candle-bearers

The archdeacon starts the commemoration: "Всѣхъ насъ православъныхъ хресътианъ да помянетъ Господь Богъ во царсътвии своемъ Небесъномъ, всегъда нинѣ и присъно и во вѣки вѣкомъ". "May the Lord remember all us Orthodox (true-believing) Christians in His heavenly kingdom, always, now and for ever and ever" (MS, pp. 32v, 33).

This is the initial and final commemoration "which is common to all traditions and is the earliest stratum of this liturgical custom"[103]. Looking closely at the Slavonic text we can find a number of interesting differences in our MS from the present accepted form of commemoration.

НАС — Us. Following the Greek text MS BL has "Нас" not "Вас", although the Slavonic Service Books of XVI-XVII cent. and later are more consistent using "Вас"[104].

ХРЕСЪТИАНЪ — older than "христианъ" is the normal form in our MS[105].

НЕБЕСЪНОМЪ — a late addition, not occuring in any other known Greek or Slavonic Service Book.

НИНѢ — instead of the Old Slavonic "нынѣ"; ВѢКОМЪ instead of the "вѣковъ" — are the forms used throughout our MS.

After the archdeacon's commemoration the archpriest commemorates the metropolitan, archbishop or bishop depending upon who is celebrating; also the whole order of priests, deacons and monks (MS, p. 32v). The commemoration is chanted aloud only by the archdeacon and archpriest; the other priests taking part in the Entrance proceed silently.

The bishop waits to meet the procession in the Royal Doors. Here the deacon puts the omophorion over his shoulders. Then the bishop incenses the diskos with the prepared gifts, accepts it from the archdeacon, "elevates it and holds it in his right hand towards the faithful" (MS, p. 32v) and chants aloud the following commemoration: "May the Lord God remember in His heavenly Kingdom the Orthodoxy of the Great Sovereign our King N. and all you (Вас) Orthodox Christians always, now and for ever and ever". Here in the bishop's commemoration the Slavonic is not consistent with the text of the archdeacon's commemoration. Here are used "Вас" and there was no commemoration of the Supreme Pontiff at this point.

Following the bishop's words "and all you Orthodox Christians" the choir sings "so that we may welcome the King of the universe" and the bishop places the diskos on the altar. Then he incenses the chalice, takes it from the archpriest and places it near the diskos. Holding the chalice in his hands he makes no commemoration, but in silence recites Ps. 23(24), 7: "Lift up your heads, O ye gates; and be ye lifted up, ye everlasting doors, and the King of glory shall come in". The archdeacon also in silence recites Ps. 117 (118), 26: "Blessed is he who comes in the name of the Lord, the Lord is God and has appeared to us".

Fr. Taft paid a great deal of attention to these extracts from Psalms 23 (24), 7 and 117(118), 26 as regards their use in the Liturgy, although he considers them as a supplement of secondary importance[106]. He says that according to the tradition of the Patriarch Philotheus the usual procedure is this: the priest (or bishop) says Ps. 23,7 (Attollite portas . . .) as he enters and the deacon, having gone into the sanctuary already and put the diskos on the altar, turns and incenses the priest as he comes in, and says: "Blessed is he who comes in the name of the Lord..." but in some MSS the converse holds[107]. The regular practice holds in MS BL and in the Service Books printed in Byelorussia and Ukraine[108]. It is possible that this usage came to Byelorussia from the Serbs, since in their first Venice edition (1519) the use of these Psalms is exactly the same as in our MS.

The bishop recites the prayer "Deal kindly, O Lord, with Sion in Your graciousness" and incenses the gifts; he then says the following interesting prayer: "Lord, Lord Lifegiver, Benefactor..." (MS, p. 34v). "The prayer is a rather poor Slavonic translation of the "inclination prayer" — Despota zoopoie, just before the dismissal of the catechumens and of the transfer of gifts in the Greek Liturgy of St. James"[109].

The codex with the Liturgy of St. James dates from the IX century. From the codex of the St. John Chrysostom Liturgy of the X cent. (Grottaferrata IV) it appears that this prayer once occupied the place now held by "Nemo dignus" — "No one is worthy", which is recited silently by the celebrant when the choir sings the Cherubic Hymn.

Still another MS of the XIV cent. (Borgia Georg. 7) of the Liturgy of St. James provides evidence that this prayer held the same place as in the codex of the IX cent., but had a title: "Oratio introitus sanctorum (donorum)"[110].

The same prayer is found in the Slavonic Service Books of the XII cent.[111], in the Liturgy of St. John Chrysostom and of St. Basil (preparation) of the XIV cent.[112], in the Service Book of the XIV cent. published by Kovaliv[113]. According to some Service Books of the XVI cent. the bishop read the same prayer while covering the holy vessels[114]. This prayer has survived in the Liturgy of St. John Chrysostom of the "jedinovercy" in their Činovnik (Moscow, 1910)[115].

All the evidence cited by Taft and others, together with MS BL, which was not available at the time they wrote, suggests that this prayer should command a greater appreciation than that bestowed upon it hitherto. Taft published this prayer in Latin translation giving at the same time variants of the different codices[116]. Below we give the same prayer from MS BL in the Latin translation of Bishop Skuminovič (MS, p. 35):

> Domine Dñe, Viuificans, benefaciens, dans nobis satietatem vitae aeternae, per hominem et Deum nostrum Iesum Christum. Dignos nos facias, ut in Sacrificio hoc perficiamus hanc Diuinam Liturgiam, ad consequendam futuram Beatitudinem. Quoniam benedictus es nunc...

5. The pre-anaphoral dialogue

After the Gifts have been carried from the prothesis to the sanctuary the bishop celebrant needs a deeper spiritual preparation before commencing that section of the Liturgy called the anaphora. There is no better preparation than an act of sincere humility, mutual support in prayer and the invocation of the help of the Holy Spirit. All this we have in pre-anaphoral dialogue between bishop celebrant and the concelebrants — deacons and priests.

The liturgical codices of the X and XI centuries already include such a dialogue although with a somewhat different wording[117]. Here is the Latin text of the MS BL, which differs both from that of the Catholic Pontificals and from that of the Russian Činovniks. There are also certain unimportant differences between the Latin and Slavonic texts of MS BL[118].

I. a) Pontifex caput inclinat: Deus propitius esto mihi peccatori.
b) Item: Veniam indulgete mihi
c) et recordemini mei Venerabiles Patres et Fratres conservientes.

II. a) Concelebrantes: gratia sua Dominus Deus veniam indulgeat,
b) et recordetur Pontificatus tui in Regno suo.
c) Depreceris pro nobis Episcope Sancte.

III. a) Pontifex: Spiritus Sanctus descendat super vos, et virtus Altissimi obumbret vos.
b) Concelebrantes: Idem ipse Sanctus Spiritus sit vobiscum et nobiscum omnibus diebus vitae nostrae.
c) Recorderis nostri Episcope Sancte.

IV. a) Pontifex: recordetur † vestri Dominus Deus, nunc &.
b) Concelebrantes: Amen.

The essence of this dialogue is the invocation of the Holy Spirit, that He by His power may sustain our frail human strength in the Holy Liturgy, the Divine drama which surpasses any human act.

The linking of the Holy Spirit with the Eucharist is even expressed by the very text of the Gospel (Lk. 1,35), according to St. John Damascene:

> "Whatever God does, he does by the power of the Holy Spirit... 'How can this be, said the Holy Virgin, for I know not man'. The archangel Gabriel replies, 'The Holy Spirit will come down upon you and the power of the Most High overshadow you'.
> You also ask now how bread becomes the body of Christ and wine and water his blood. And I say to you that the Holy Spirit comes again, and accomplishes what is inconceivable and incomprehensible"[119].

III a) = Lk. 1,35, but it is a different mood and tense: instead of the future indicative, as in the Gospel, in MS BL there occurs the present subjunctive. The Slavonic text concerning the Holy Spirit is the same as in the Service Books of XVI-XVII centuries and of those in present use.

The major differences in the text concern sections I and II of the dialogue. Some Service Books add to the text a prayer not only asking for the Holy Spirit but also beseeching that He should "remain with us and concelebrate with us all the days of our life"[120].

Below we give two versions of this dialogue: A = MS BL; B = Suprasl Pontifical.

A MS BL p. 34v	B Suprasl Pontifical p. 12-12v
I. а) Аръхиерей поклонъ творытъ. Боже милосътивъ буди мне грѣшъному.	I. а) Стitель споклономъ глетъ г.Бже млтивъ буди нам грѣшнымъ. Бже очисти грѣхи нша и помлуй нас.
б) Таже. Просътитѣ мя	б) Таж преклонь главу глетъ: Простѣте мя чтнiи Оцы,
ц) и помяните мя честъные отцы и братия Сослужитѣли.	ц) и блгословѣте и помолѣтеся о мнѣ грѣшном.
II. а) Сослужытели. Благодатию своею Господь Богъ да просътитъ	II. а) Iереи отвѣщают: Дхъ С. найдетъ на тя, и сила вышняго осѣнитъ тя.
б) и помянетъ Аръхиерейство твое во царсътвии своем.	б) Iереи: Помяни насъ Влко стый.
ц) Помолися о нас Владыко Святый.	
III. а) Аръхипрей: Духъ Святый найдет на вы, и сила вышъняго осѣнитъ вы.	III. Стitель блгословляя рукою глетъ: Да помянетъ вас Гдь Бгъ въ цртвiи своемъ Небесномъ: нинѣ, и прно, и въ вѣки вѣкомъ, Аминь.
б) Сослужытели: Самъ той Святый Духъ да будетъ свами и с нами во вся дни жывота нашего.	
ц) Помяни насъ Владыко Святый.	
IV. а) Да помянетъ васъ Господь Богъ во царстъвии своемъ нинѣ . . .	
б) Сослужытели: Аминь.	

The versions of the dialogue A and B are clearly similar: A Ia) b) = B Ia) b); A IVa) b) = B III, but not identical; the most important differences being between A IIIa) b) and B IIa).

A IIIa): the bishop prays that the Holy Spirit may come down upon the concelebrants. According to the Suprasl Pontifical (B IIa) the concelebrants pray that the same Holy Spirit come down upon the bishop only and the bishop does not reciprocate.

A Ib) = B Ib) — the same rite of forgiveness as occurs in the MS BL at the beginning of the Liturgy (p. 9v).

It seems that this dialogue between the bishop-celebrant and the concelebrants combined two factors: 1) a request by the bishop to remember him: "and remember me, venerable fathers and brethren concelebrants" (A Ib) and 2) a prayer to the Holy Spirit. The first proposition seems to be substantiated by the fact that according to MS BL during the Great Entrance when the bishop receives the gifts from the archdeacon and from the archpriest he is not remembered by them, or they by him, as occurs in the parallel place in the Russian Činovnik[121].

The dialogue ends with the bishop's blessing with the trikirion and the invocation: "Lord, Lord look upon us from heaven..." and then with the Cross and the prayer: "Save, O God your people..." The choir sings "Is polla eti despota". A similar ceremony is also found in the Russian Činovniks with this difference that the bishop-celebrant gives the blessing with the trikirion and dikirion simultaneously and does not recite any prayer. The choir sings the same "Is polla eti despota".

According to MS BL, if ordinands for the priesthood are present, the rite of ordination follows, otherwise the deacon comes out and stands before the Royal Doors and there follows the ektenia of supplication: "Исъполънимъ молитъвы (plur.) наша Госъподеви". In modern Service Books: молитву (sing.)[122].

RITES AND PRAYERS ACCORDING TO MS BL AND ACCORDING TO THE ARCHIERATICA DURING THE GREAT ENTRANCE

Features held in common:

1) The Cherubic Hymn and prayer "Nemo dignus".
2) The bishop-celebrant remains in the Sanctuary.
3) Lavabo.
4) Bishop-celebrant incenses the diskos and the chalice before placing them on the altar.
5) The bishop places the holy vessels himself.
6) The bishop incenses the offered Gifts and recites Ps. 50(51), 18.

Specific to MS BL:

1) Commemoration of the king (the government) while the bishop holds the diskos in his right hand. No commemoration with the chalice.
2) Ps. 23(24), 7 recited by bishop; Ps. 117 (118), 26 by archdeacon.
3) The archpriest and another priest pass the great veil over the bishop-celebrant's head and then place it over the gifts.
4) The prayer: "O, Lord, Lord..." said by bishop.
5) No commemoration of Pope.

Common to the Suprasl, Lvov, Rome Archieratica:

1) Commemoration of the Pope by bishop-celebrant holding the chalice in his right hand. No commemoration with the diskos.
2) The verses of Psalm 23(24), 7; 117(118), 26 are not recited.

Specific to the Russian Činovniks:

1) The bishop-celebrant bows ("metanije") and kisses the diskos and chalice receiving them from the protodeacon and priest respectively.
2) Commemorations holding the diskos, then the chalice.
3) Psalm 117(118), 26 recited by bishop-celebrant only.
4) Protodeacon and priests, giving to bishop the holy vessels, repeat: "May the Lord God remember your bishopric (archijerejstvo) in his Kingdom".

Specific to the Roman Archieraticon, 1975:

1) Commemoration by the priest, who carries the chalice in the procession, of His Beatitude Major Archbishop and Metropolitan, or Archbishop and Metropolitan or God-loving Kir-Bishop[123].
2) Commemoration by the bishop-celebrant only once, holding the chalice, of Pope, his Beatitude Major Archbishop and Metropolitan, Government, armed forces, founders of the church etc.

The prayer before the kiss of peace

The Liturgy continues. During the litany of supplication the bishop silently recites the prayer: "O Lord, almighty God...", and then the ecphonesis: "By the mercies of Your only-begotten Son", and "Peace to all!" The deacon says: "Let us love one another", the choir replies: "The Father, the Son and the Holy Spirit..." The bishop recites the prayer before the kiss of peace: "O Lord Jesus Christ Creator of love . . ."

The same prayer is found in the Service Books of the XIV and XVI centuries, in the Moscow Service Book 1602: "Молитва пред цѣлованіемъ" and in the Suprasl and Lvov Archieratica[124].

Here are the texts of the prayer in Slavonic (MS, p. 36v) and in Latin (MS, p. 37):

> Госъподи Ис Хе любъви творъче, дѣлателю благимъ, даждъ намъ рабомъ твоимъ любити другъ друга, яко ты возълюби насъ, да вѣрою и любовию единомысъленъно и единодушъно ко тебѣ Богу прыближымъся, и прычасътимъся Святыхъ твоихъ таинъ, и царъствию твоему досътойны будемъ. И тебѣ славу возъсылаемъ, Отъцу, и Сыну и Святому Духу нинѣ...
> *Таже Иереи сослужытели вси присътупуютъ ко Аръхиерею, целующе престолъ десъницу, и ланиту десъную его.*
> *Аръхиерей:* Христосъ посърѣдѣ насъ.
> *Сослужытели:* Есть и будетъ.
>
> Domine Jesu Christe Charitatis Creator, bonorum operator, concede nobis famulis, ut diligamus nos invicem, prout tu dilexisti nos, ut per fidem et caritatem ad te Deum approximemus et participes fiamus SS. tuorum Sacramentorum, et Regno tuo digni efficiamur. Et tibi gloriam damus, Patri et Filio et Spiritui Sancto nunc &.
> *Tunc Sacerdotes concelebrantes omnes accedunt ad Pontificem osculantes Sacram Mensam, manum dextram et genam illius dextram.*
> *Pontifex:* Christus in medio nostrum.
> *Concelebrantes:* Est et erit.

Commemoration of the Pope

In accordance with the terms of the Union of Brest, as conceived by its initiators, the inviolability and immutability of the Eastern rite were to be preserved. This principle was accepted by Rome with the proviso that it should contain nothing contrary to the Catholic faith.

The commemoration of the Pope, since the Byelorussian and Ukrainian Bishops had broken their connection with the Patriarch of Constantinople, was the most obvious new liturgical need. The current practice, as given in our modern Catholic liturgical books, did not come into effect at once; rather it evolved gradually. MS BL gives a picture of the period between the Union of Brest (1596) and the Chapter of the Basilian Fathers (Žyrovicy 1661), at which the question of the commemoration of the Pope in the Liturgy was discussed and finally decided[125].

It appears that until this Chapter the Metropolitan made a commemoration of the Pope only when the Gifts were carried in from the prothesis to the altar during the Great Entrance. Each priest commemorated his own Bishop and the Bishop commemorated the Metropolitan[126].

Before MS BL the only Catholic Service Book in Byelorussia was that of Mamonič

(Vilna 1617). The latter does not include the commemoration of the Pope, since it was intended for priests; therefore, where today the priest or deacon does commemorate the Pope, the Mamonič text simply gives a commemoration of the Bishop by the priest.

MS BL prescribes four commemorations of the Pope. The first time it occurs during the ektenia "Rcem vsi" (p. 22v Slavonic text, p. 23 Latin text) after the archdeacon's petitions for King and Metropolitan. Then the Metropolitan holding the dikirion in his right hand and the staff in his left blesses the congregation and recites: "O Lord, save † our Ecumenical Pontiff and hear him in the day that he calls upon Thee".

The rubric makes it clear: this commemoration is included only if the Metropolitan is celebrating, otherwise the celebrant Bishop commemorates not the Pope but the Metropolitan.

This is the older and more traditional form of commemoration of the Pope, which was fairly soon to be changed owing to criticism from the Latinists against the Uniates[127], who said that the latter were neglecting to commemorate the Universal Pontiff sufficiently, and as a result of the decision of the Basilian Congregation in Žyrovicy (1661). Thus the Suprasl Pontifical (1716) commemorates the Pope, not the Metropolitan; it is the archdeacon who makes the commemoration, the additional title "Most Holy" is added and the commemoration of the Pope now takes the first place, before the King and the Celebrant-Bishop.

The next commemoration of the Pope according to MS BL is prescribed during the preparation of the Holy Gifts on the prothesis. Here the Pope is commemorated twice: 1) when the Metropolitan puts a particle under the Lamb and prays for the living, and 2) when he prays for the dead.

1) (Be mindful, O Lord) of every Orthodox Bishop: His Holiness the Universal Pontiff N., of our Metropolitan (if the celebrant is not the Metropolitan himself), of the honourable priesthood..." (MS, p. 29v).

After the commemoration of the Pope follow those of the King, the Council (Палата) and the Armed Forces. The order of the commemorations is somewhat different from that in the ektenia "Rcem vsi".

2) The Pope is commemorated a second time during the oblation, when the Bishop prays for the dead (MS, p. 30v). Here he mentions the Universal Pontiffs (in the plural), in the first place before Patriarch, Archbishops, Bishops, Kings etc.

During the Great Entrance, when the prepared Gifts are carried from the prothesis altar to the sanctuary there is no commemoration of the Pope. After the invocation by the archdeacon, the archpriest makes a commemoration of "the Orthodoxy of our Sovereign Lord the King N." (MS, p. 33v).

The next explicit commemoration of the Pope occurs in MS BL (p. 42v) at the same place as is customary to-day: when the choir has finished the hymn in honour of Our Lady, the Metropolitan intones:

"First of all remember, o Lord, our Ecumenical Pontiff, His Holiness N., preserve him for Thy churches..." But before this commemoration there appears the rubric: "The Bishop if he is a Metropolitan intones". This means that our MS assumes that if the celebrant is a Bishop, he commemorates the Metropolitan but not the Pope, while if he is a priest, he prays for his Bishop.

The fourth and most solemn commemoration of the Supreme Pontiff "if a feast of great solemnity is being celebrated" (MS, p. 43v) occurs after the invocation and blessing by the Metropolitan: "And may the mercies of our great God and Saviour Jesus Christ be with you all" and before the litany prayer: "After commemorating all the Saints..." This is the rite of eulogy which we have already noted. (See p. 166)

From this, it seems that even before the Chapter of Žyrovicy (1661), the Pope was commemorated in the Liturgy at least four times, but that the commemoration was to be made only by the Metropolitan.

Naturally, Skuminovič who dedicated the whole second chapter of his book *Przyczyny* (Vilna, 1643) to the Pope and to the links between the Eastern Church and the Roman See, would be careful to specify precisely in his MS those places where the Pope was to be commemorated. This was a result not only of Skuminovič's personal faith and convictions, but of the Union of Brest itself, by which the whole Byelorussian and Ukrainian Churches became Catholic and hence the liturgical commemoration of the Pope followed as an external sign of faith. This in no way changed the rite of the Liturgy, but rather enriched it[128].

Some other features of MS BL

In this last chapter, we should like to draw attention to some other characteristic parts of the Liturgy of St. John Chrysostom of MS BL, about which we have not yet spoken.

1. Our MS does not give the full text of *the Creed,* and therefore we cannot make any certain assertions about the "Filioque". It would seem, however, that had the full text been included, it would not have contained the "Filioque", which was definitively introduced during the time of Metropolitan Gabriel Kolenda (1666-74)[129].

MS BL states that *the Creed* should be read by a lector, but insists that he read it "with a very loud voice"[130].

When *the Creed* is recited, the bishop, together with the concelebrant priests, waves the large veil over the paten and chalice. Other Pontifical Service Books order the concelebrating priests to wave the veil over the head of the bishop[131]. At the end of *the Creed,* the bishop kisses the veil and says: "Holy God, Holy mighty"; the archdeacon opens the Royal Doors and the deacon makes the exclamation: "Let us stand aright..." (MS, p. 37v).

2. We can see the Serbian influence in the wording of the Preface, particularly in the last words, which are usually sung: Побѣдную пѣснь поюща, вопиюща, взывающа и глаголюща. (MS, p. 38v). Exactly the same is found in the Service Book of Metropolitan Isidore[133] and in some other Service Books, e.g. Serbian 1519 and Vilna 1583.

3. MS BL (p. 39v) states that all the particles, and not the Agnus only, should be consecrated. It further states that the bishop alone should say aloud the words of consecration, and that all the other concelebrants should recite them secretly.

The words for consecrating the bread have the conjunction "i" (=and) against all Gospel texts (Mat. 26,26; Mk. 24,22; Lk. 22, 19). The same is found in the Sophia MS of the XII century[134], in the Service Books of Stratyn (1604), Vilna (1617 Mamonič), and in a book that is very rare today, in the Polish language, *Wykład Liturgiey świętej y Modlitwy z Doktorów SS,* Vilna, 1624, p. 93.

For the consecration of the bread, our MS (p. 39v) uses "се", and for the consecration of the wine "сия". The Basilian Chapter of 1668 in Vilna accepted for universal use "се" instead of "сия" for the consecration of the wine[135].

After the consecration, MS BL (p. 39v) has "помняще" (remembering): *Помняще* убо спасительную сию заповѣдь... The same word is found in Metropolitan

Isidore's Service Book[136], of Vilna 1617. In today's Service Books, as in that of Vilna 1583, the word "поминающе" is used. English translations of both do not reveal any great difference.

4. In our MS the epiclesis is preceded by the invocation of the Holy Spirit. This prayer is a later addition, and is not found in the oldest Greek Codex (Barberini, Vatican). Some printed Service Books (Vilna, 1583; Moscow, 1602) include it but leave its use to the *ad libitum* of the celebrant[137], while others give it in brackets (Kiev 1646, 1653; Lvov 1646, 1691). Nevostrujev-Gorskij gives some manuscript Service Books of the XV, XVI, and XVII centuries[138] which contain the invocation. De Meestre expresses surprise that modern Greek Service Books have omitted this prayer[139].

5. After the hymn to Our Lady "It is indeed fitting to glorify you" (MS, p. 41v), the bishop prays in silence: "Through the virtue of the precious and life-giving Cross, through the intercession of the precious Spiritual Powers..."

The dead are commemorated in almost the same way as they are today in the litanies for the dead.

6. After the prayer "O Lord Jesus Christ, Our God, look down from Your dwelling place..." before Holy Communion, the deacon and the candlebearers bring water to the bishop and he washes his hands (MS, p. 46v). All the concelebrating priests and deacons wash their hands during the Communion of the bishop.

7. When dividing the large host (the Lamb), the bishop says: "Your disciples, Lord, have known You in the breaking of bread (Lk. 24,35). Grant that we too may come to know You in eternal life" (MS, p. 46v). The same beautiful prayer, not in use today, is found in the older Slavonic Service Books: of St. Barlaam of Chutyn (XII cent.)[140] and in the Service Books of the XIV and XVI centuries[141].

8. Before pouring the hot water into the chalice, the bishop blesses it with some peculiar words[142]. The rubrics state: "The archdeacon pours a little of the water into the holy chalice" (MS, p. 46v).

9. When the priests receive a particle of the Consecrated Bread from the bishop, they kiss his hand and his cheek. The bishop says: "Christ is among us", and the priest answers: "He is and will be" (MS, p. 48v)[143]. It is the bishop who gives the Consecrated Wine to the priests and also to the deacons.

10. The archdeacon puts into the chalice, with the help of the sponge, all the remaining particles (MS, p. 49v), because all have been consecrated and not only the Lamb.

11. The prayer outside the sanctuary (заамбонная малітва) is said "with a loud voice" by the priest who is oldest in dignity: the archpresbyter (MS, p. 51v).

12. The concluding chant of the choir seems not to include "Многая лета".

13. The bishop takes off his robes at the same ambo where he was vested with them.

* * *

NOTES

1) De Meester, 'Les origines', pp. 296-300. See also 1.c. after p. 358: Tableau synchronistique des modifications du texte grec de la Liturgie de S. Jean Chrysostome. — Petrovski, 'Histoire de la rédaction slave', pp. 859-928. — Hanssens, *Institutiones,* t. III, pp. 3-6. — Muretov, *Istoričeskij obzor,* pp. 117-118. — Dmitrievskij, *Bogosluženije,* pp. 57-74. — Kucharek, *The Byzantine-Slav Liturgy,* pp. 218-233.

2) *Bogosluženije,* pp. 57-74. A. Dmitrievskij has used the material which was described by Nevostrujev-Gorskij *(Opisanije Slavjanskich Rukopisej,* otdel 3, č. 1, Moscow, 1869); included in this material there are two Pontifical Service Books of XVI-XVII centuries, Nr. 366, 367.

3) Dmitrievskij, *Bogosluženije,* p. 58. Petrovski, 'Histoire de la rédaction slave', pp. 886, 891. — Goar, *Euchologion,* p. 48. The same prayer appeared in the Service Books (= Služebniki) of the Venice edition: 1519, 1554, 1570.

4) E.g. in the Moscow edition of the Service Book of 1602.

5) *Bogosluženije,* pp. 59-60. See also: Rud, 'Liturhija', p. 171.

6) In the Entrance Prayers given by A. Dmitrievskij, 1.c. p. 60, where he describes schematically the Vilna Service Book of 1583, there are certain defects, e.g. in the prayers before the church doors; in the troparia for a saint instead of "Holy (man) of God" there is "Holy God", and the prayer: "Come, let us bow down" is omitted. He gives also the prayer: "You, O Lord, created me..." (Создавый мя Господи), which does not appear in the Vilna edition of 1583 at all. — There are some inaccuracies or a tendency for the ukrainization of the Old Slavonic text by Rud, 'Liturhija', p. 171. He says, quoting the Vilna Service Book, 1583, "Непроходимая врата", but this should be "Непроходимая двери". He says "Пречистому твоему образу", but this should be "Пречистому ти образу". He always puts "i" instead of "ѣ" or "e".

7) *Bogosluženije,* pp. 69-71.

8) *Činovnik Archierejskago Svjaščennosluženija* published in Warsaw, 1944 and in USA by the Russian Orthodox Church Abroad, Jordanville, 1965.

9) To the author of these notes the Archieraticon published in Univ, 1740, was not available. From Chojnackij, *Zapadnorusskaja C. Unija,* pp. 131-212, one can be sure (at least in this matter) that there are no differences between the Archieratica of Suprasl (1716) and that of Univ (1740). As to Greek and Slavonic Archieratica see: *DACL,* t. I, p. 2, col. 2736-39. — Korolevskij, 'Le Pontifical', pp. 202-215. — Petruševič, *Archijeratikon Kijevskoj Mitropolii s poloviny XIV st. po spisku s konca XVI st.,* Lvov, 1901. Offprint of *Bohosl. Vistnik,* I-II, 1900-1901. — Makarij, *Istorija R.C.,* t. IX, SPb 1879, pp. 295-97. — Dolnyckyj, *Pidručnik,* pp. 101, 107.

10) Mantija — the robe worn by a bishop of Eastern Rite. Klobuk — a monk's cowl, hood. Klobuk is mentioned in MS BL not at the beginning of the bishop's procession, but later when he comes before the Royal Doors (MS, p. 2v).

11) The place of the bishop's residence in Suprasl Archieraticon (1716) is indicated as "kelija", the cell.

12) There are three similar names: кадильница — the thurible, the censer; кадило — the thurible, the censer or the incense; фимиям — the incense. See: Nikolskij, *Posobije,* p. 81.

13) On the scheme below A7. This prayer is composed of excerpts of the different Psalms: 72(73), 2; 121(122), 1; 65(66), 13; but mostly 5, 8-9. It is found in the MSS. of the XV c. (Petrovski, 'Histoire de la rédaction slave', p. 892); in the manuscript Service Books of the XVI c. (Dmitrievskij, *Bogosluženije,* groups 4-7, p. 70), and also in the published Service Books in Vilna 1583, 1598; in the Moscow S. Book of 1602 and in Archieratica: Suprasl (1716), Lvov (1886) and Rome (1975).

14) This is a part of Ps. 5, 8-9, which in MS BL is joined with the previous prayer "My feet lead me in the path" (See note 13). Dmitrievskij seems to consider it as a separate prayer, because explaining "My feet lead me in the path" he does not mention Ps. 5, 8-9. Today nearly the whole of Ps. 5 is recited by the priest when he has finished the prayers before the iconostasis and enters into the sanctuary. Instead ČAD (Moscow 1668) and the contemporary Russian Archieratica prescribe the recitation of this prayer by the bishop during the Little Entrance after the protodeacon's exclamation "Wisdom. Stand up!" and the choir's "Let us come and bow down".

15) On the scheme below A9. This prayer to Our Lady is found in the MSS of the Service Books in XIV c. *(Izvestija AN,* t. VII, part 8, p. 269; Petrovski, 'Histoire de la rédaction slave', p. 879; Kovaliv, *Molitovnik-Služebnik,* pp. 160-161); in XV c. (Petrovski, l.c. p. 891) and in XVI c. (Dmitrievskij, *Bogosluženije,* groups 4-7, pp. 63-70). In the Vilna published Service Books 1583, 1598; Moscow, 1602, and in the Archieratica: Suprasl, Lvov, Rome. Also as the "theotokion" (baharodzičen) in the funeral service for priests. *(Trebnik,* part 2, Rome, 1946, p. 184). According to MS BL and to the Archieratica of Suprasl and Lvov the bishop says this prayer advancing to the church. Other sources present rather a large variety of directions:

1. standing in the doors of the church (Vilna 1598; 7th group at Dmitrievski's *Bogosluženije);*
2. at the porch of the church in front of the western church doors (One-hundred Chapters Council = Stoglavyj Sobor);
3. crossing the threshold of the church (5th group in Dmitrievskij's *Bogosluženije);*
4. during the opening of the doors of the church (Vilna, 1583);
5. entering the church doors (Service Book of XVI c., Nevostrujev-Gorskij, *Opisanije,* p. 57);
6. entering the church (Service Book of XIV c. and Archieratica of the XVI c.).
7. The Roman Archieraticon (1975) keeping the traditional prayers has changed radically one rubric: all prayers of the procession, including "The impassable door" and the Psalms 14(15), 22 (23) and 23(24), should be recited in the bishop's residence. After "The impassable door" there is also the dismissal prayer (apolysis). For the procession of the bishop there remain two exclamations of the protodeacon: "Be you blessed by the Lord of Sion" and "Blessed be the name of the Lord" or instead of the latter "It is indeed fitting to glorify you". Then the bishop recites Ps. 5 and enters the church.

16) Ps. 22(23) was and is in frequent liturgical use, particularly in relation to the eucharistic rite (See: Pravilo k Božestvennomu pričaščeniju, Nikolskij, *Posobije,* p. 357, note 1). According to a Service B. of the XIV c. it was said by the priest kneeling together with Psalms 14(15) and 50(51). Kovaliv, *Molitovnik-Služebnik,* pp. 1ab, 161. According to the Vilna Service Book (1598) the priest recited Psalms 14 and 22 after the kissing of icons and he then entered the sanctuary, while the Moscow Service Book (1602) prescribes just the opposite: the priest should recite the same Psalms before kissing the icons. The Pontificals of Suprasl (1716) and of Lvov (1886) give the Psalms 14, 22, 23, which the bishop should recite silently during his procession to the church.

17) Chojnackij *(Zapadnorusskaja C. Unija,* p. 134), stressing the difference between the Uniate and the Orthodox rite, says: "The Orthodox bishop standing at the ambo over the eagle (= the little carpet with the eagle) begins: Blessed be our God". It would be more interesting for us if the author had given us the origin of the use of this carpet with an eagle and the city of Jerusalem. Today the "eagle" is used in the Byzantine-Slavonic Rite at the consecration of a bishop, and it is also sometimes used when the bishop celebrates. MS BL makes no mention of it, nor do the Moscow ČAD (1668) or the Uniate Pontificals. It is true that Dmitrievskij *(Bogosluženije,* p. 71) says that the bishop before vesting is standing on the estrade on the "eagle".

18) Here are two prayers: the first one "Lord, remove from me all my transgressions" (on the scheme below C32) is known through the Service Books in XV (Petrovski, 'Histoire de la rédaction slave', p. 891) and XVI centuries (Dmitrievskij, *Bogosluženije,* p. 70). The other one (on the scheme C33): "O Lord, our God, send down Your hand", most probably older than the first one, without doubt is of Greek origin and reached the Slavs with the Order of Philotheus Kokkinos, Patriarch of Constantinople (1353-4, 1364-76) in XIV c. (Goar, *Euchologion,* p. 48; Petrovski, l.c. pp 886, 891). The same prayer is found in Venice editions of the Service Books 1519, 1520, 1554. Today it is in all modern editions and is recited by priest and bishop when they enter the sanctuary.

19) In spite of its being said here "the prothesis being already completed" the bishop will still perform the greater part of the prothesis before the Great Entrance (MS, pp. 28v-31v).

20) *Служебникъ Святительскій.* This name was generally accepted and later became established in the printed editions. So far four published Archieratica with this name are known:

1. Pontifikal si jest Služebnik Svjatitelskij, Suprasl, 1716
   (Petrov, *Slavjanskija knigi,* Nr. 451. — Golenčenko, *Bibliograf. spisok,* Nr. 333).

2. Služebnik Svjatitelskij... v obiteli unevskoj... roku 1740. (Petrov, l.c. Nr. 576. — Svencickij, *Kataloh knih*, Nr. 228).

3. Služebnik Svjatitelskij, edition of Bačynskyj, Lvov, 1886. (Svencickij, l.c. Nr. 231).

4. Archieratikon ili Služebnik Svjatitelskij, Rome, 1973-75.

The full name of the two first Archieratica is also given by Chojnackij (*Zapadnorusskaja C. Unija*, 131).

21) Novostrujev-Gorskij, *Opisanije*, p. 1. — Golubinskij, *Istorija R.C.*, p. 355 note 1).

22) *Molitovnik-Služebnik*, pp. 2-4.

23) Dmitrijevskij, *Bogosluženije v R. C.*, p. 70.

24) "Amvon" = the ambo has two meanings: 1) pulpit, i.e. the place from which readings are made and sermons are delivered; 2) platform, i.e. the place where the bishop is vested and remains until the Little Entrance. Nikolskij, *Posobije*, p. 27. — Kucharek, *The Byzantine-Slav Liturgy*, pp. 414, 423-24.

25) It is found in: ČAD (1668), Suprasl (1716), in Archieratica published in Warsaw (1944) and in USA (1965).

26) It may be considered as one of the features of MS BL. The Archieratica mentioned above (note 25) do not have it. — Chojnackij (*Zapadnorusskaja C. Unija*, p. 136) says: "The Uniate bishops are vested not by subdeacons, as with us, but by the archdeacon, who at the same time says the prayer for vesting". See also Schweigl (*Archijerejskoje služenije*, Rome, 1959, p. 14).

27) According to MS BL the vesting prayers are said by the bishop himself and the archdeacon helps him to robe. The Russian Archieratica (ČAD, Warsaw and USA) prescribe that deacons should robe the bishop. Chojnackij is not exact and often exaggerates in his anti-uniate zeal.

28) The prayer in putting on the "naplečnik": "Set upon my head the helm of salvation so that I may vanquish the devil's snares". The English text is from the occasional booklet *Ceremony of Consecration and the Pontifical Divine Liturgy of N. N. Savaryn*, Toronto, 1943, p. 19. The same prayer is found in the Archieratica of Suprasl, Lvov, but not in the Roman.

29) *Ukazatel dlja obozrenija Moskovskoj Patrijaršej Riznicy*, Moscow, 1863, p. 12. Ib. p. X, nr. 51 the picture of the paraman used by the Metropolitan Photius. — See: Sreznevskij, *Materialy dlja slovarja*, t. II, SPb 1895, col. 879-80. — Nikolskij, *Posobije*, p. 746.

30) Hieronymus, *Translatio Regulae S. Pachomii*, Migne, PL 22, 64.

31) Savva, *Ukazatel*, p. 12.

32) Braun, *Die Liturgische Gewandung*, pp. 22, 49-52.

33) Braun, op. cit., p. 237. About sakkos pp. 302-305.

34) Golubinskij, *Istorija R. C.*, t. I, p. 265.

35) Savva, *Ukazatel*, p. 15.

36) Neselovskij, *Činy chirotonesij i chirotonij*, p. 349.

37) *Bullarium Dipl. et Privilegiorum S. Rom. Pontificum*, Edit. Taurinensis 1865, t. X, p. 252-54.

38) Bylanych, *Synodus Zamostiana an. 1720*, Rome, 1960, p. 14.

39) Savva, *Ukazatel*, p. 15.

40) Nevostrujev-Gorskij, *Opisanije*, p. 93.

41) The Roman Archieraticon (1975) made no mention of it either.

42) The Vilna Service Book (1583) has a particular prayer for vesting of the epitrachelion (the stole): "They took Jesus and bound him and delivered him to Pontius Pilate, the governor. Through your passion you have saved yourself, so save us also from passions, our life and resurrection, glory to you". The first part is found also at the vesting of the epitrachelion in the Moscow Service Book (1602). The Gospel texts which are recited during the vesting by priest or bishop are in the following Service Books: Kiev edition 1629, 1639, 1653; Lvov 1691 and all three Archieratica: Suprasl, Univ, Lvov.

43) Nevostrujev-Gorskij, *Opisanije*, pp. 1-2. — Petrovski, 'Histoire de la rédaction slave', pp. 862-63.

Taft, *The Great Entrance*, p. 266 note 40: "Note that Slavic sources put the prothesis prayer *after* the initial blessing of the liturgy". This is incorrect at least so far as MS BL is concerned.

44) Taft, op. cit., p. 270.

45) Muretov (*Istoričeskij obzor činosledovanija proskomidii*, p. 23) seems to have mentioned the same prayers of the Great Entrance.

46) See note 43.

47) See note 43.

48) Dmitrievskij, *Bogosluženije v R. C.*, p. 81.

49) Nevostrujev-Gorskij, *Opisanije*, p. 93.

50) All Vilna Service Books, including the *Liturgikon* of the Metropolitan Žochowski (Vilna 1692, Suprasl 1695), have a clear Byelorussian pronunciation (accent): pomólimsia (e.g. Supr. Liturgikon pp. 100, 116 etc.). Because there grew up a legend, without reasonable foundation, that the old Byelorussian liturgical editions accepted the Ukrainian pronunciation (accent), it is useful in order to clarify the question to draw attention to the copy of the Liturgikon of the Metropolitan Žochowski, which is found in the Francis Skaryna Byelorussian Library in London. This copy does not contain the original text of the Liturgy of St. John Chrysostom, which has been replaced by a copy of the same Liturgy edited in Vilna in 1773 by the Metropolitan Wolodkovič, between pages 80 and 100 of the original book. It is true that the Liturgy of the Metropolitan Wolodkovič has the Ukrainian pronunciation, but the original text of Žochowski's edition, which is also available to us, bears witness to the contrary. From the Liturgikon of the Metropolitan Žochowski until the Service Book of the Metropolitan Wolodkovič 80 years went by. It is true that before the liquidation by the Tsar of the Catholic Church of Eastern Rite in Byelorussia (1839) Ukrainian influence was there perceptible. See: Ohijenko, 'Rozmežuvannia pamiatok ukrainskich vid biloruskich', *Zapiski ČSVV*, č. 1-2, 1935, p. 264. — Karskij, *Belorusy*, t. II, vyp. 1, pp. 393-444; The same: *Trudy po belorusskomu i drugim slavjanskim jazykam*, pp. 492-496. — Veselovska, *Naholos u schidno-slovjanskich movach*, Charkiv, 1970.

51) In the Pontifical Service Books nothing is said about it. According to ČAD (Moscow 1668) each ecphonesis is said by a different priest.

52) So far as is known all Service Books, both manuscript and printed, in Byelorussia and the Ukraine in XVI-XVII centuries had the ecphoneseis ending "vo veki ve*kom*". This was also so in Russia up to the time of Patriarch Nikon. When "vo veki ve*kov*" was introduced, is difficult to ascertain. It seems that the Suprasl Pontifical Service Book (1716) belongs to the transition period. But it is also known that some books published later still have "vekom", e.g. *Alfa i Omega*, Vilna, 1786, pp. 10v, 300v, 302v. — *Kniga glagolemaja Zlatoustago*, Vilna, 1798, pp. 334 etc.

53) Palata — "In the old litanies of the Church of England, the word *palace* was used as an equivalent to the Lords of the Council and all the nobility as it stands in the present litany", King, *The Rites and Ceremonies of the Greek Church in Russia*, London, 1772, p. 64.

54) Archieratica Suprasl (1716) and Lvov (1886) prescribe that the bishop should stand without mitre until "et incarnatus est", then he is seated. In the Russian Archieratica nothing is said about the mitre, but require the bisop to stand throughout he whole "Jedinorodnyj" (Monogenes). Chojnackij (*Zapadnorusskaja Cerk. Unija*, p. 139) adds that the bishop should stand the whole time wearing his mitre.

55) For those expert in old manuscripts and prints this is quite important; also it avoids the difficulty of raising questions about the pronunciation and the accent, which are not always clear. (See note 50). Some authors reproducing the Old Slavonic text use "i" instead of "jat" (ѣ), which is contrary to scientific method and inaccurate. In Byelorussia "ѣ" was pronounced as "e", not as the Ukrainians do as "i".

56) E.g. ČAD III,15 "and elevates the Holy Gospel and makes a little Cross". So also Warsaw (p.5) and USA (p. 14). In the Moscow Service Book of 1602 there is just the opposite rubric: the deacon having said "Wisdom. Stand up!" does not make the sign of the Cross. Maybe this is only proof that the Moscow Service Book of 1602, of pre-Nikon date, contains the rite of the Kievan province.

57) In the same place the rubric of the Roman Archieraticon (p. 38) seems to be incorrect: "Having

completed the last troparion, the protodeacon proceeds to the middle..." etc. The choir or the reader has just sung the third antiphon but not the last troparion. The troparia are sung or read *after* the protodeacon's exclamation.

58) According to the Lvov Archieraticon (1886) after the bishop's blessing the deacon answers: "Amen. Wisdom. Stand up!" and he enters the sanctuary and puts the Gospel on the altar. This prayer of the Trisagion is found also in other Archieratica: II,9; III,18, but not in the same place. In MS BL it occupies the same place as is indicated in modern Service Books.

59) The bishop "takes in his hands two candles and reads the prayer: Christ our God, the true Light". Dmitrievskij, *Bogosluženije v R. C.*, p. 105.

60) Dmitrievskij, l. c., pp. 105, 107.

61) Nevostrujev-Gorskij, *Opisanije*, p. 94.

62) Dmitrievskij, l. c., p. 106.

63) Nikolskij, *Posobije*, p. 438 note 3. See also pp. 388, 439.

64) Heraclius Lisoŭski, the Archbishop of Polack (1784-1809), known because of his efforts to purify the Byzantine-Slavonic rite from Latin influences, among other things considered that it was a latinization to chant the ecphonesis "For You are holy, O our God" facing the people and with hands open. To do so was prescribed by the rubrics in the Service Books published after the Synod of Zamość (1720). Solovij (*De reformatione liturgica Heraclii Lisowskyj Archiepiscopi Polocensis* (1784-1809), Rome, 1950, pp. 44-45) thinks that the Liturgikon of the Metropolitan Žochowski was the first to introduce such a rubric. With this assertion of both Archbishop Lisoŭski and Solovij one cannot agree, because the rite of chanting the ecphonesis towards the people is earlier and not necessarily a latinization. It could be just the result of Greek influence.

65) Krasnoselcev, *Materjaly dlja istorii činoposledovanija Liturgii Sv. Ioanna Zlatoustago*, p. 108. — Kucharek, *The Byzantine-Slav Liturgy*, p. 384 note 7.

66) Rud, 'Liturhija', p. 181.

67) The deacon says: "Bless, Master, the holy prothesis" and the bishop answers thereto: "Blessed be the prothesis of our Lord God and Savour Jesus Christ". Dmitrievskij, *Bogosluženije v R. C.*, p. 103.

68) Kucharek, *The Byzantine-Slav Liturgy*, p. 423.

69) The Service Books prescribe the same as MS BL: Venice 1519; Vilna 1583, 1617; Ješje 1641; Kiev 1639. As concerns the Kiev Service Book, Rud, 'Liturhija', p. 180, is mistaken, because according to that the deacon himself takes the Gospel from the altar.

70) On the insistent ektene see: Kucharek, *The Byzantine-Slav Liturgy*, pp. 446-457.

71) Archieraticon of Habert, p. 73: The patriarch blesses the people with the trikirion silently. Dmitrievskij (*Bogosluženije v R. C.*, p. 111) gives the same prayer which has some linguistic differences: "uslyšy ny". "prizovem". According to Dolnyckyj, (*Pidručnik ceremonij*, p. 107), the deacon commemorates emperor and pope.

72) Dmitrievskij (*Bogosluženije v R. C.*, p. 112) makes this remark: "Eternal memory should be performed on the days of the universal commemoration. On this occasion the priests sometimes sang eternal memory ("viečnaja pamjat")". Today it is sung during the office for the dead and on the "licija" after the apolysis. (*Typikon*, chapter 14. Nikolskij, *Posobije*, pp. 757-58, 766).

73) Iliton (from Greek) — unconsecrated corporal. It is mentioned in Barberini's MS of IX c. (Brightman, *Liturgies*, Vol. I, pp. 316, 369); in the Service Book of Barlaam of Chutyn (Nevostrujev-Gorskij, *Opisanije*, p. 2), XII c. — See Nikolskij, *Posobije*, pp. 415, 471, 806. — Kucharek, The *Byzantine-Slav Liturgy*, 464-65. — *Slovnik Jazyka Staroslovenskego*, Praha, 1973, p. 124. — In MS BL there is no mention of the antimension (the consecrated corporal) at all. In the first half of the XVII c. in Byelorussian and Ukrainian Catholic Churches the custom was introduced of covering the antimension by the iliton and upon this were put the paten (diskos) and the chalice. As a result of controversy and objections on the part of the Latins (Sakovič, etc.) Mohila wanted the iliton also to be blessed and this blessing one finds in his *Euchologion*, Kiev, 1646, part II, pp. 90-92.

74) Taft. *The Great Entrance*, p. 4. Also notes 3, 4, 5. As concerns the modern Greek use see: De

Meester, *La Divina Liturgica,* Rome, 3rd ed. 1925, p. 51; p. 127 note 44. — *La Divina Liturgia di S. Giovanni Crisostomo,* Grottaferrata, 1960, pp. 64-67.

75) Brightman, *Liturgies,* Vol. I, pp. 377-79. — Hanssens, *Institutiones Liturgicae,* t. III, pp. 272-73, 286. — Taft, *The Great Entrance,* pp. 119-148.

76) When Patriarch Nikon changed the liturgical texts some objected that he had altered "Trisvjatuju pesn prinosjašče" to "pripevajušče" as do Latins when accompanying organs with the voice. Kartašev, *Očerki po ist. Russkoj Cerkvi,* Paris, 1959, p. 169.

77) Beljajev, *Praktičeskij kurs izučenija drevnej russ. skoropisi,* p. 35. Sreznevskij, Materijaly, t. I, pp. 1027-29.

78) Sreznevskij, l. c., p. 1367.

79) Sreznevskij has no such form. "Jaka", may be an example of the Byelorussian akańnie.

80) Taft, *The Great Entrance,* p. 58.

81) Taft, l. c., pp. 58-59.

82) "Originally there was only a single alleluia at the end of the Cherubicon, as we see in all early sources", Taft, l. c., pp. 57-58.

83) Goar, *Euchologion,* pp. 87, 92.

84) Taft, l. c., p. 54.

85) Maximilianus Princeps Saxoniae, *Praelectiones,* p. 75: De personis liturgicis.

86) Dmitrievskij, *Bogosluženije,* p. 116.

87) ČAD (Moscow 1668) does not have it. The Činovnik from 1798 is quoted by Taft, *The Great Entrance,* p. 172 note 98.

88) Taft, l. c., p. 167.

89) Goar, *Euchologion,* p. 659. *Trebnik,* part III, Rome, 1951, p. 182.

90) Goar, l. c., p. 364.

91) About this prayer Dmitrievskij *(Bogosluženije v Russ. C.,* p 100) says that when the Liturgy was celebrated by the bishop, then before the apolysis at the end of the hours, according to the Serbian custom, he read it. The Serbian practice is established in the Service Books of 1519, 1554, 1570. The same prayer is found in the Service Books of the Liturgy of St. Basil: The priest's prayer before the Liturgy. Orlov, *Liturgija Sv. Vasilija Velikago,* pp. 11-13.

92) Bocian ('De modificationibus in textu slavico', p. 953) says that in the Service Book of the Metropolitan Cyprian it was provided by a rubric that instead of nine particles the celebrant could put on the diskos one only. But it is not clear which Service Book Bocian had in mind. One described by Nevostrujev-Gorskij *(Opisanije,* pp. 11-17) does not support Bocian's assertion.

93) Hanssens, *Institutiones Liturgicae,* t. II, pp. 182-196; t. III, pp. 17-18, 28-30, says nothing about the Cross and Angels. The Service Books of Vilna (1583) and Stratyn (1604) have the beginning of the prothesis as in MS BL. The Service Book of Mamonič (1617) mentions neither Cross nor Angels. Again the Service Book of Mohila (1639) requires the commemoration of Angels, but omits the Cross. So also in the Service Book of Kiev (1653). — The Service Book of the Metropolitan Wołodkovič, Vilna 1773, prescribes the commemoration of the precious life-giving Cross and the heavenly bodiless Powers. — Bocian, 'De modificationibus in textu slavico', p. 954: "Sanctorum commemorationem quod spectat, in antiquioribus missalibus occurentia verba „Virtute venerandae et vivificae crucis et venerandarum coelestium virtutum incorporearum" a Synodo Leopoliensi cum provocatione ad antiqua exemplaria et euchologium Benedicti PP. XIV ex missali eliminata sunt", The Greek Service Books — both the Orthodox (from 1838) and Catholic — after the commemoration of Our Lady prescribe placing a particle from a third prosphora "in honour and memory of the great captains of the angelic armies, Michael and Gabriel, and of all the heavenly bodiless powers", *Byzantine Daily Worship,* Alleluia Press, 1969, p. 256. See: *La Divina Liturgia di S. Giovanni Crisostomo.* Testo Greco e Italiano, Grottaferrata, 1960, p. 18. — De Meester, 'Les origines', p. 311. — Mandala, P.M., *La Protesi della Liturgia nel Rito Bizantino-Greco,* Grottaferrata, 1935, p. 124 etc.

K. Nikolskij *(Posobije,* pp. 365-66, notes 2,7) gives the reason why Angels should not be commemorated: because they never have sinned therefore they have no need of redemption by Christ. Recently the same question has been discussed by Archbishop Basil Krivocheine in his article: 'Nekotoryje Bogoslužebnyje osobennosti u Grekov i Russkich i ich značenije', *Vestnik Russkago Zapadno-Jevropejskogo Egzarchata,* Paris, 1975, Nr. 89-90, pp. 77-78. He considers a theological problem: does the redemption concern only men or the Angelic Powers too? The Greek way — according to Archbishop Basil — puts the stress more on the cosmic aspects while the Russian practice expresses rather the anthropocentric aspect of redemption. It seems this "deep" theology is out of place. First of all because not only the Greek but also many Slavonic Service Books have the same text with the Cross and Angelic Powers. Secondly, a long time ago Simeon of Thessalonica gave a theological reason why the particles of prosphora should be put on the diskos during the preparation: "quia Incarnationis mysterio ipsae ministraverunt", because they (the Angelic Powers) rendered their service to the mystery of Incarnation. (P. M. Mandala, o.c. p. 166.).

94) Martinov, *Annus Ecclesiasticus,* p. 124: colitur 8 Maii.

95) Martinov, l. c., p. 81: Phalelaeus eremita, colitur 27, 28 Februarii.

96) The Service Book of Vilna (1583) has only the name of St. Anthony of Kiev; Vilna (1593) gives the Moscow thaumaturgists Saints Peter, Alexy and Jonah; the Rostov thaumaturgists Bishops Leontius, Isaiah, Ignatius and Jacob; the martyrs of Kiev Boris and Gleb. See: Archimandrite Leonid, *Bibliografičeskaja zametka,* p. 12.

97) E.g. Service Book of Mohila 1693, Lvov Liturgiaron (1712), which is the Catholic one!

98) Bocian, 'De modificationibus in textu slavico', p. 952: "Vocationes diaconi... absunt". — Rud, 'Liturhija', p. 173, says that all Prayer Books indicate a dialogue with the deacon. This is often said but it is incorrect.

99) E.g. Kiev Service Books from 1629, 1639 and Lvov from 1646. See Rud, 'Liturhija', p. 175.

100) About the use and place of the Ps. 50(51) see: Taft, *The Great Entrance,* pp. 223-225. Dmitrievskij, *Bogoslužnije v Russ. C.,* p. 116.

101) Goar, *Euchologion,* ed. 1647, p. 98. — Nevostrujev-Gorskij, *Opisanije,* pp. 2, 21. — Petrovski, 'Histoire de la rédaction slave', p. 920. — Dmitrievskij, *Bogosluženije v Russ. C.,* p. 112. — Taft, *The Great Entrance,* p. 254.

102) *Bogosluženije v Russ. C.,* p. 116.

103) Taft, *The Great Entrance,* pp. 220-222.

104) Taft, l. c., p. 227. "The first euchology in which we have found a commemoration of the Great Entrance is the 13th century *British Museum Harl. 5561.* As the priest enters he says to himself... May the Lord God remember us in his kingdom and all Christians", l. c., p. 229. — Goar, *Euchologion,* ed. 1730, p. 59. The Vilna Service Books (1583, 1598, 1617) have "vsech vas".

105) Aničenka *(Bielaruska-ukrainskija piśmovyja suviazi,* p. 218) says that " хрестиан" is an indication that a manuscript is Byelorussian, but "хрестіан" that it is Ukrainian.

106) Taft, l. c., pp. 234-241.

107) Taft, l. c., p. 235, note 69.

108) According to Vilna Service Books (1583, 1593) the priest himself recites the Psalms. According to Vilna 1583 the exit with the prepared Gifts begins after "Jako cara vsech podjemlušče" (p. 64v). According to the Kiev and Lvov Service Books the deacon says "Blessed be he who comes", and the priest "Lift up your gates, princes". See: Petrovski, 'Histoire de la rédaction slave', pp. 888-889. — Dmitrievskij, *Bogosluženije v Russ. C.,* p. 117. — Taft, *The Great Entrance,* p. 236.

109) Taft, l. c., p. 255.

110) Taft, l. c.

111) Nevostrujev-Gorskij, *Opisanije,* p. 1.

112) Nevostrujev-Gorskij, l. c., pp. 21, 23.

113) pp. 19-19v. See also Nevostrujev-Gorskij, *Opisanije,* pp. 21, 23.

114) Dmitrievskij, *Bogosluženije v Russ. C.,* p. 117. — Taft, *The Great Entrance,* p. 225 note 168.

115) Činovnik, Moscow, 1910, quoted by Taft, l. c., p. 256.

116) Taft, l. c., p. 256. Should be "bonum" or "bonus"?

117) Raes, 'Le dialogue après la grande entrée', pp. 38-51. — Taft, l. c., pp. 285-310. — Kucharek, *The Byzantine-Slav Liturgy*, pp. 504-507.

118) Ia): Pontifex caput inclinat = Bishop bows his head; in Slavonic: "Poklon tvoryt" = makes a deep bow. — IVa): After "recordetur" in the Latin text there is a cross: †, no doubt indicating where the bishop gives the blessing. In the Slavonic text the cross is omitted, most probably by a scribal error.

119) De fide orthodoxa 4, 13. Migne, PG 94, 1141. Taft, l. c., pp. 288-89.

120) In some Service Books (e.g. Stratyn, 1604) there is mentioned the concelebration of the Holy Spirit. Taft, l. c., p. 294, says: "The interpolation for the concelebration of the Spirit had never won a permanent place in the old redaction".

121) See: Warsaw (1944, p. 9v); USA (1965, pp. 32, 32v).

122) In the recent Service Books "molitvu". In old ones — "molitvy": Vilna 1583, 1598, 1617, 1773; Suprasl 1716; Kiev 1653; Lvov 1691; Moscow 1602.

123) It seems that this commemoration is made *sotto voce*, corresponding therefore to the Russian rite: "May the Lord God remember your bishopric..." said by protodeacon and priests.

124) Nevostrujev-Gorskij, *Opisanije*, pp. 21, 23, 58, 66, 81. — Taft, l. c., pp. 393-96.

125) *Archeogr. Sbornik*, XII, pp. XXXIX note 2, 72, 91. — Praszko, *De Ecclesia Ruthena Catholica*, p. 258.

126) Goar, *Euchologion*, ed. 1730, p. 124. — Bylanych, *Synodus Zamostiana an. 1720*, p. 50.

127) Praszko, l. c., p. 258.

128) Bocian, 'De modificationibus in textu slavico', pp. 936-38.

129) *Čtenija obšč. istorii i drevnostej*, kn. I, 1871, p. 167. — *Archeogr. Sbornik*, t. XII, Vilna, 1900, pp. 96-97.

130) Dmitrievskij, *Bogosluženije v Russ. C.*, pp. 120, 122 note 4. — Taft, *The Great Entrance*, pp. 416-418.

131) Taft, l. c., pp. 418-423. — Rud, 'Liturhija', pp. 191-193.

132) See: Nevostrujev-Gorskij, *Opisanije*, pp. 15, 47. — Dmitrievskij, l. c., p. 119. — De Meester, 'Les origines', pp. 335, 337. — Bocian, 'De modificationibus', p. 960. — Taft, l. c. p. 423–425.

133) Horbač, *Try tserkovnoslovjans'ki liturhični rukopysni teksty*, p. 54.

134) Orlov, *Liturgija Sv. Vasilija V.*, SPb, 1909, p. 393.

135) *Archeogr. Sbornik*, t. XII, Vilna, 1900, p. 96.

136) Horbač, l. c., p. 55.

137) Nevostrujev-Gorskij, l. c., p. 15.

138) Nevostrujev-Gorskij, l. c., pp. 47, 107, 205.

139) De Meester, l. c., p. 288 note 1, p. 341.

140) Nevostrujev-Gorskij, l. c., p. 7.

141) Nevostrujev-Gorskij, l. c., pp. 22, 36, 67. — Dmitrievskij, *Bogosluženije v Russ. C.*, p. 123.

142) See: Dmitrievskij, l. c., p. 124.

143) See: Dmitrievskij, l. c., p. 125.

TABLE OF CONTENTS OF THE ORIGINAL TEXT OF THE MS BL

INDEX

to the introduction, bibliography and biography of Bishop Theodore Skuminovič together with explanatory liturgical notes.

C

D

H

I

J

K

L

T

U

V

W

Y

Z

CONTENTS

Page	Misprint	Corrigendum
6/1	Nevostrujev-Gorski	Nevostrujev-Gorskij
116	Recontioris	Recentioris
125	Tyškievč	Tyškievič
145	the	The
151/78	clarum	claram
169	мі ру	мі тру
169	Евалаемъ	Евалиемъ
189	bisop	bishop
189	he	the
191/93	sunt,	sunt.
192/97	Liturgiaron	Liturgiarion
199	Collectioni	Collection
201	Liturgiaron	Liturgiarion
202	Ryaa	Ryan

* * * * *